Radical Thought in Italy

Edited by

Sandra Buckley

Michael Hardt

Brian Massumi

THEORY OUT OF BOUNDS

...UNCONTAINED

BY

THE

DISCIPLINES,

INSUBORDINATE

PRACTICES OF RESISTANCE

...Inventing,

excessively,

in the between...

PROCESSES

OF

HYBRIDIZATION

Radical Thought in Italy

A Potential Politics

Paolo Virno and Michael Hardt, editors

Maurizia Boscagli, Cesare Casarino, Paul Colilli,
Ed Emory, Michael Hardt, and Michael Turits, translators

Theory out of Bounds   *Volume 7*

University of Minnesota Press

Minneapolis • London

Published by the University of Minnesota Press
111 Third Avenue South, Suite 290
Minneapolis, MN 55401-2520
Printed in the United States of America on acid-free paper

LIBRARY OF CONGRESS CATALOGING-IN-PUBLICATION DATA
Radical thought in Italy : a potential politics / Paolo Virno and
Michael Hardt, editors.
p.   cm. — (Theory out of bounds ; v. 7)
ISBN-13: 978-0-8166-4924-2
ISBN-10: 0-8166-4924-3
1. Radicalism — Italy.   2. Italy — Politics and government — 1945–
I. Virno, Paolo, 1952–   . II. Hardt, Michael.   III. Series.
HN490.R3R33   1996
303.48'4 — dc20
96-11842

Contents

O N E

Introduction: Laboratory Italy

Michael Hardt

In Marx's time revolutionary thought seemed to rely on three axes: German philosophy, English economics, and French politics. In our time the axes have shifted so that, if we remain within the same Euro-American framework, revolutionary thinking might be said to draw on French philosophy, U.S. economics, and Italian politics. This is not to say that Italian revolutionary movements have met only with great successes in recent decades; in fact, their defeats have been almost as spectacular as those suffered by the French proletariat in the nineteenth century. I take Italian revolutionary politics as model, rather, because it has constituted a kind of laboratory for experimentation in new forms of political thinking that help us conceive a revolutionary practice in our times.

This volume is not intended primarily, then, as a history of the recent political movements or an explanation of the current crises of the Italian political system. The primary focus is rather to present a contemporary Italian mode of thinking revolutionary politics. The difference of Italian thought, however, cannot be grasped without some understanding of the difference marked by the history of Italian social and political movements. The theorizing, in fact, has ridden the wave of the movements over the past thirty years and emerged as part of a collective practice. The writings have always had a real political immediacy, giving the impression of being composed in stolen moments late at night, interpreting one day's political struggles and planning for the next. During extended periods many of these authors were theorists on the side and kept political activism as their day job. Althusser was fond of quoting Lenin as saying that without revolutionary theory there can be no revolutionary practice. These Italians insist more on the converse relation: revolutionary theory can effectively address only questions that are raised in the course of practical struggles, and in turn this theorizing can be articulated only through its creative implementation on the practical field. The relationship between theory and practice remains an open problematic, a kind of laboratory for testing the effects of new ideas, strategies, and organizations. Revolution can be nothing other than this continually open process of experimentation.

It will be necessary, then, in the course of this volume, to give some indications of the nature of the political movements in Italy over the past thirty years.[1] The practices in the 1960s and 1970s of the Italian extraparliamentary Left, independent of and more radical than the Italian Communist Party, did indeed constitute an anomaly with respect to other European countries and certainly with respect to the United States, in terms of its size, intensity, creativity, and long duration. Some like to say that whereas 1968 lasted only a few months in France, in Italy it extended over ten years, right up until the end of the 1970s. And the Italian experiences were no weak echo of Berkeley in the 1960s or May in Paris. The movements in fact went through a series of stages, each with its own experiments in democratic political organization and radical political theory.

A first long season of political struggles extended from the early 1960s to the early 1970s, in which factory workers constituted the epicenter of the social movements. The attention of revolutionary students and intellectuals was focused on the factories, and a significant portion of the militant workers saw the struggle for communism and workers' power as leading through independent political organizations, outside the control of and often opposed to the Communist Party and its trade unions. The most significant radical political theorizing of this period dealt with the emerging autonomy of the working class with respect to capital, that is, its power to generate and sustain social forms and structures of value independent of capitalist relations of production,[2] and similarly the potential autonomy of social forces from the domination of the State.[3] One of the primary slogans of the movements was "the refusal of work," which did not mean a refusal of creative or productive activity but rather a refusal of work within the established capitalist relations of production. The anticapitalism of the worker and student groups translated directly into a generalized opposition to the State, the traditional parties, and the institutional trade unions.

A second stage of the movements can be defined roughly by the period from 1973 to 1979. In general terms, the focus of radical struggles spread in this period out of the factory and into society, not diluted but intensified. Increasingly, the movements became a form of life. The antagonism between labor and capital that had developed in the closed spaces of the shop floor now invested all forms of social interaction. Students, workers, groups of the unemployed, and other social and cultural forces experimented together in new democratic forms of social organization and political action in horizontal, nonhierarchical networks.[4] The Italian feminist movement gained a significant role during this period, with its activities focused on the referenda on divorce and abortion. This is the period too when terrorist groups such as the Red Brigades emerged from this same social terrain. One should not, however, let the dramatic exploits of the terrorist groups, in particular the 1978 kidnapping and assassination of the prominent politician Aldo Moro, eclipse the radical social and political developments of a wide range of leftist movements. Across the social spectrum there were instances of political antagonism and diffuse forms of violence mixed with social and cultural experimentation. The political theory that emerged from these movements sought to formulate alternative, democratic notions of power and insisted on the autonomy of the social against the domination of the State and capital. Self-valorization was a principal concept that circulated in the movements, referring to social forms and structures of value that were relatively autonomous from and posed an effective alternative to capitalist circuits of valorization. Self-valorization was thought of as the building block for constructing a new form of sociality, a new society.

Beginning at the end of the 1970s, the Italian State conducted an enormous wave of repression. The magistrates sought to group together and prosecute the terrorist groups along with the entire range of alternative social movements. Thousands of militants were arrested under extraordinary statutes that allowed for extensive preventive detention without any charges being made against those arrested and without bringing them to trial for extended periods. The courts were given wide powers to obtain convictions merely on the basis of the association of the accused with political groups charged with certain crimes. Large numbers of political activists went into hiding and then into exile, and thus by the early 1980s the political organization of the social movements was all but destroyed. Most of the contributors to this volume, in fact, lived this period either in prison or in exile. At the same time, Italian capital embarked on a project of restructuring that would finally destroy the power of the industrial working class. The symbolic defeat took place in 1980 at the Fiat auto plant in Turin, which had for decades been a central site of workers' power. Fiat management succeeded in shrinking the workforce, laying off tens of thousands of workers, through the computerization of the production plants.[5] These were the years of winter for the social movements, and the radical political theorizing too lived a kind of exile, as if it had gone underground to weather the bleak period. The Italian economy experienced another boom in the 1980s, largely powered by new forms of diffuse and flexible production, such as that characterized by Benetton. But the social terrain was typified by a new conformism, nurtured by opportunism and cynicism. Marx might say that his beloved mole had gone underground, moving with the times through subterranean passages, waiting for the right moment to resurface.

All three of these periods—the intense worker militancy of the 1960s, the social and cultural experimentation of the 1970s, and the repression of the 1980s—made Italy exceptional with respect to the other European countries and the United States. Radicals outside of Italy might have admired the audacity and creativity of the social movements and mourned their brutal defeats, but the conditions of Italian revolutionary practice and thought seemed so distant that their lessons could not be applied and adapted to other national situations. I believe, however, that in the 1990s, despite sometimes dramatic and sometimes ludicrous headlines that make Italian politics seem increasingly eccentric, Italian exceptionalism has in fact come to an end, so that now Italian revolutionary thought (as well as reactionary developments) can be recognized as relevant to an increasingly wide portion of the globe in a new and important way. The experiments of laboratory Italy are now experiments on the political conditions of an increasing large part of the world.

This new convergence of situations might be linked to two general processes. It is due partly, no doubt, to the capitalist project of globalization, in which in certain sectors throughout the world, capital is moving away from dependence on large-scale industries toward new forms of production that involve more immaterial and cybernetic forms of labor, flexible and precarious networks of employment, and commodities increasingly defined in terms of culture and media. In Italy as elsewhere, capital is undergoing the postmodernization of production. At the same time, on an equally global scale, neoliberal policies (imposed when necessary by the IMF and the World Bank) are forcing the privitization of economic sectors that had been controlled by the State and the dismantling of the structures of social welfare policies. The Reagan and Thatcher governments may have led the way, but the rest of the world is fast catching up.

In political and cultural terms, too, the Italian condition is moving toward a convergence with other countries, sometimes in rapid, dramatic leaps.

Certainly the cynicism, fear, and opportunism that have recently characterized the culture of the institutional Left in Italy are factors that we in the United States have come to know well. One might say that the conditions of Italian politics have become Americanized. Certainly, the meteoric rise of the media magnate Silvio Berlusconi as a major political figure in the mid-1990s, emerging from outside and in opposition to traditional political structures, cannot but seem strangely familiar from the perspective of the United States. In a way, Berlusconi combines the political entrepreneurship of a Ross Perot with the media entrepreneurship of a Ted Turner. In any case, it is a small step in the developing form of rule, call it mediocracy or teleocracy, from a bad actor as president to a media tycoon. Furthermore, the Italian political condition has approached what Fredric Jameson has identified as a defining aspect of U.S. Left culture in recent years, that is, the condition of theorizing without movements. This does not mean that radical theorizing might now take place without reference to political practice—of course, revolution can be theorized only through interpretation and extension of really existent forces immanent to the social field. It means, rather, that radical theory is deprived of the coherent movements and the firmly consolidated collective social subjects that once animated the terrain of revolutionary practice. Theorists must now interpret the prerequisites of emergent conditions and the nascent forces of political subjectivities and communities coming to be. In such conditions, political theorizing in general might be forced to take on a more highly philosophical or abstract character to grasp these potentialities. To a certain degree, then, postmodernization of the economic realm and Americanization of social and cultural fields are the two faces of a general convergence. This is why the experiments conducted in laboratory Italy are now experiments of our own future.

The convergence of social conditions, reducing the gap of Italian exceptionalism, has brought Italy close to us and thus made the essays in this volume relevant for us in a way Italian theorizing could not be before. There remain, however, important differences marked by the kind of political thought presented here, perhaps as the accumulated wealth of its exceptional past. First of all, there is a communist theorizing bent on the abolition of the State and the refusal of political representation that we seldom find elsewhere. The refusal of the State also brings with it an attack on hierarchical organizations in party structures, trade unions, and all forms of social organization. Antagonism to the State is the centerpiece of a generalized insubordination. The abolition of the State, however, does not mean anarchy. Outside the constituted power of the State and its mechanisms of representation is a radical and participatory form of democracy, a free association of constitutive social forces, a constituent power. Self-valorization is one way of understanding the circuits that constitute an alternative sociality, autonomous from the control of the State or capital. Some of the contributors to this volume outline a project, for example, whereby the social structures of the Welfare State might be transformed so that the same functions are supported no longer from above but now from below, as a direct expression of the community. The effort to constitute a community that is democratic and autonomous, outside of political representation and hierarchy, is a continual project of these theorists.

Combined with the radical critique of the State is a sustained focus on the power of labor. Marx agreed with the capitalist economists that labor is the source of all wealth in society, but it is also the source of sociality itself, the material of which all our social relations are woven. Throughout these essays there are attempts to understand the way that laboring practices have changed in recent years and how these new forms of labor might carry new and greater potentials. New concepts such as "immaterial labor," "mass intellectuality," and "general intellect" all try to capture the new forms of cooperation and creativity involved in contemporary social production—a collective production defined by cybernetic, intellectual, and affective social networks. The affirmation of the powers of labor found in the work of these theorists, however, should not be confused with any simple call that we go to work or enjoy our jobs. On the contrary, any affirmation of labor is conditioned first by the "refusal of work" inherited from the workers' movements of the 1960s. Radical workers (in Italy as elsewhere) have always tried to get out of work, to subtract themselves from exploitation and the capitalist relation. The social movements translated this into a form of life in the realm of nonwork, outside the relations of waged labor. In the contemporary essays in this volume, this tendency is theorized in a more general way as a mass defection or exodus, a line of flight from the institutions of the capitalist State and the relations of waged labor. The authors' affirmation of labor, then, refers not simply to what we do at work for wages but rather generally to the entire creative potential of our practical capacities. These creative practices across the range of terrains—material production, immaterial production, desiring production, affective production, and so forth—are the labor that produces and reproduces society. The seeds of a communist society already exist in the virtual paths that potentially link together this labor in new collective articulations.

What is perhaps most attractive about these Italian theorists and the movements they grow out of is their joyful character. All too often, leftist cultures have identified a revolutionary life with a narrow path of asceticism, denial, and even resentment. Here, however, the collective pursuit of pleasures is always in the forefront—revolution is a desiring-machine. Perhaps this is why, although these authors follow many aspects of Marx's work, they seldom develop either the critique of the commodity or the critique of ideology as a major theme. Although certainly important projects, both of these analyses run the risk of falling into a kind of asceticism that would predicate revolutionary struggle on a denial of the pleasures offered by capitalist society. The path we find here, in contrast, involves no such denial, but rather the adoption and appropriation of the pleasures of capitalist society as our own, intensifying them as a shared collective wealth. This is far from a vision of communism as equally shared poverty, and much less a reference back to precapitalist communal forms. Communism, rather, will emerge out of the heart of capitalism as a social form that not only answers the basic human needs of all but also heightens and intensifies our desires. Corresponding to this focus on joy, there is also permeating the work of these authors a distinctive kind of optimism, which might appear naive to some at first sight. At various points in the 1970s, for example, their writings made it sound as if revolution was possible and even imminent. Even during the bleak periods of defeat and political repression, there is still an optimistic reading. In the final essay of this volume, for example, Paolo Virno interprets the counterrevolution of recent years as an inversion and redeployment of revolutionary energies, as if it were the photonegative of a potential revolution. These authors are continually proposing the impossible as if it were the only reasonable option. But this really has nothing to do with simple optimism or pessimism; it is rather a theoretical choice, or a position on the vocation of political theory. In other words, here the tasks of political theory do indeed involve the analyses of the forms of domination and exploitation that plague us, but the first and primary tasks are to identify, affirm, and further the existing instances of social power that allude to a new alternative society, a coming community. The potential revolution is always already immanent in the contemporary social field. Just as these writings are refreshingly free of asceticism, then, so too are they free of defeatism and claims of victimization. It is our task to translate this revolutionary potential, to make the impossible real in our own contexts.

The Essays

The essays in this collection are organized into four groups that function more or less as one continuous narrative.[6] Part I constitutes an attempt to cure ourselves of the poisonous culture of the 1980s, what some might call the culture of postmodernism, which certainly has remained dominant thus far through the 1990s. The essays by Paolo Virno and Massimo De Carolis take stock of and critique the emotional and political climate of the culture that is dominated affectively by fear and resignation and politically by cynicism and opportunism. The point is not simply to lament the poverty of our contemporary political culture, but rather to find in it positive elements that can lead to a new cultural transformation. We can learn to redirect some of the powers that drive cynicism and opportunism, and learn in the process how to combat fear. Adelino Zanini then gives a brief overview and critique of "weak thought," identifying it squarely with an Italian version of postmodern ideology that emerged from the tragic social condition of the 1980s. Finally, Rossana Rossanda, who belongs to a somewhat different tradition from the other authors in this volume, reconsiders the Marxist and communist tradition after the fall of the Berlin Wall. The defeats of the Left in the late twentieth century are not a result of "too much" Marxism or communism, she argues, but, on the contrary, of a failure to redeploy creatively the resources of these traditions.

The essays in Part II analyze the economic and social conditions of contemporary capitalist production. Carlo Vercellone and Alisa Del Re discuss the consequences of the crisis and dismantling of the Welfare State in Italy. Vercellone traces the history particular to the Italian case, focusing on the alternative forms of welfare that have been generated by different social movements, and Del Re insists on the special position women hold in relation to welfare policies. Both analysts seek to identify social forms of welfare that could constitute a new alternative network, independent of State control. The remaining essays in Part II trace the recent migration of capitalist production out of the factory and toward more diffuse social forms. Marco Revelli takes stock of the anthropolitical and sociological consequences of the mass layoffs of workers following the restructuring of production at the large factories, in particular the enormous Fiat auto plant in Turin. Franco Piperno and Maurizio Lazzarato follow this with analyses of the effects of the new technologies and the new, immaterial forms of labor that have come to play a dominant role generally in contemporary capitalist production.

The essays in Part III propose new concepts for political theorizing today, adequate to our social conditions. Giorgio Agamben offers a philosophical investigation of the "form-of-life" that might animate our coming political community, outside of any Statist notion of politics. He proposes the figure of the refugee as the paradigmatic political subjectivity of our era. Augusto Illuminati discusses the potential and pitfalls of a nonrepresentative form of democracy, along with its implications for our modern conceptions of citizenship and community. Paolo Virno attempts to discern the outline of new revolution in our contemporary political conditions that appears as a kind of engaged exodus or constructive withdrawal from the structures of wage labor and State control. Finally, Antonio Negri complements this proposal with the notion of a constituent republic, which would mark an alternative to the State and give form to the continuously open expression of the revolutionary energies of the multitude.

The two essays that make up the appendix are intended as a historical overview to situate and complement the theoretical essays in the rest of the volume. They fill the same role as the last part of volume 1 of *Capital*, on primitive accumulation: they detail the historical developments that in one country have laid the conditions for the preceding theoretical analysis of a general situation. In this sense, the appendix may be read profitably before the rest of the volume. "Do You Remember Revolution?" was written in 1983 by eleven authors who were then in prison, including Paolo Virno and Antonio Negri. The essay sketches the history of the social movements in Italy from the late 1960s up to the late 1970s and the time of the authors' arrest. Paolo Virno's "Do You Remember Counterrevolution?" provides the sequel, analyzing the political and social developments through the 1980s and into the 1990s that led to the collapse of the traditional party structure and the dissolution of the First Republic, which had defined Italian govenment since the end of World War II.

The reader will notice that several unfamiliar concepts, such as constituent power, general intellect, and exodus, reappear continually throughout the different essays, taken for granted, as if they were already common terms. In effect, these authors understand the invention and articulation of new concepts to be a collective project. When one author introduces a new term, the others take it up immediately, giving it their own interpretations and feeling no need to cite where it came from. Before long, the original source of the concept is forgotten and it is adopted as a common part of the vocabulary. For the convenience of the reader, we have added a glossary at the end of this collection that explains the most important of these newly invented concepts.

The essays in this volume, then, demonstrate not only the anomaly of recent Italian history, in terms of its material situation and political climate, but also the convergence it has experienced toward a common global economic and political condition. These Italian authors bring to this new world order a wealth of revolutionary experience and desire. *Laboratory Italy* refers no longer to a geographic location, but to a virtual space of hope and potential that may be actualized anywhere; better, it refers to a specific modality now available to all of us, of experimenting in revolution.

Notes

1. During this same period there developed an original and powerful tradition of feminist theory in Italy. In English, see the Milan Women's Bookstore Collective, *Sexual Difference: A Theory of Social-Symbolic Practice* (Bloomington: Indiana University Press, 1990); Paola Bono and Sandra Kemp, eds., *Italian Feminist Thought: A Reader* (Oxford: Basil Blackwell, 1991). There are aspects that this feminist tradition shares with the tradition presented in this volume, in particular the focus on autonomy and the construct of alternative social structures, but in practice the movements seldom enjoyed much contact and were at times antagonistic toward one another.

2. The classic text is Mario Tronti, *Operai e capitale* (Turin: Einaudi, 1966, enlarged ed. 1971). Parts of this book have been published in English as "The Strategy of Refusal," in "Autonomia: Post-political Politics" (special issue), *Semiotext(e)* 3, no. 3 (1980): 28–34; "Social Capital," *Telos*, no. 17 (Fall 1973): 98–121; and "Workers and Capital," *Telos*, no. 14 (Winter 1972): 25–62.

3. See Antonio Negri's essay "Keynes and the Capitalist Theory of the State," which appears in English as chapter 2 of *Labor of Dionysus: A Critique of the State-Form* (Minneapolis: University of Minnesota Press, 1995), 23–51.

4. See the excellent description of the movements by Franco Berardi (Bifo), "The Anatomy of Autonomy," in "Autonomia: Post-political Politics" (special issue), *Semiotext(e)* 3, no. 3 (1980): 148–71.

5. Marco Revelli has perhaps most thoroughly analyzed the restructuring of the Fiat plant and the defeat suffered by the workers in political and sociological terms. This volume includes his essay "Worker Identity in the Factory Desert." See in Italian his full-length study, *Lavorare in FIAT* (Milan: Garzanti, 1989), in particular 84–129.

6. Several important authors who are part of this tradition have not been included in this volume for reasons of space or other considerations. One of the most significant of these is Franco Berardi (Bifo), who has written recently on the new potentials of cyberspace and cybertime, both as a field for democractic social organization and as a weapon for new means of social control. Sergio Bologna's latest work investigates autonomous forms of labor that are organized and reproduced outside of directly capitalist control. Finally, Giuseppe Cocco has made valuable contributions on the relationships between social movements and the economic strategies of flexible production.

PART I

Antidotes to Cynicism and Fear

T W O

The Ambivalence of Disenchantment

Paolo Virno

An examination of the emotional situation of recent years constitutes neither a light-hearted literary diversion nor a recreational hiatus amid otherwise rigorous research. On the contrary, such an approach aims at the most pressing and concrete issues, at relations of production and forms of life, at acquiescence and conflict. It is an "earthly prologue" deaf to all angelic rustlings, intent instead on settling accounts with common sense and with the ethos that emerged from the 1980s.

By *emotional situation*, however, I do not mean a group of psychological propensities, but those modes of being and feeling so pervasive as to be common to the most diverse contexts of experience, both the time given over to work and that dedicated to what is called life. We need to understand, beyond the ubiquity of their manifestations, the *ambivalence* of these modes of being and feeling, to discern in them a "degree zero" or neutral kernel from which may arise both cheerful resignation, inexhaustible renunciation, and social assimilation on the one hand and new demands for the radical transformation of the status quo on the other. Before coming back to this essential and ambivalent nucleus, however, we must pause and consider the real expressions of the emotional situation in the years following the collapse of the great mass political movements—extremely harsh and unpleasant expressions, as we know.

What is involved here is a conceptualization of the field of *immediate coincidence* between production and ethics, structure and superstructure, between the revolution of labor processes and the revolution of sentiments, between technology and emotional tonality, between material development and culture. By confining ourselves narrowly to this dichotomy, however, we fatally renew the metaphysical split between "lower" and "higher," animal and rational, body and soul—and it makes little difference if we boast of our pretensions to historical materialism. If we fail to perceive the points of identity between labor practices and modes of life, we will comprehend nothing of the changes taking place in present-day production and misunderstand a great deal about the forms of contemporary culture.

Marked by intensified domination, the post-Fordist productive process itself demonstrates the connection between its own patterns of operation and the *sentiments of disenchantment*. Opportunism, fear, and cynicism—resounding in the postmodern proclamation of the end of history—*enter into production*, or rather, they intertwine with the versatility and flexibility of electronic technologies.

Sentiments Put to Work

What are the principal qualities demanded of wage laborers today? Empirical observation suggests the following: habitual mobility, the ability to keep pace with extremely rapid conversions, adaptability in every enterprise, flexibility in moving from one group of rules to another, aptitude for both banal and omnilateral linguistic interaction, command of the flow of information, and the ability to navigate among limited possible alternatives. These qualifications are not products of industrial discipline so much as results of a socialization that has its center of gravity *outside of the workplace*, a socialization punctuated by discontinuous and modular experiences, by fashion, by the interpretations of the media, and by the indecipherable *ars combinatoria* of the metropolis intertwining itself in sequences of fleeting opportunities. It has recently been hypothesized that the "professionalism" supplied and demanded today consists of skills gained during the prolonged and precarious period preceding work.[1] This delay in adopting particular roles, typical of youth movements in decades past, has today become the most prominent of professional qualifications. Looking for a job develops those generically social talents—as well as the habit of developing no durable habits at all—that function as true and proper "tools of the trade" once work is found.

This development involves a double movement. On the one hand, the process of socialization, the interweaving of the web of relations through which one gains experience of the world and oneself, appears independent of production, outside the initiatory rituals of the factory and the office. On the other hand, continuous change in the organization of labor *has subsumed* the complex of inclinations, dispositions, emotions, vices, and virtues that mature precisely in a socialization outside of the workplace. The permanent mutability of life enters the productive process by way of a "job description": habituation to uninterrupted and nonteleological change, reflexes tested by a chain of perceptive shocks, a strong sense of the contingent and the aleatory, a nondeterministic mentality, urban training in traversing the crossroads of differing opportunities. These are the qualities that have been elevated to an authentic productive force.

The very idea of "modernization" and the framework of oppositions on which it depends have been demolished: the blows of the new against the immobility of a preexisting order, artificiality versus seminaturalness, rapid differentiation versus consolidated repetitiveness, renewal of a linear and infinite temporality versus the cyclicality of experience. This mass of images, forged on the terrain of the first industrial revolution, has been stubbornly applied—whether by inertia or a repetitive compulsion—to every successive new wave of development. Its inadequacy is complete.

The change now under way, far from opposing itself to the lengthy stasis of traditional societies, is taking place on a social and cultural stage already completely modernized, urbanized, and artificial. We may wonder how the most recent eruption of unforeseen events will combine with a certain habituatedness to the unforeseen, and with an acquired responsiveness to transformation without pause. How will the most recent deviation from the known accumulate and interfere with a collective and individual memory riven with sudden changes in direction? If we still want to talk about a revolutionary destruction of social foundations, we can only mean a destruction taking place where there is no longer any real foundation to destroy.

The crucial point is that today's productive revolution exploits, as its most valuable resource, everything that the project of "modernization" counted among its effects: uncertain expectations, contingent arrangements, fragile identities, and changing values. This restructuration uproots no secure tradition (no trace remains of Philemon and Baucis dispossessed by the entrepreneur Faust), but rather *puts to work* the states of mind and inclinations generated by the impossibility of any authentic tradition. So-called advanced technologies do not so much provoke alienation, a scattering of some long-vanished "familiarity," as reduce the experience of even the most radical alienation to a professional profile. Put in fashionable jargon: nihilism, once the dark side of technology's productive power, has become one of its fundamental ingredients, a prized commodity in the labor market.

The Offices of Chatter

This turbulent uprooting has been variously described and diagnosed by the great philosophers of our century. For philosophy, however, the particular traits of this experience, impoverished and deprived of any solid skeletal structure, appeared for the most part *at the margins* of productive practice, a skeptical and corrosive complement to the processes of rationalization.

The emotional tonalities and ethical dispositions that best reveal the drastic lack of foundation afflicting action seemed to show up at the end of the workday, after the time clock had been punched. Think of Baudelaire's dandyism and spleen, or Benjamin's distracted spectator who refines his sensibility by means of completely artificial spatiotemporal constructions, that is, at the movies. Think too of Heidegger's two famous figures of "inauthentic life": "idle talk" and "curiosity." Idle talk, or "chatter," is groundless discourse incessantly diffused and repeated, transmitting no real content but imposing itself as the true event worthy of attention. Curiosity is the pursuit of the new for its own sake, a "pure and restless seeking," an incapacity for reflection, an agitation without end and without goal. Both of these figures announce themselves, according to Heidegger, at the very moment that serious and grave "concern" with the tools and goals of a job is interrupted, when pragmatic and operational relations to the surrounding world fade away.

Now the conspicuous novelty of our age lies in the fact that these modes of "inauthentic life" and stigmata of "impoverished experience" have become autonomous and positive models of production installed at the very heart of rationalization. Groundless discourse and the pursuit of the new as such have gained, in striking relief, the status of operational criteria. Rather than operating only after the workday, idle talk and curiosity *have built their own offices.*

Productivity's subsumption of the cultural and emotional landscape of irremediable uprooting appears in an exemplary fashion in *opportunism.* The opportunist confronts a flux of interchangeable possibilities, keeping open as many as possible, turning to the closest and swerving unpredictably from one to the other. This style of behavior, which characterizes the dubious morality of many contemporary intellectuals, has a technical side. The possible, against which the opportunist is measured, is utterly disincarnate. Although the possible may take on this or that particular guise, it is essentially the pure *abstraction of opportunity*—not an opportunity for something, but rather opportunity without content, like the odds faced by a gambler. The opportunist's confrontation with an uninterrupted sequence of empty possibilities is not, however, limited to a particular situation. It is no parenthesis to be closed at will in order that one may move on to a more "serious" activity with a rigid concatenation of means and ends, with a solid compenetration of forms and contents. Opportunism is a game with no time-outs and no finish.

This sensitivity to abstract opportunities constitutes the professional requirement of post-Taylorist activity, where the labor process is regulated by no single goal, but by a class of equivalent possibilities redefinable in every particular instance. The computer, for example, rather than a means to a univocal end, is a premise for successive "opportunistic" elaborations of work. Opportunism is valued as an indispensable resource whenever the concrete labor process is pervaded by diffuse "communicative action," when work is no longer identified as solitary, mute, "instrumental action." Whereas the silent "astuteness" with which tools make use of natural causality demands people of linear character, a character submitted to necessity, computational chatter demands "people of opportunity," ready and waiting for every chance.

The phantasmagoria of abstract possibilities in which the opportunist acts is colored by *fear* and secretes *cynicism*. It contains infinite negative and privative chances, infinite threatening "opportunities." Fears of particular dangers, if only virtual ones, haunt the workday like a mood that cannot be escaped. This fear, however, is transformed into an operational requirement, a special tool of the trade. Insecurity about one's place during periodic innovation, fear of losing recently gained privileges, and anxiety over being "left behind" translate into flexibility, adaptability, and a readiness to reconfigure oneself. Danger arises within a perfectly well known environment. It grazes us. It spares us. It strikes someone else. Even with regard to concrete and circumscribed questions (posed short of any metaphysical concern), we experience at every step of our intellectual labors either the feeling of decimation or the euphoria of being spared — being the ninth or eleventh in line. In contrast to the Hegelian relation between master and slave, fear is no longer what drives us into submission *before* work, but the active component of that stable instability that marks the internal articulations of the productive process itself.

Cynicism is strictly correlated to this stable instability. Cynicism places in full view, both at work and in free time, the naked rules that artificially structure the parameters of action, that establish groups of opportunities and sequences of fears. At the base of contemporary cynicism is the fact that men and women learn by experiencing rules rather than "facts," and far earlier than they experience concrete events. Learning the rules, however, also means recognizing their unfoundedness and conventionality. We are no longer inserted into a single, predefined "game" in which we participate with true conviction. We now face in several different "games," each devoid of all obviousness and seriousness, only the site of an immediate self-affirmation—an affirmation that is much more brutal and arrogant, much more cynical, the more we employ, with no illusions but with perfect momentary adherence, those very rules whose conventionality and mutability we have perceived.

Cynicism reflects the location of praxis at the level of operational models, rather than beneath them. This location, however, in no way resembles a noble mastering of our condition. On the contrary, intimacy with the rules becomes a process of adaptation to an essentially abstract environment. From the a priori conditions and paradigms that structure action, cynicism picks up only the minimum of signals needed to orient its struggle for survival. It is no accident, therefore, that the most brazen cynicism is accompanied by unrestrained sentimentalism. The vital contents of emotion—excluded from the inventories of an experience that is above all else an experience of formalisms and abstractions—secretly return, simplified and unelaborated, as arrogant as they are puerile. Nothing is more common than the mass media technician who, after a hard day at work, goes off to the movies and cries.

Time and Chances

By analyzing the ethos of recent years, the dominant sentiments and styles of life, we hope to begin to grasp a form of socialization, a formation of subjectivity that is essentially completed outside of the workplace. Its modalities and inflections are what today actually unify the fragmented whole of wage labor. The "vices" and "virtues" developed in this extralabor socialization are then *put to work*. In other words, they are subsumed in the productive process, reduced to professional qualifications. This is true, however, only, or principally, at those points where innovation has completely penetrated. Elsewhere such "vices" and "virtues" are no more than accidental characteristics of forms of life and social relations in a broader sense.

In contrast to Taylorism and Fordism, today's productive reorganization is selective; it develops spottily, unevenly, flanking traditional productive patterns. The impact of technology, even at its most powerful point, is not univocal. Rather than determine a univocal and compulsory mode of production, technology keeps alive myriad distinct modes of production, and *even resuscitates those that are obsolete and anachronistic.* Here is the paradox. This particularly vigorous innovation involves only certain segments of the workforce, constituting a sort of "umbrella" under which is replicated the entire history of labor: islands of mass workers, enclaves of professionals, swollen numbers of the self-employed, and new forms of workplace discipline and individual control. The modes of production that over time emerged one after the other are now represented synchronically, almost as if at a world's fair. This is precisely because cybernetic and telecommunications innovations, although directly involving only a part of active labor, nonetheless represent the background condition of this synchrony of different patterns of work.

So what unites the software technician, the autoworker at Fiat, and the illegal laborer? We need the courage to respond: *nothing* unites them any longer with respect to the form and content of the productive process. But also: *everything* unites them regarding the form and content of socialization. What is common are their emotional tonalities, their inclinations, their mentalities, and their expectations. The "life world" is constituted by this homogeneous ethos, which in advanced sectors is part of production itself and delineates a professional profile for those employed in traditional sectors — as well as for the marginal workers who daily oscillate between employment and unemployment. Put simply, the point of suture can be found in the opportunism of labor and the opportunism universally encouraged by the urban experience. From this point of view — underlining, that is, the unitary character of the socialization unleashed by the productive process — the theory of the "society of two-thirds" (two-thirds of society protected and guaranteed, one-third impoverished and marginal) seems misleading. To indulge this theory is to risk limiting oneself bitterly to repeating that life is no bed of roses, or to conducting fragmented and unconnected analyses, re-creating in this way a mottled social topography that carries no real explanatory value.

Both this seemingly anachronistic fragmentation of productive activities and the significant consonance among styles of life are expressions of the tendency that has characterized the past two decades: the end of the society of work. The reduction of necessary work to a nearly negligible portion of life, the possibility of conceiving wage labor as an episode in a biography instead of as a prison and source of lasting identity — this is the great transformation of which we are the sometimes unconscious protagonists and the not always reliable witnesses.

The direct expenditure of labor has become a marginal productive factor, a "miserable residue." In the words of Marx himself, the most extreme and tormented Marx, work now "steps to the side of the production process instead of being its chief actor." Science, information, general knowledge, and social cooperation present themselves as "the great foundation-stone of production and of wealth" — they alone are the foundation, and no longer the workday.[2] And yet our working hours, or at least their theft, remain the most visible measure of social development and wealth. The end of the society of work thus constitutes a contradictory process, a theater of furious antinomies and disconcerting paradoxes, a tangled weave of chances and foreclosures.

The workday may be an accepted unit of measure, but it is no longer a true one. The movements of the 1960s pointed out this untruth in order to shake up and abolish the status quo. They signaled their opposition, their utter disagreement with objective tendencies. They vindicated the right to nonwork. They enacted a collective migration out from the regime of the factory. They recognized the parasitic character of working for a boss. Nevertheless, in the 1980s the status quo triumphed in its untruth. In what seems like an all-too-serious joke, the *end of the society of work has occurred in the very forms prescribed by the social system of wage labor itself*: unemployment resulting from reinvestment, flexibility as despotic rule, early retirement, the task of managing all the free time created by the absence of full-time work, the reappearance of relatively primitive productive sectors alongside innovative and driving sectors of the economy, and the revival of archaic disciplinary measures for controlling individuals no longer subordinated to the rules of the factory system. All this stands before us.

These developments recall what Marx wrote about common-share corporations, in which the surpassing of private property is achieved *on the terrain of private property itself*. Here, too, the surpassing is real, but it is also accomplished on the same old terrain. To think both of these theses at once, without devaluing the former as merely imaginary and without reducing the latter to an extrinsic husk — this is the unavoidable difficulty. The decisive issue is no longer the aggregate contraction of the workday, the achievement of which forms the common background both to present practices of domination and to eventual demands for their transformation. There will always be free time; it is the form this excess takes that is at stake. The traditional political Left, however, is completely unequipped to compete in this contest. The Left found its raison d'être in the permanence of the society of work and in the internal conflicts of labor's particular articulation of temporality. The end of that society and the consequent possibility of a battle about time decrees the end of the Left. We must recognize this end without satisfaction, but also without regrets.

The effective exhaustion of "productivism," or the central focus on work, is apparent in the modes of feeling and experience prevalent today: a profound sense of belonging to a temporal spatiality deprived of definite direction, detachment from every progressive conception of historical movement (that is, from that linear causal nexus of past, present, and future that has its very model, precisely, in work), and a familiarity with states of things that essentially consist of systems of opportunities. As mentioned earlier, we can recognize in these modes of feeling and experience the ground of a substantial homogeneity between those workers with so-called dependable jobs and the newly marginalized, between the computer technician and the most precarious of the precarious, between those in the top two-thirds and those outside of it.

Still, inasmuch as it takes place according to the rules of wage labor, the sunset of work is evident mainly in the emotional tonality of fear and in the attitude of opportunism. The sense of belonging to unstable contexts crops up only as a perception of one's own vulnerability to change, as unlimited insecurity. In the opacity of social relations and the uncertainty of roles that follow the loss of the centrality of work, it is fear that takes root. The absence of any authentic historical *telos* capable of univocally directing practice makes itself known, paradoxically, in the feverish spirit of adaptation of the opportunist, a spirit that grants the dignity of a salvational *telos* to every fleeting occasion. The opportunism we have come to know in recent years lies in the application of the logic of abstract labor to "opportunities." Chance becomes an inescapable goal to which we submit without resistance. The criterion of maximum productivity is extended to what appears specifically in the now predominant experience of nonwork. Spare time takes the form of urgency, tempestuousness, ruin: urgency for nothing, tempestuousness in being tempestuous, ruin of the self. The rapid acquiescence of the opportunist turns the imaginary struggle over the workday, over time, into an exhibition of a universal timeliness.

General Intellect

The sentiments of disenchantment, and among them cynicism in a special way, should be highlighted against the background of a new and different relation between knowledge and "life." The split between hand and mind, and thus the autonomy of the abstract intellect, has become something irreversible. The self-propelled growth of knowledge separate from work makes certain that every immediate experience is preceded by innumerable conceptual abstractions incarnated in techniques, artifices, procedures, and rules. The before and after have been reversed. Abstract knowledge, which in its groundless constructedness is little concerned with the evidence of direct experience, comes before every perception and any given operation; it accumulates before experience, like an antecedent before its conclusion.

This reversal of positions between concepts and perceptions, between knowledge and "life," is a decisive issue whose comprehension demands a brief detour. As usual, in order to be concise, I find it necessary to digress. This particular digression pertains to one of Marx's texts, both famous and controversial, the "Fragment on Machines" from the *Grundrisse: Foundations of the Critique of Political Economy*. What does Marx maintain in these pages? He presents a not very "Marxist" thesis: that abstract knowledge—in the first place scientific knowledge, but not only that—begins to become, precisely by virtue of its autonomy from production, nothing less than the principal productive force, relegating parcelized and repetitive labor to a peripheral and residual position. Knowledge is objectified in fixed capital, transfused into the automatic system of machinery and granted objective spatiotemporal reality. Marx utilizes a highly suggestive image to indicate the totality of abstract cognitive schemes that constitute the epicenter of social production and together function as the ordinating principles of all of life's contexts. He speaks of a general intellect: "The development of fixed capital indicates to what degree general social knowledge has become *a direct force of production*, and to what degree, hence, the conditions of the process of social life itself have come under the control of the general intellect and have been transformed in accordance with it" (706). It is not difficult today to expand this notion of general intellect well beyond the idea of knowledge materialized in fixed capital. The "general intellect" includes the epistemic models that structure social communication. It incorporates the intellectual activity of mass culture, no longer reducible to "simple labor," to the pure expenditure of time and energy. There converge in the productive power of the general intellect artificial languages, theorems of formal logic, theories of information and systems, epistemological paradigms, certain segments of the metaphysical tradition, "linguistic games," and images of the world. In contemporary labor processes there are entire conceptual constellations that function by themselves as productive "machines," without ever having to adopt either a mechanical body or an electronic brain.

Marx connects to the prominence of the general intellect an emancipatory hypothesis quite different from those, better known, that he develops elsewhere. In the "Fragment on Machines," the incidence of the crisis is no longer imputed to an inherent disproportion in a mode of production *actually* based on the labor time attributed to single individuals. The existence of a decisive contradiction is recognized between, on the one hand, a productive process that makes direct and exclusive use of science and, on the other, a measure of wealth still coincident with the quantity of work incorporated in products. The divergence of these two tendencies would lead, according to Marx, to the breakdown of "production based on exchange value" (705) and, thus, to communism.

Of course, things did not happen this way. What is striking now is the complete factual realization of the tendency described in the "Fragment" without any emancipatory or even conflictual outcome. The specific contradiction that Marx tied to the advent of communism has become a stable component, if not in fact *the* stabilizing component, of the existing mode of production. Rather than induce a crisis, the "qualitative imbalance between labour...and the power of the production process it superintends" (705) has constituted the solid foundation on which domination is articulated. Separate from its demand for a radical transformation, the "Fragment" is nothing but the last chapter of a natural history of society, an empirical reality, the recent past, something that has already been. Notwithstanding this, or precisely because of this, the "Fragment" allows us to focus on several aspects of the ethos of the present day.

Inasmuch as it effectively organizes production and the world of everyday life, the general intellect is indeed an abstraction, but a *real abstraction*, equipped with a material operability. In addition, because it consists of paradigms, codes, procedures, axioms—in short, because it consists of the objective concretizations of knowledge—the general intellect is distinguished in the most peremptory way by the "real abstractions" typical of modernity, by those abstractions that give form to the principle of equivalence. Whereas money, the "universal equivalent" itself, incarnates in its independent existence the commensurability of products, jobs, and subjects, the general intellect instead stabilizes the analytic premises of every type of practice. Models of social knowledge do not equate the various activities of labor, but rather present themselves as the "immediate forces of production." They are not units of measure, but they constitute the immeasurability presupposed by heterogeneous operative possibilities. They are not "species" existing outside of the "individuals" who belong to them, but axiomatic rules whose validity does not depend on what they represent. Measuring and representing nothing, these technico-scientific codes and paradigms manifest themselves as constructive principles.

This change in the nature of "real abstractions"—the fact, that is, that abstract knowledge rather than the exchange of equivalents gives order to social relations—reverberates in the contemporary figure of the cynic. The principle of equivalence, which stands at the foundation of the most rigid hierarchies and the most ferocious inequalities, guarantees nonetheless a certain visibility of social connections, a commensurability, a system of proportionate convertibility. This is so much so that there is bound to it, in a shamelessly ideological and contradictory way, the prospect of unlimited reciprocal recognition, the ideal of universal and transparent linguistic communication. Conversely, the general intellect, destroying commensurabilities and proportions, seems to make everyday life and its forms of communication intransitive. Although the general intellect ineluctably determines the conditions and premises of a social synthesis, it nevertheless occludes its possibility. It offers no unit of measure for an equation. It frustrates every unitary representation. It dissects the very bases of political representation. Today's cynicism passively reflects this situation, making of necessity a virtue.

The cynic recognizes, in the particular context in which he operates, the predominant role played by certain epistemological premises and the simultaneous absence of real equivalences. To prevent disillusion, he forgoes any aspiration to dialogical and transparent communication. He renounces from the beginning the search for an intersubjective foundation for his practice and for a shared criterion of moral value. He dismisses every illusion regarding the possibility of an equitable "reciprocal recognition." This decline of the principle of equivalence, a principle intimately connected to commerce and exchange, can be seen in the cynic's behavior, in his impatient abandon of the demand for equality. He entrusts his own affirmation of self to the multiplication and fluidification of hierarchies and unequal distributions that the unexpected centrality of knowledge in production seems to imply.

Contemporary cynicism both reflects and brings to an irreversible conclusion the inversion of knowledge and "life." Immediate familiarity with one or another set of rules and a minimized elaboration of their essential contents—this is the form taken by cynicism's reactive adaptation to the general intellect. Furthermore, as negatively as possible, cynicism attests to the illusory character of an "ethics of communication" that seeks to found the sociality of science on the basis of a transparent dialogism. In the ashen light of cynicism, the complete inadequacy of such linguistic free exchange is made clear. Science is *social* because it predetermines the character of the cooperation involved in work, not because it presupposes an equitable dialogue. It is social because it is the form in which everyone's activity is inscribed, not because it postulates the need to welcome and harmonize rationally each person's arguments and claims.

In the figure of the cynic, as well as in that of the opportunist, there is an atrophy of the salient traits with which the metaphysical tradition invested the dignity of the subject: autonomy, the ability to transcend the particularity of individual contexts of experience, the fullness of self-reflection, and "intentionality." This atrophy takes place at the moment that these traits, and precisely these, have found complete fulfillment in the effective power of abstract knowledge and its technical apparatus. Autonomous, separate, "unalterable," self-referential, always exceeding determinate contexts, capable of complete detachment from the tenacious "life worlds"—this is the general intellect. It factually realizes the complex plot of metaphysical subjectivity. Above all, it realizes the self-transcendence from which derives the political and ethical tension with the "completely other." This technical realization, however, is also a release and an absolution. Today's ethos, both in its most horrible and most adaptable figures and in its potential demands for radical change, is nonetheless consigned to the "here and now."

Degree Zero

At this point we must ask ourselves whether there is anything in the emotional constellation of the present that shows signs of refusal or conflict. In other words, is there anything good in opportunism and cynicism? Naturally the answer is no, and there must be no misunderstanding here. These regrettable and sometimes horrible figures, however, bear indirect testimony to the fundamental emotional situation from which they derive, but of which they are not the only possible result. As mentioned earlier, we must reconsider those modes of being and feeling that lie at the center of opportunism and cynicism like a neutral kernel, and yet are subject to a completely different development.

To avoid any equivocation and any pretext for malicious misinterpretation, I should clarify what I mean by the "neutral kernel" or "degree zero" of an ethically negative behavior. There must be no artful transvaluation such as, "What seems most evil is the true good," nor any complicitous wink to the "ways of the world." Our theoretical challenge lies instead in the identification of a new and important *modality of experience* through the forms in which it may for the moment be manifest, without, however, reducing that experience to them.

For example, the "truth" of opportunism, what might be called its neutral kernel, resides in the fact that our relation with the world tends to articulate itself primarily through possibilities, opportunities, and chances, instead of according to linear and univocal directions. This modality of experience, even if it nourishes opportunism, does not necessarily result in it. It does, however, comprise the necessary background condition of action and conduct in general. Other kinds of behavior, diametrically opposed to opportunism, might also be inscribed within an experience fundamentally structured by these same possibilities and fleeting opportunities. We can discern such radical and transformative behavior, however, only by tracing in the opportunism so widespread today, the specific modality of experience to which this behavior might indeed be correlated, even if in a completely different way.

In short, the sentiments of disenchantment and today's adaptive modes of behavior specify the emotional situation, the modality of experience, that represents their degree zero. This is what I have tried to show, case by case, in the preceding pages. What must be emphasized are both the *irreversibility* and the *ambivalence* of this emotional situation. As for irreversibility: we are not faced here with a passing condition, with a simple social or spiritual conjunction in response to which we might hope for the restoration of some other, earlier order. Because what is in question is not a long, dark parenthesis, but a profound mutation of the ethos, of culture and its modes of production, it is misguided to ask how far we have lasted through the long night, as if expecting an imminent dawn. Every light we will ever find is already here in the so-called darkness. We need only accustom our eyes. As for ambivalence: a modality of experience is not one and the same thing with its present manifestations. Rather, it is open to radically conflicting developments. Irreversibility and ambivalence exist together. This conclusion is just the opposite of current theoretical discussions in which whoever criticizes the status quo believes he or she has exorcised its irreversibility, and whoever recognizes this irreversibility is anxious to erase any trace of its ambivalence.

What, then, are the modes of being and feeling that determine the common emotional situation of both those who adapt and those who resist? In the first place, obviously, are the modes of being and feeling inherent to the end of the society of work. Let us briefly recall those themes examined earlier in detail, paying particular attention now, however, to the one that has become most important—the degree zero and its inherent ambivalence. As soon as it ceases to be the epicenter of all relations, work no longer offers any lasting orientation. It ceases to channel behavior and expectations. It no longer leads the way, nor does it extend a safety net capable of reducing or concealing the unfounded and contingent character of every action. Put another way, in contrast to its position in the recent past, work no longer functions as a powerful surrogate for an objective ethical framework. It no longer takes the place of traditional forms of morality that have long since been emptied or dissolved. The processes of the formation and socialization of the individual now unfold outside the productive cycle, in direct contact with the extreme fragility of every order and as training for confronting the most diverse possibilities, for the habit of having no habits, for a responsiveness to continual change, to change without end or goal.

In these attitudes and propensities are visible the degree zero of the sentiments connected with the end of the society of work. As we have seen, however, this "end" takes place under the aegis of and according to the rules of wage labor, and therefore against the background of specific relations of domination. The production of commodities thus subsumes and valorizes the emotional situation typical of nonwork. The salient characteristics of a socialization occurring outside of the workplace—a singular sense of contingency, acceptance of alienation, and direct connection to a network of possibilities—are transformed into professional qualifications, into a "toolbox." Not only does work no longer function as a surrogate for morality, but it incorporates the consequences of the dispersion of every substantial ethos. It makes explicit use of our lost familiarity with particular contexts and determinate modes of operation. In the contemporary organization of labor, even the irreversible crisis of the "work ethic" is put to use. Reduced to the logic of abstract labor, pervaded by the homogeneous and infinite time of commodities, the radical feeling of contingency manifests itself as opportunism and timeliness.

Nevertheless, and this is what counts, the emotional situation intrinsic to the end of the society of work can take on a completely different inflection. I want to be clear on this point. The ambivalence of which I am speaking cannot be examined exhaustively in its "virtuous" sense. To do so would be to misunderstand the practical character of ambivalence. It is not only a question of a new intellectual conception that reveals what already is, but of new phenomena, different forms of life, different material and cultural products. What we can do is broadly define the terms of a conceptual lexicon, circumscribe an absence, point out a chance, and indicate the "place" of something that may come. It goes without saying that in compiling an intellectual lexicon we accept the inconvenience of a certain rarefaction of discourse, a higher degree of abstraction.

More than a merely negative determination, the growing sphere of nonwork is filled with clear-cut operational criteria, with *other* forms of praxis almost completely opposed to those that operate upon commodities. It is a strip of coastline revealed in its variety and richness by the retreat of the sea. It is a fullness, a convexity. It is, above all, a place in which an activity that elides and supplants wage labor can be situated. Such activity, far from reconstituting an artisanlike rapport between concrete product and the means adopted to realize it, grants a completed form, and thus a limit, to the indefinite number of possibilities by which activity is measured time and time again.

How can this antinomy between work and activity inscribed in present-day modes of being and feeling be more completely articulated? Whereas wage labor understands the possible as a shower of atoms, infinite and indifferent, absent of any *clinamen*, the activity to which I have alluded configures the possible always and only as a possible world. A "world" is a system of correlations from which no single element can be extracted without losing its proper signification; it is a saturated and completed unity to which nothing may be added and from which nothing may be subtracted. It is a delimited whole, prerequisite and indispensable to the representation of any of its parts. A "possible world" is the proleptic correlation, the saturated unity, the delimited whole, that activity continually institutes within a chain of possibilities.

In this idea of activity there is an echo of Leibniz's conception of a single possibility comprehensible only within a complete "possible world." To this Leibnizian notion of a "possible world" it may be useful to apply the opposition, delineated by Heidegger, between "world" and "simple presence" (*Vorhandenheit*). The "world," as the essential context for belonging, is experienced before any cognitive objectification. Simple presences (*Vorhandene*) are, instead, entities or facts inasmuch as they are placed "before" the subject of representation. On this basis we can better determine the difference between work and activity with respect to their relations to opportunities and chances—decisive relations, of course, for both.

Abstract labor arranges the chain of possibilities as an infinite series of *simple possible presences*, all equivalent and interchangeable. Conversely, activity makes of the possible a concluded and finite world. It subtracts from the limitless flux of individual chances, examining each chance from the point of view of a totality of connections, from a context. This totality of connections is configured by the activity itself; it is not previously assigned to it in the manner of an exterior finality. Moreover, such a totality of connections is itself only a possibility. A "possible world," determined by nonwork as activity, is not something that can ever resolve itself in factual reality. Even were innumerable particular chances to be transmuted into "completed facts," their connection, or rather the "world" in which they inhere, would in no way lose its prerogative of being only possible. Facts themselves remain comprehended only as radical contingencies, grasped against the background of their mutability and understood in terms of the alternatives with which they remain pregnant. Neither limbo nor latency, the "possible world" does not stand waiting in the wings, aspiring to "realization." Rather, it is a real configuration of experience whose reality resides in always keeping in full view, like the scarlet letter, a sign of its own virtuality and contingency.

Exodus

We should ask again, What are the modes of being and feeling that characterize the emotional situations both of those who bow obsequiously to the status quo and of those who dream of revolt? Another answer to this question resides in the modes of being and feeling coextensive with the predominant role played by abstract knowledge, by the general intellect, in every vital context and every operation. We should recognize here, too, not only the characteristic of these modes as modalities of experience, but also their ambivalence.

I have already treated extensively the background condition of which contemporary cynicism constitutes a specific modulation. This condition involves immediate familiarity with rules, conventions, and procedures; adaptation to an essentially abstract environment; knowledge as the principle force of production; and the crisis of the principle of equivalence and the deterioration of the corresponding ideal of equality. Now, in order to illustrate the emotional situation inherent to this background condition, I must resort to a humble "parable," attributing exemplary value to this experience, in itself banal and marginal.

A person stands at the edge of the sea, intent upon nothing. He hears the sound of the waves, noisy and continuous, even though after a certain time he is no longer listening. That person perceives, but without being aware of it. The perception of the uniform motion of the waves is no longer accompanied by the perception of self as perceiving subject. This perception does not at all coincide with what in philosophical jargon is called apperception, or the consciousness of being in the act of perceiving. At the graying edge of the waves, the person standing there absorbed is one with the surrounding environment, connected by a thousand subtle and tenacious threads. This situation, however, does not pass through the filter of a self-reflexive "subject." Rather, this integration with the context is that much stronger the more the "I" forgets itself. Such an experience, however, clashes with what has become the point of honor of modern philosophy, that is to say, with the thesis that perception is inseparable from apperception, that true knowledge is only the knowledge of knowledge, that reference to something is founded upon reference to oneself. The experience of the person on the beach suggests, rather, that we belong to a world in a material and sensible manner, far more preliminary and unshakable than what seeps out from the little we know of knowledge.

This discrepancy between perception and apperception is the distinctive trait of a situation, our situation, in which, in Marx's words, "the conditions of the process of social life itself have come under the control of the general intellect and have been transformed in accordance with it" (706). The superabundance of minuscule perceptions becomes systematic in an environment of artificial actions. In a workplace dominated by information technologies, thousands of signals are received without ever being distinctly and consciously perceived. In a completely analogous way, our reception of the media does not induce concentration, but dispersion. We are crowded with impressions and images that never give rise to an "I." This surplus of unconscious perceptions is, in addition, the mark of every *uprooting* that we suffer. Exiles and emigrants, our sense of identity is bitterly tried, precisely because the flow of perceptions that never take root in the self-reflective conscience is growing disproportionately. This perceptive *surplus* constitutes, moreover, the operative way of taking one's place in an unknown environment. But uprooting no longer evokes actual exile or emigration. It constitutes, rather, an ordinary condition that everyone feels because of the continual mutation of modes of production, techniques of communication, and styles of life. Uprooting foregrounds that "hearing without listening" that for the person at the edge of the sea is a marginal phenomenon. The most immediate experience articulates itself, today, through this disproportion. But how can we conceive this experience?

Along the parabola of modern philosophy that stretches from Descartes to Hegel, only Leibniz valorizes an experience that depends on what falls outside of the self-reflective subject: "There are hundreds of indications leading us to conclude that at every moment there is in us an infinity of perceptions, unaccompanied by awareness or reflection."[3] For Leibniz, it is these "little perceptions," the opaque side of the spirit, that connect each individual to the complete life of the universe. But this is an exception. According to the model of subjectivity that has prevailed in modernity, perception is rooted in a specific environment, whereas the simultaneous, inevitable consciousness of perception (apperception) is the source of transcendence, the opening onto the universal. Perceiving myself perceiving, I look at myself in a certain sense *from outside*, from beyond the particular context in which I move about, and perhaps, from outside of being-in-context itself.

This dominant model accounts for an empirical nexus that is often not fully recognized: having particular and definite *roots*—in a place, in a tradition, in work, in a political party—not only does not present an obstacle to transcendence, but rather is the most important prerequisite of casting a detached glance "from the outside" onto one's own finite condition. Let us examine this surprising complicity more closely. The fundamental lever of every sort of transcendence is the fullness of the self-referential moment, the basic and conclusive temporal character attributed to knowing oneself while one is experiencing. Today, a similar fullness seems to be obtained when one's relationship with a context is so specific, stable, and monotonous as to be always and completely rechanneled into self-reflection and resolved in a lasting identity. This rooting, a form of univocal belonging to a particular environment, constitutes the concrete background of a harmonic unity of perception and apperception. But this unity, conferring special dignity on self-reflection, is in turn the source of transcendence, that look "from outside," and a reactionary spiritual apprenticeship, just as much as it is a source of progressive optimism.

A process of uprooting without end, engendered by the mutability of contexts marked for the most part by conventions, artifices, and abstractions, overturns this scheme and submits it to an inexorable practical critique. The concretizations of social knowledge, having become immediate if ever-changing environments, overcome the consciousness of the individual. The individual hears more than he or she listens to, and perceives more than he or she apperceives. Because today self-reflective consciousness is always in default with respect to the network of "little perceptions," it finds in them its own limit: it cannot "look from outside" at what always exceeds it. When I perceive myself perceiving, I pick up only a small part and perhaps not even the most important part of the "self that I perceive." Mobility, attenuation of memory (whether natural or traditional), shocks produced by continual innovations—we adapt to all these things today by means of "little perceptions." Consciousness of the self is always comprehended and delimited within a horizon delineated by this perceptual excess, an excess that locates us within an environment that is never "our own."

This irreparable lack of roots reshapes and circumscribes the role of self-referential subjectivity in the most severe way. Curiously, the more abstract the contexts in which we operate, the more important is our material and sensual location within them. By shrinking apperception with respect to perception, the systematic uprooting incited by the general intellect excludes access to that no-man's-land from which we might cast our gaze back at our own finite condition, like the frame a film director sees, detached and completely comprehensive. It excludes, as we have seen, that impulse toward transcendence that instead is coupled with univocal identities and solid roots.

Today's modes of being and feeling lie in an *abandonment without reserve to our own finitude*. Uprooting—the more intense and uninterrupted, the more lacking in authentic "roots"—constitutes the substance of our contingency and precariousness. The "formalization of the world" provokes an unmitigated awareness of its transitory quality. Nevertheless, abandonment to finitude is not the same as its lucid representation, as its clarification, as "looking it in the face." The conscious gaze that seeks to clarify its own limits always presupposes a margin of possible externality to the situation in which it is confined. That gaze sublimates or diminishes the evanescence of the world, and tries to overcome it.

The existential, or more generally the secular, evocation of mortal destiny remains diametrically opposed to our current sensibility, because in effect it adumbrates a radical attempt at transcendence. From the representation of mortality derives the impulse to project an "authentic life." This conscious consideration of provisionality produces "decisions," definitive identities, and fundamental choices. Death, so to speak, is put to work. Although existentialism boasts of the sober conclusions it draws from recognizing the incontrovertible state of things, in reality that incontrovertible state is appropriated as an existential "tool"; it is transcended and redeemed. Conversely, the radical abandonment to finitude that characterizes the contemporary emotional situation demands that we submit ourselves to finitude as a limit that cannot be contemplated "from outside," that is unrepresentable and thus truly untranscendable. It is an unusable limit that can be employed neither as a motivator of "decisions" nor as the skeleton of a well-structured identity.

The abandonment to finitude is inhabited by a vigorous *feeling of belonging*. This combination may seem incongruous or paradoxical. What kind of belonging could I mean, after having unrelentingly insisted upon the unexpected absence of particular and credible "roots"? True, one no longer "belongs" to a particular role, tradition, or political party. Calls for "participation" and for a "project" have faded. And yet alienation, far from eliminating the feeling of belonging, empowers it. The impossibility of securing ourselves within any durable context disproportionately increases our adherence to the most fragile instances of the "here and now." What is dazzlingly clear is finally *belonging as such*, no longer qualified by a determinate belonging "to something." Rather, the feeling of belonging has become directly proportional to the lack of a privileged and protective "to which" to belong.

It is here, in the neutral kernel of today's emotional tonality, that ambivalence once again makes its appearance. Pure belonging deprived of any "to which" can become an omnilateral and simultaneous adhesion to every present order, to all rules, to all "games." This is what happened in the 1980s. The contemporary cynic demonstrates this tendency in strategies of self-affirmation and, more often, simple social survival. Nevertheless, the feeling of belonging, once freed from all roots or any specific "to which," entertains a formidable critical and transformative potential as well.

This potential was already visible in the not-too-distant past. On more than one occasion, youth movements and new labor organizations chose defection and "exodus" over any other form of struggle. As quickly as possible, they sought to abandon their roles and throw off their oppressive chains rather than confront them openly. Along these lines of flight there began to be delineated a realm of experience felt to be their own, a "custom" that had no other foundation than the experience in which it was forged. The traditional European Left never figured out how to regard this development, so it bitterly denigrated these strategies of defection and "flight." In fact, exodus — exodus from wage labor and toward activity, for example — is not a negative gesture, exempt from action and responsibility. On the contrary, because defection modifies the conditions within which conflict takes place, rather than submit to them, it demands a particularly high level of initiative — it demands an affirmative "doing."

Today defection and exodus express the feeling of pure belonging that is typical, in Bataille's terms, of the community of all of those who have no community. Defection moves away from the dominant rules that determine individual roles and precise identities, and that surreptitiously configure the "to which" of belonging. Exodus moves toward an "accustomed place" continually reconstituted by one's own activity, an "accustomed place" that never preexists the experience that determines its location, nor that, therefore, can reflect any former habit. Today, in fact, habit has become something unusual and inhabitual, only a possible result, and never a point of departure. Exodus, therefore, points toward forms of life that give body and shape to belonging as such, and not toward new forms of life to which to belong. Exodus, perhaps, is the form of struggle best suited to demands for a radical transformation of the status quo — demands that may transform, and overthrow, the experience of the 1980s.

Opportunism, cynicism, and fear define a contemporary emotional situation marked precisely by abandonment to finitude and a *belonging to uprooting*, by resignation, servitude, and eager acquiescence. At the same time, they make that situation visible as an irreversible fact on whose basis conflict and revolt might also be conceived. We must ask whether and how signs of opposition might be discerned that reflect the same affection for the fragile "here and now" that today primarily produces opportunism and cynicism. We must ask whether and how both opposition and hope might emerge from the uprooting that has given rise to a euphoric and self-satisfied nihilism. And we must ask whether and how our relationship to changing opportunities might not be "opportunistic" and our intimacy with the rules not be "cynical." Any person who detests contemporary morality is precisely the person who will discover that every new demand for liberation can do nothing but retrace, if under an opposing banner, the paths along which the experiences of the opportunist and the cynic have already run their course.

Translated by Michael Turits

Notes

1. Aris Accornero and Fabrizio Carmignani, *I paradossi della disoccupazione* (Bologna: Il Mulino, 1986).

2. Karl Marx, *Grundrisse: Foundations of the Critique of Political Economy*, trans. Martin Nicolaus (New York: Random House, 1973), 705. Page numbers for further references to this volume appear in text in parentheses.

3. Gottfried Wilhelm Leibniz, *New Essays on Human Understanding*, trans. and ed. Peter Remnant and Jonathan Bennet (Cambridge: Cambridge University Press, 1981), 53.

THREE

Toward a Phenomenology of Opportunism

Massimo De Carolis

Those Who Can and Those Who Cannot

It is a peculiar fact that in different languages, corresponding terms can at times acquire diametrically opposed meanings. A noteworthy example is the word *self-conscious*, which corresponds exactly to the Italian *autocosciente* and which in every-day American English functions as a synonym for *awkward* or *unnatural*. For a European with some philosophical background, this coincidence cannot but have a certain impact, given that our tradition from Descartes to Hegel has always found in self-consciousness (*autocoscienza*) not only the apex of spirituality, but the premise of that reflective attitude that presides over every free and responsible action. Conversely, for the average American, behavior that is free is before all else *unself-conscious*, that is, unconstrained, unreflective, natural. This idea of a spontaneity that coincides with unself-consciousness may not at first glance seem very interesting, or, at most, may simply indicate Americans' scarce propensity for reflection, their proverbial pragmatism. On further consideration, however, it soon becomes obvious that even among us Europeans a certain ideal has begun to emerge, if only in subterranean form: the ideal of behavior that is free because it is confident and unconstrained, an agile and effortless movement about the world, an ideal that is the antithesis of traditional models of freedom and responsibility based, by contrast, on a reflective consciousness of one's own roles and ideals. One example that is particularly apt, because of the very terms in which it is expressed, may be the way in which in the feminist movement the ideal and practice of consciousness-raising, or self-consciousness, has clearly lost prominence, while a thematics of comfort and ease has been increasingly affirmed. In a more general sense, however, an analogous tendency can be found in the social strata that until recently stood at the center of the great mass political movements: the desire to make oneself a subject, to acquire full consciousness of one's own identity, has been replaced by the need to insert oneself successfully into social structures, even at the cost of rendering identity fluid, malleable, and elusive.

In its current form, this tendency has been judged and rejected primarily as the appearance of widespread *opportunism*. In theory, such a definition is fundamentally irrefutable: What else is opportunism if not the flexible adaptation of one's own identity to continually changing circumstances? The label of opportunism, however, does not succeed in grasping the problem. This becomes obvious when we consider a fact that at first glance may seem surprising: that today's so-called opportunism seems to be spreading with particular force throughout the same social strata and groups that in decades past voiced demands for radical ethical and political change. In broad terms, in other words, opportunism is spreading primarily among the mass intelligentsia of large urban centers. Naturally, this fact can be explained in sociological terms by the drastic transformation of the productive system imposed by modern technologies, the growing conditions of alienation and isolation marking emerging social structures, and the crisis of the major ideologies that this transformation has brought about. Still, it seems unlikely that even this rapid a historical process could so quickly have eradicated ethical principles that seemed unquestionably alive and profound until a few years ago. The possibility exists, absurd as it may sound, that today's opportunistic tendencies are fundamentally propelled and motivated by *these very same radical demands*, and exactly for this reason they are asserting themselves primarily among the social subjects most prone to them. To what extent is this possibility reinforced by the fact, as we have just seen, that there runs through opportunism some kind of a need for freedom, and thus for something that in every modern society is a fundamental goal and supreme ethical value? What can opportunism have to do with an ethical demand? Can opportunism teach us something about freedom and its relation to self-consciousness?

In our European philosophical tradition, freedom has always been conceived above all as *autonomy*: autonomy from every influence and every external constriction and, at the same time, autonomy from every passion and natural inclination. It should come as no surprise, therefore, that self-consciousness and reflection figure in this model as the greatest guarantees of freedom. Only the pure rational subject is free, the subject that gives its own law to itself and remains alien to every involvement and form of abandonment to the world. A substantial *detachment from the world* figures in this picture as the most obvious corollary to freedom, whether the freedom of an individual, a group, or an entire nation. It is only in establishing a rigid separation between *self* and *other* that full identity and self-mastery, and along with them true autonomy, can be attained.

This necessity of separating oneself, locating oneself elsewhere, has been strong in all movements of liberation, alongside the need to affirm a consciousness of one's self. This is not at all to say that this conception actually succeeds in fully articulating the demands and requirements implicit in the idea of freedom. To reach the opposite conclusion, one need only think about the current everyday meaning of the word *free*. In everyday language, being free means having at one's disposal particular concrete possibilities, possessing the power and the actual ability to complete or not to complete particular actions. Such power, however, requires participation in the world, an intimacy with the context of one's actions that turns into familiarity and then into the effective capacity to act. To learn to swim you cannot be afraid to jump into the water, to gain political power you have to be part of public life, and so forth. In direct contrast to the idea of autonomy, this concept of freedom as practical power (*potentia*, or possibility) finally tends to suppress every detachment, confuse in a more or less profound way the subject and the environment, and dignify the interaction with the world without which, by definition, practical power cannot exist. According to this definition, someone is free who possesses the ability, the competence, or simply the good fortune to be able to recognize and exploit the innumerable chances offered by the world. Every opportunistic tendency in the modern world is motivated, in the final instance, by the will to *belong* to one's own world, to move through it like a fish through water, and it is exactly *this* idea of freedom that is expressed in the American glorification of *unself-consciousness*. A natural, unreflective detachment in action is in fact the clearest sign of an effective mastery of the means at one's disposal—perhaps the most ancient mark of those who can.

Although, at least superficially, struggles for autonomy seem today to have regained a certain political currency, there are good reasons to suppose that in contemporary society the ideal of freedom as practical power is destined to acquire an ever greater dominance over the ideal of freedom as autonomy. In the first place, at least in Western countries, the autonomy and independence of diverse social groups have become increasingly less an issue the more the strong and well-defined cultural identities on which past demands for autonomy were based have tended to dissolve into a general and *intransitive uniformity* in which such demands are out of place from the start. At the same time, the growing complexity of society has ensured that a condition of detachment and isolation appears not only unrealistic, but above all highly undesirable because of its coincidence with an objective condition of marginalization. Above all, however, technical and social development has given a completely new meaning to the question of the possible. The number of possibilities, the number of *chances* offered by the modern world, is growing disproportionately. Access to these possibilities, however, is ever less guaranteed and demands on the contrary—time after time and in ever-growing amounts—wealth, competence, preparation, and other particular qualities. In other words, *access to possibilities is reserved for those who can, and thus in practice, for those who already have it.*

The eternal conflict between those who have power and those who do not thus assumes the form of a fundamental opposition between *those who can* and *those who cannot*—a much more fractured arrangement that takes on different contours in every social sector and, above all, invests not only the political sphere but society as a whole. It must be emphasized, however, that this conflict is particularly contorted, because *the possible* is by nature a self-reflective concept that aims at and presupposes only itself.

In part we have already seen how possibility presupposes itself in that it is granted only to those who already possess it. Whoever is instead excluded, even if only slightly, from access to possibilities is pushed with ever greater force to the margins of social interaction. Even maintaining old possibilities becomes ever more exhausting, until the very *will* to halt this process fades away. In contrast to those who simply lack power—and for this reason *want* it—those who cannot become attached to their own impotence as a particular identity, as a particular niche. This is what distinguishes the defeated and socially marginalized of today from the oppressed masses of epochs past, who were ever anxious for revolt and redemption. The possible aims at nothing but itself. Freedom constitutes, in fact, in modern society, the ultimate ethical value. Once it is translated into practical power or possibility, no criterion for measuring the success of an action can exist but the accumulation of ever greater potential. In other words, access to the possible aims at nothing but opening up new possibilities ad infinitum. Forms of behavior such as opportunism and cynicism derive from this infinite process in which the world becomes no more than a supermarket of opportunities empty of all inherent value, yet marked by the fear that any false move may set in motion a vortex of impotence.

There is no reason to conceal the unhappiness and suffering implicit in this abandonment to the possible; it is just as fruitless to apologize thoughtlessly for this new opportunistic scenario as it is to condemn it hastily. We must admit, however, that the self-reflectiveness of the figures of the opportunist and the cynic is a real problem — not just a case of false consciousness — and that the modern world has only brought to light a contradiction that has always been internal to our culture, in which the possible has systematically and hastily deferred to the real. Appealing again to the ethical principle of self-consciousness risks merely displacing the problem. It is within the experience of the possible itself, within its labyrinthine twists and turns, that a new strategy and a new demand for salvation must be sought. For this reason, the concrete figures that combine demands for freedom and participation in the world with unself-consciousness and renunciation should be watched with an attentive and unprejudiced eye. In their ambiguity is expressed the self-reflexivity of practical power, the key to all its contradictions. We must determine whether this self-reflexive structure does not conceal within itself a radical demand for salvation, an extreme possibility that, once expressed, might put an end to the vacuity of chances and redeem those who cannot from impotence. For this reason, contemporary critical thought cannot exempt itself from the task of a *phenomenology of opportunism*.

Opportunism and Fear

Opportunism is a style of life that conditions not only relations with the external world, but also the most intimate and private states of mind. Drawing even a rough map of the emotions and sentiments typical of opportunism demands that we first distinguish between two of its varieties that are often confused. On one side, there is the opportunism traditionally associated with dominating, sovereign power: the Machiavellian art of the prince who knows how to manipulate the rules of the game, who can bend to his or her advantage what to others seem like universal and necessary laws. There prevails in the emotional background of this figure the ancient quality of *hubris* — the arrogance of trying to derail the natural course of things — which vies with *melancholy* for a world reduced to pure instrumentality, a plaything without weight or consistency. Beside this sovereign opportunism there has always existed, however, the opportunism of the disinherited, those without defense or protection who are caught in a web of opportunities and assaulted from every angle, forced to improvise a defense, to squeeze through the links of destiny in search of some escape route. Notwithstanding its plebeian connotation, this second attitude can boast of a no less ancient, and in its own way no less noble, tradition than the first. The first theorists of opportunism, the Sophists of ancient Greece, were usually exiles deprived of every right of citizenship, hobos of knowledge hunted by the law and institutions. Diogenes, the founder of ancient cynicism, personally knew both exile and slavery. It is said, in fact, that Diogenes conceived his doctrine while observing the course of a mouse, admiring the animal's blind ability to take advantage of every opportunity for salvation—an illuminating comparison that demonstrates how the dominant sentiment in this second type of opportunism is none other than *fear*, the anxiety of an animal in flight.

Of these two figures, the second has for quite a while been the more timely. Although the ancient arrogance of the prince has today disappeared into the Buddha-like countenance of some half-smiling State bureaucrat, the binomial of opportunism and fear has come to life again in the precariousness, the permanent tension, and the wilderness of unpredictable chances that, particularly in large cities, defines the everyday lives of thousands of people. This does not lessen the fact, however, that between these two figures there exists a whole range of hybrids and connections. Fear compels the imitation of power, which in turn, behind the patina of its arrogance, conceals the anguish of a rabbit caught in a trap. There is a methodological reason, however, for insisting on the distinction. What unites opportunists of every type and species is their opposition to people of principle, those moral individuals who direct their actions toward projects and ideals of a greater scope and who affirm in this way their autonomy from the ephemeral opportunities of the moment. Now, it would be a case not only of opportunism but of bad taste if we were to misconstrue the ethical dignity of this figure and dismiss with a simple shrug of our shoulders the entire tradition of morality. It would also be too simple, however, to embrace this tradition obtusely, ignoring the unease and the crisis that for decades has shaken its foundation. According to our hypothesis, the fulcrum of this moral crisis is the idea of detachment from the world implicit in the traditional model of morality. This idea is *also* presupposed in sovereign opportunism. Only on the basis of such a detachment from the world can sovereign opportunism become an instrument that is controllable and manipulable at will. Rather than an alternative to morality, the arrogance of the prince represents morality's own will to autonomy, if in an inconsistent and parodistic form, destined *a fortiori* to succumb to the very same crisis. If, therefore, the goal of our reflections is to discover some sign indicating a way out of this crisis, the sparse remains of sovereign opportunism have little to offer. The question is, rather, What does *fear* have to teach us?

A good way of approaching the problem may be to reexamine the distinction between anxiety (*Angst*) and fear (*Furcht*) proposed by Heidegger and later taken up by all existentialist literature. It is significant that this entire tradition assigned to the experience of anxiety a specific ontological value, but only on the condition that it be distinguished from the simple fear of a concrete and particular threat. Nothing demonstrates the break between our own historical situation and even our recent past better than the reversal of this relationship. Today we are instead compelled to recognize in fear a concrete exemplarity, and the anxiety described by writers such as Sartre and Camus at times seems like a literary fiction never confirmed in our actual existence. From the existentialist point of view, anxiety is not oriented toward a concrete danger, but rather reveals the constitutive finitude of the existence into which we are thrown. It is always, in other words, an anxiety before Nothingness in which the entire world suddenly seems deprived of sense, wrapped in a veil that forbids our access. Anxiety confines the subject to a metaphysical elsewhere, rendering him or her extraneous, indifferent even to the concrete dangers that arise within the world. From the experience of anxiety one thus gains a greater capacity for resisting real danger, a type of shield against fear. Confined in his or her elsewhere, the anxious subject looks almost with indifference at horrors and threats too extraneous and profane to incite apprehension. On close inspection, therefore, it seems that in anxiety there is reestablished the superior detachment, the autonomy with respect to the course of the world, that has always stood at the foundation of a moral outlook. It is thus more than understandable why in the past anxiety was presented as the irrefutable threshold of an authentic and complete existence.

Precisely this protective location elsewhere is what is lacking in simple fear. In fact, not only does fear arise before some particular thing, but—according to Freud—before some familiar and accustomed thing (in German, something *heimlich*) that suddenly appears menacing and disturbing (*unheimlich*) without, however, ever ceasing ineluctably to pertain to everyday experience. Fear does not revolutionize experience, it only renders it uncertain and precarious. We are not made more resistant by fear, but infinitely more fragile and insecure before real dangers. Rather than feeling extraneous to the world, the person who fears recognizes him- or herself irrevocably immersed in the world, exposed and without refuge from its dangers. Because what we fear never ceases to be part of the most common and vulgar everyday experience, we manage to live with its threat, but without pretense and with no illusions about reaching some richer and more authentic experience.

In other words, at the base of fear lies the experience of being fully and irremediably exposed to the world. For a phenomenology of opportunism it is crucial to realize the *critical* potential of this experience. Forgoing any possible appeal to an elsewhere, such an experience dismantles at the outset the myth of a pure subject, the myth that supported both the moral individual's need for autonomy and the will to power expressed by sovereign opportunism. More profound still, however, the experience of fear unhinges the opposition between those who can and those who cannot from which modern opportunism derives its reason for being. In fear these two groups are objectively united, driven to recognize in each other their own specular images. This happens, however, not only in the sense of a negative fraternization around a common anxiety. What is more important is that from this reciprocal recognition the fundamental demand for participation and access to the possible gets pushed toward some new resolution. Neither escape into one's own impotence nor passive abandonment to the marketplace of undifferentiated chances can address the most pressing concerns of the person who lives in fear: how to reestablish a relationship of familiarity with a world now laced with danger, how to render *heimlich* what has already become *unheimlich*.

In ancient times, questions of this nature were entrusted to a special type of wisdom directed not at establishing universal laws, but at discovering the sense of what is accidental, material, and unrepeatable. This practical wisdom was often represented in animal form — as a mouse or an octopus. The hunted animal must, in order to save itself, extend its knowledge, learn to recognize traces, paths, escape routes. What is revived in the opportunist is therefore precisely this *animal* knowledge, a knowledge of the senses and not the intellect, constructed from subtleties of color, sound, and odor. Like a connoisseur of wines, the opportunist must learn to distinguish and conjecture only a possible signification. Were the moral individual one evening to allow him- or herself to be led by the opportunist into the metropolitan labyrinth of chances, he or she would discover there an unknown universe of hints, signs, and wisdoms. It is not only aesthetic appreciation, however, that confers on this world a special power of fascination. In reality, without getting this close to things, without being schooled in the tactile and the olfactory, we will never be able to reinsert ourselves into the world and, in this way, to stop being afraid.

The World Turned Environment

At the outset of this essay, I advanced the seemingly paradoxical hypothesis that contemporary opportunism is born from the very same radical demands that in the past translated into ethical and political engagement. Naturally, this implies an internal transformation and at least in part a reshaping of these demands. It is undeniable as well that a decisive push in this direction has been provided by the outcomes of recent social struggles, which have seemed to imply the failure of every proposal for radical change. It would be simplistic, however, to try to explain everything as the inevitable disenchantment of defeat. The observations made thus far have shown in a sufficient way, I believe, that adjacent to this negative aspect there is a positive one. If the idealistic goals of the 1960s and 1970s have undergone a drastic transformation, this is due above all to the fact that the way they were originally expressed now appears partial and inadequate *independent* of their eventual political failure or success. It is not because of a defeat, but because of its own internal logic that the desire for freedom has now brought to light the problem of practical power along with a new will to belong to one's world. It is not only to adapt to a context become static and impoverished that the call for salvation—once aimed at broad programs of political revolution—is measured today by the need to grant fullness to contemporary ways of life that would otherwise be condemned to being no more than instruments for the realization of some possible future.

This is not to say that this change in mentality does not imply a change in the actual conditions of existence; it is precisely in the experience of fear that the traces of such a transformation become visible. In this experience there is implicit a sort of contradiction. The world that surrounds me appears extraneous, inimical. And yet I feel myself ineluctably assigned to this same world, with room neither to move nor to escape. It is easy to see that this contradiction is typical of contemporary opportunism as I have described it, from the moment that the demand for belonging is addressed to *that same world* whose radical, threatening extraneousness has already been felt. This interlacing of extraneousness and belonging is unthinkable within a traditional social order in which *on one side* lies the ethical community of which I feel myself an integral part and that therefore surrounds me like a protective shell, and *on the other side* lies the environment external to this shell, at times sublime, at times menacing, but always obviously and naturally extraneous. The clear and precise distinction between these two regions—which was marked in an exemplary way by the walls of the ancient city—was a fundamental requirement of every social subject in the past, as well as for communities, classes, and groups whose borders did not coincide with those of political society. It is clear, for example, that the ascendancy of autonomy within the liberation movements implied an analogous requirement and sought to institute within a *single* social system a precise border between an inside and an outside, between the horizon proper to a particular community (determined by specific codes of belonging) and the rest of the social system, which was effectively reduced to being a simple environment. One of the most incisive effects of recent technological development has been to subvert this distinction between community and environment—first by rendering ever weaker the ties of the community, then by colonizing the environment in an ever more massive way, and finally by generating theoretical and practical paradigms capable of being applied indiscriminately to social reality no less than to the environment, that is, to nature.

Nothing is more revealing of this process than the speed and success with which the concept of the *Umwelt*—literally, the world-environment—has emerged from the biological context in which it was originally conceived to acquire a prominent role in the human sciences, philosophy, and even the contemporary political debate. What is expressed here is the decisive fact that *the world is now for us only an environment*, something beyond any distinction between internal and external, culture and nature. In this synthetic formula we seek to combine a complex network of historical transformations, relatively independent from each other but in fact connected at an objective level, that are contributing to changing the relationship between human beings and the world in a particular way. A full understanding of the weight and sense of these transformations is particularly difficult to achieve, because we are dealing with processes that are far from complete. Still, their general description, if only approximate and provisional, is completely indispensable because it is precisely in this network of transformations that we find the *historical* index from which contemporary opportunism derives both its direction and its timeliness.

The first aspect of this reduction of world to environment that we can point out at the level of social existence is the progressive *dissolution of traditional ethics*—that is, the web of habits, beliefs, and values that in the past directly permeated every individual by the sole fact of his or her belonging to a particular society: a collection of cultural acquisitions, in other words, that constituted a second nature no more easily shed than one's own skin. Today, in a world turned environment, this immediate adhesion to the community is prevented by the simple fact that an indefinite number of communities with different traditions and origins are forced to coexist and interact in an ever closer way within the apparatus of the mass media, which for its part can function only on the condition that it neutralize traditional values and codes. I should note in passing that this unhinging of every concrete ethics forms the basis for today's global extension of the dominant systems of practice, from the international market to the worldwide information system to the technico-scientific exploitation of natural resources. The most immediate and obvious consequence of this process at the existential level is the liquidation of every authentic experience of *exoticism* — that is, of every direct confrontation with a full and concrete alterity — from the moment that access to every phenomenon is mediated and guaranteed by the same apparatuses, independent of geographic or cultural distance. Moreover, the fact that the entire earth constitutes an environment in no way reconstitutes the sense of an intimate belonging to the world that derived from traditional ethics. It is true that the communications apparatuses that structure contemporary experience possess their own codes and functions. For the most part, however, these are not *ethical* principles but simply *functional rules*. They demand no identification from the individual, only adaptation, and exhibit in clear terms their own status as *contingent possibilities*, indicating the modes and conditions of their own eventual revision (just as every legitimate scientific theory is held to indicate the conditions under which it can be falsified).

Although these mass apparatuses prestructure and orient the action of individuals in a no less profound way than traditional ethical systems, they remain something contingent and *extraneous* into which the individual feels him- or herself irremediably thrown, but without any particular sense of belonging, just as a species of animal is assigned to its environment by biological destiny, but without any moral solidarity. It is for this reason — and not because of any resurgence of nineteenth-century biologism — that contemporary opportunism continually invokes animalistic images and metaphors.

This apparent naturalization of the social environment constitutes, however, only one side of the process I am describing. The opposite side is nature itself, which, becoming environment, radically changes its mode of being. On the basis of the ancient conception of practice as the realm of the *possible*, nature — as the realm of necessity — in the past always had the value of a presupposition or a frame, a *limit* to human action. This does not mean that a natural phenomenon could not be comprehended, investigated, and eventually exploited by humans. Its naturalness, however, referred in every instance to a necessary structure, to a *given fact* independent of any possible external interaction. The transformation of nature into environment implies the dissolution of this factuality, as much at the level of scientific theory as at the level of technical practice. In principle, therefore, every given fact comes to be conceived as a *possibility*, whose subsistence depends on a complex network of interactions with an entire system of other contingencies and on the basis of rules that are in turn themselves completely contingent and revisable under determinate conditions. Not only, therefore, is it in principle almost always possible to intervene in a practical way in this network of possibilities, but the intervention of humanity or reason now ceases to appear as a sort of invasion from the outside that must be legitimated. When human action itself becomes just one possibility among others, and as such always already forms part of the network of interactions in which it operates, it shares that network's rules and modes of being and becomes substantially indistinguishable from it at the ontological level.

Alongside the contradictory dialectic between extraneousness and belonging to the world, the second decisive trait of opportunism—the dominance of the possible over every factual necessity and thus over every absolute principle—reveals itself as deriving from a specific historical scenario. In its individual traits opportunism may sometimes reproduce models of behavior as old as humanity, but in its comprehensive *sense* it is something absolutely new, something that can be adequately comprehended and evaluated only in relation to historical transformations incisive enough to make useless the paradigms that once seemed irrefutable and secure. From this perspective, the ambiguities and contradictions of opportunism take on the value of a litmus test for a series of questions that none of us can view with indifference. What is the best way to live in a world turned environment, a world in which everything shuffles along as a mere possibility, intimately familiar and yet threateningly extraneous at the same time? What possibilities and strategies can be found in this world that will satisfy the most profound and authentic demands of human beings? And finally, what particular form can these demands assume in a world so radically transformed?

Possibility and Power

In our cultural tradition the experience of the *possible* has always had a subordinate value, both from the point of view of common sense—*factual reality* has always been the only thing that truly counts for common sense—and at the level of morality and science, united in their veneration of the *necessity* expressed by laws. The most incisive expression of the historical rupture that marks our era may be the reversal of this subordination, a reversal that tends to make possibility the dominant category of every fundamental sphere of existence. Thus in the sciences, the necessary now presents itself as the limit-case of the possible and the concept of law itself is redefined in terms of *probability*. Analogously, on the psychological level, the experience of factual reality is revealed as a secondary construction that emerges from the projection and selection of possibilities. Ultimately, the very principles of practical action acquire the status of rules for a variety of games in which it is always possible, in theory, to identify a metarule that suspends or changes the rules in force. What rules the possible is in turn a possibility, a contingency, and so on and so forth, an infinite chain that in principle will never discover its necessary end or foundation. In short, as the first theoreticians of nihilism rightly intuited, the most disturbing experience of the contemporary era is that *everything has become possible,* where the emphasis, however, falls not on the *everything,* but rather on the character of nonnecessity or contingency into which everything has collapsed.

In this menacing sea of possibilities, opportunism is an instinctive and at bottom naive attempt to navigate by simply following the current, knowing full well that no land is in sight and thus that staying afloat matters more than maintaining a precise course. But what does staying afloat really mean? Or rather, metaphors aside, what does the opportunist really *want*? It would be remarkably naive to take literally the concrete goals of opportunistic behavior in any given instance. Money, success, in extreme cases survival—whether one is aware of it or not, none of these objectives is desired in itself. Their positive value is once more not a necessary and objective given fact, but precisely a contingency, an option selected on a case-by-case basis from a network of circumstances and purely conventional rules. To these rules the opportunist adapts without resistance, but with instinctive awareness of their conventionality and contingency. In other words, a true opportunist cannot believe in the value of money, power, or success any more than he or she can really believe in a political ideal or moral principle. In either case it is just a question of opportunities, evanescent and provisional chances about which it would make no sense to become too impassioned. Desire and passion, in this scenario, know only two possible objects, both of which came up at least partly earlier in these reflections: on one hand, *the rules themselves* in their abstract and formal beauty, in their capacity to assume a new form in every new game, to give birth to a logical and coherent order amid the most chaotic movement, and to redistinguish each time the winning and virtuous moves from the rough and the inopportune; on the other hand, the *singular experience in its concrete materiality,* freed henceforth from any subordination to presumed universal principles and thus able to express and vindicate its own irreducible fullness. These, then, definitively, are the new demands that today find their expression in opportunism, even if, as it is easy to see, in a form that is instinctive, unreflective, and inevitably condemned to failure.

Sooner or later, in fact, every opportunist is destined to the bitter discovery that simply following the current will not suffice to keep either of these passions afloat. The reason for this insufficiency lies, in the final analysis, in the self-reflective structure of possibility from which, as we know, contemporary opportunism draws its reason for being. As I have already indicated, in a world in which everything is possible the efficacy and value of any possibility can be measured only according to the new possibilities that it opens up, and thus according to the *quantum* of potential or power that it is able to produce. This calculation, which reduces every experience to a simple *opportunity for the increase of potential*, is in principle always possible and always maintains the same formal structure, whatever the internal rules of an individual game or context of action may be. On top of these rules is inevitably superimposed a *universal metacode of potential* of a purely abstract and formal nature, substantially indifferent as much to material content as to the internal forms and functions of individual fields of actions, and thus profoundly extraneous to both of the passions that animate the opportunist. Nevertheless, the abstract universality of this code renders it particularly adept at regulating and structuring the mass communication structures of a world turned environment. The more, therefore, that the world of experience is permeated and dominated by these structures, the more the dominant current flows in a direction precisely opposite to the radical demands to which opportunism gives expression. Its brilliant capacity for exploiting every rule and the tiniest variant of any given game gets buried by the brutal simplicity of the universal mechanisms of power. Its instinctive openness to the concrete materiality of every individual occasion becomes no more than a useless archaism in an environment completely dematerialized and rendered inaccessible to every kind of sensibility.

Between the new radical demands that lie at the bottom of opportunism and the code of potential or power that no opportunist can escape, there inevitably arises a conflictual tension. This tension is all the more ambiguous and complex given that in the final analysis the two poles of the conflict are rooted in the same soil: the primacy of the possible in a world turned environment. Within this tension the opportunist remains captured in a sort of double bind: either bend to the prevailing current, renounce your passions, and become just a dull administrator of sovereign power — which implies, on the existential level, a failure deprived of any acceptable compensation — or remain faithful to your passions, *resist* the current, and effectively abandon your opportunistic propensity. In either case, the tension will be resolved only when opportunism yields to a new figure.

For its part, critical thought can have no other interest than to radicalize this tension and transform ambivalence into open conflict. Such an operation cannot take place from the outside, however, but must respond to the internal development of the figures in question, assembling the demands and tensions they express. This is the only way to avoid confining these phenomena to a conventional scheme, far from the reality of things. This is the only way, above all, to pose adequately the crucial question of the relationship between ethics and politics, to ask oneself, in other words, whether in their current form such radical demands may be translated into a new kind of politics, or whether instead their most authentic expression is destined to be located elsewhere, in a space that politics can never reach. This is a theoretical task that demands reflection and awareness. Theory will go nowhere, however, unless it stays in touch with the forms of life in which this question demonstrates its complexity and urgency.

Translated by Michael Turits

F O U R

Weak Thought between Being and Difference

Adelino Zanini

Condition and Ideology

The appearance of a "minimalist" or "weak" thought in Italy cannot be attributed to a will, but rather should be recognized as the fruit of a social condition. That is why it is so difficult to talk about it. What is chosen for it often does not belong to it, and what is proper to it is only the caricatural aspect—an ugly frame surrounding a tragic pseudorepresentation. Weak thought cannot be brought back to a single "site" of philosophical reflection, in any case, however often it touches base there. The modern condition has exhausted an expansive cycle of thought. Any philosophical project that has sought some form of human liberation from limitation has had to confront a double crisis: on one hand, the ungovernability of the object that it helped create, and on the other hand, the insubordination of the subjects that often have anticipated its development. Thus the more the modern condition has expressed a high level of socialization and rationalization, the more it has generated "sites" of difference, which have withered not due to any conditions but due to relations—not with respect to the power that constitutes them, but with respect to the power that dominates them. On the other hand, then, in this residual formation and this multiplication of powers, the completion of the cycle is transformed into a continual deferral. The modern is a constant residue of being, and difference expresses power and generates history as residue.

Effectively, between Nietzsche and Heidegger the completion of the modern philosophical project seemed definitively confirmed, while it had been led outside of any dialectic. In fact, what was confirmed was not any phenomenological and existentialist humanism, but precisely *being as deferral*. In a general sense, what Bataille said about the relation between Nietzsche and communism referred to this same paradox: tragedy can be *mine*, but only communism has continued to be able to formulate the problem of the object and the subject as *our* problem. In other words, postmodern ideology is entirely prefigured in the impossible completion of the modern. As such, it is certainly more properly understood as an ambiguous condition than as an ideology. We should not assume, however, that such a condition is adequately expressed or expressible in terms of "weak" or "soft" thought.

This ambiguity came to the fore in Italian philosophical thought in the 1980s. It expressed above all a singular situation: perhaps no other European society in recent history has been so conflictual as Italian society in the 1970s, and no other society has given expression to such a radical theory of social change, centered on the demand for communism as a minimum objective. In the same way, precisely in Italy the "weakness" of thought has gone beyond the condition, even the tragic condition, of the defeat of social struggles. The condition has become an ideology, and in response to the effective and total transparency of domination in society there is only the sentiment of disenchantment. They say, then, *amor fati*— that is, what appears no longer has anything "proper," to it, or rather, everything "proper," while it inheres to a subject, represents in a reactive way every "presence." Better and more clearly, we may say that this is a way of "adjusting to the times."

Metaphysical Clarity and Domination

Why is it that the "renunciation of foundation" (the lack of foundation and at the same time the breaking through of the foundation) takes away the possibility of an "other" foundation? Nietzsche would say that it is thus with God and Man; Heidegger would say it is thus with being as foundation of the existent; Wittgenstein would say it is thus with sign and sense. No "weakness," however, is implicit in all this. "This-thus" excludes an "other-than"—with respect to what follows, however, there is no "softness." Naturally, nonetheless, "weak" thought boasts its reasons. A knowledge without foundations seems to it a knowledge that can always be nostalgic for reason. In this sense, the considerations developed on the terrain of the so-called crisis of reason do not seem sufficient for weak thought to exorcise the presumed specter of the irrational. Pretending to "save" an "other" reason, they do not conduct any renunciation of foundation. In Nietzsche, for example, an equivalent rationalizer dissolves his or her own figure. But what follows can take much weaker forms—a poetizing thought, caught between aesthetics and rhetoric.[1]

Gianni Vattimo reminds us that the dialectical critiques of the twentieth century, basing themselves on Marxian thought, have both completed the dialectic and produced its own dissolution. Precisely at the point where humanity has reached its summit, there its human dignity is complete—in other words, finished. Every feeling of redemption, every historical rationality, every teleology is complete. The mystery of the dialectical *aufhebung* has definitively realized a static state of being in its modern will to redemption. Modernity and historicity constitute the cradle in which every *subjectum* has pretended to master the world; the failure of every governed history, in which the resentment of the subject is nothing but a reactive spirit, has testified to the fact that this cannot be true. Vattimo argues that any attempt to restore this *hypokeimenon*—that is, the subject and the truth-foundation—is blind to the fact that the postmodern condition is a condition of "the end of history." The decline of the West is not only a romantic myth. It sanctions the loss of the unity of the human narrative and it exhausts the time gauged according to a *Prinzip Hoffnung*.

This is the danger that weak thought warns against: seeking to reestablish the progressive and enlightening unity of the human narrative, seeking to reestablish being and thus the subject and thus metaphysics. Hence they have recourse to *difference*, and that is, following Heidegger, the ontological difference between being and the existent. Being is not, it occurs, temporally. Toward being we grasp a recognition that is always a leave-taking. According to the Heideggerian *Verwindung*, this is a going beyond that is proper to being, a kind of "taking up again." There is no presence to being, but only a remembrance. Thinking being is thinking the canon, not the exception or the illumination. No *Grund*, no ground assures any reason, no recovery from an illness, but rather the assumption of a destiny, which is really a taking up again of destiny. With respect to being as remembrance, *pietas* (not recovery) is the adequate attitude of decay, confirming the decay of being and its becoming "thinner." With this recognition, it seems, the dialectic and difference are brought together as "weak thought."

Here, on the other hand, is where we find the strict relationship between metaphysical clarity and domination. There is war, exploitation—so why bother denying it? In the metaphysical clarity domination is explicit, but it does not lead to a redemption of being, always and simply leading toward a diverse that is finally the same: submissive alienation, ignorant degradation, implicit domination.

The world is not demystified. We adopt rather a more friendly attitude toward appearance, *Lichtung*. A hermeneutic becomes possible that proceeds according to the simple traces in the remembrance of being. *An-danken* and *Berwindung* are seen as openings for history and destiny, and thus weak ontology becomes hermeneutics.

It would be useless to speak of the violation of reason, or of lost rationality, or a silenced history, but why not? It is perhaps better to speak of a poetizing and redundant "breaking through." Nonetheless, why should there be *this* weakness in the act of remembrance? That being is not but that it rather occurs is a subtle distinction, but why should it be "weak"? Consider the following exchange in Wim Wenders's film *Kings of the Road* (Im Lauf der Zeit):

> *"Who are you?"*
> *"I am a pederast."*
> *"I didn't ask you for your history."*
> *"But I am my history."*

And yet there is no weakness in this history, not because "everything as to be changed" (while the totality is not given) but rather because the tragedy belongs to me in this body that is not "humanistically" displayed. On the other hand, it is not the "weakness" that shows me that it belongs to me, but its tragic character. One has the impression that there is an aesthetics of the tragic (which Jean-François Lyotard, who is a reference point for weak thought, describes best), and that there is an ethics of the tragic, which, however, is strong, certainly not an "almost nothing." The relationship between being and difference is all played out here. Being is power precisely because it can occur; it is not withering because it has occurred but strong because it is ungraspable. Here postmodern ideology has nothing to say: the condition humiliates the ideology, even without any transcendental *Diskurs*.

Once Again: Being and Difference

Should Deleuze and Foucault be considered nostalgic for metaphysics simply for the fact that they do not reach the forgetting of being? This is the charge that "weak thought" levels against them. The glorification of simulacra and "disqualified" powers—there is truth in it but not metaphysics, or rather not more than elsewhere. What is this surpassing, this rewritten language, if it is not also a simulacrum? And it is a simulacrum of being because since it continues to do metaphysics. What Deleuze and Foucault have shown, rather, is the unforgettable character of being, which occurs because it suffers, because the deployments that support it are historically embodied. There is a small difference, however, in that the instance proper to destiny is given, here and now, as a tragedy. This is so not so much because being is a withered, impalpable presence, but because it is an entity whose suffering forms the world. In this sense, it cannot not occur. It should not be considered "weak" for its occurring, but rather it occurs because in its occurring resides its tragic character. In other words, it seems to me that both Deleuze and Foucault demonstrate the trick implicit in the omnipotence of the Cartesian *cogito*, without making it, however, a smoke screen. It is useless to vent one's furies on the question of the determinability of the subject. No one really believes any longer in the mise-en-scène of any omnipotence whatsoever. If there is a truly totalitarian (albeit illusory) determination of "presence," it is given as a pure dimension of the domination over subjects—and with respect to "resentment" the roles are completely reversed. It seems to me, in short, that the point of attack can easily become a pretext. This, obviously, is also true in the converse: it would be irreverent to be blind to the difference that separates the respective reflections of Deleuze and Foucault from any philosophy of the subject. It would be irreverent to try to construct, *with them*, an "other" philosophy of subjects. There is no simulation of positive freedom, but there is the expression of communities that have subtracted themselves as becomings: lines of flight rather than contradictions, a "whatever" being, we could say, if that really holds for the community of those without community.[2] Toni Negri is thus right to look for a tragic element in Deleuze and Guattari's *A Thousand Plateaus*.[3]

This is, then, the contemporary tragic condition of the subject, or rather its contingency. *Here* is where being occurs, but because its suffering does not exhaust time, it makes it into a duration. An aesthetics of tragedy the results of which could become paradoxical is not far from "weak thought." The difference that expresses the power engendered by history only as residue, an aesthetics of tragedy, instead *completes time*, because it emphasizes the weakness, not the tragedy, of the contingency. What cannot be determined positively about this contingency is its cause, and thus it seems to have no redemption. It is simply the expression of an imperfect being, a collective body tragically displayed. Its aesthetics, insofar as it fixes its goal in the image of the completion of time, dissolves time: being occurs in nothingness. It seems instead essential to think of the contingent not as a tragic image, an instant that dissolves time, but as tragic duration, which is linked as much as possible to the safeguard of a memory of the future. Ethics can be a memory of the future: a community of those without community. Here, clearly, the postmodern chatter has few alternatives. Being is a continual deferral because the tensions that the modern set up in it have not all been dissolved. This resort to a "post-" of

Nietzsche and Heidegger is hardly convincing. Theirs is "only" an *extreme* condition, but as such it belongs irreducibly to the modern and speaks to us only about the modern. The more it tries to go beyond being, the more it is caught within it.

The 1980s

In Italy more than elsewhere, perhaps, the weight of the 1980s was devastating. What resisted was not a "memory" (even if its loss was often fruit of a deliberate refusal), but rather an invention of the everyday. Everything but resentment produced this difference. And yet it was a tragic difference. There where it gave rise to an aesthetics it was effectively the most authentic filiation of a "weakness": widespread and open repentance. There where it could be expressed without any mediation, it even brushed against cynicism and opportunism—attitudes that are not at all noble and in any case passive (but not necessarily so) with respect to a fatality without hope.

Now, what is the result of this occurrence of being, this being whose occurrence is precisely a differing that does not complete time but multiplies it? Weak thought arrived at the formulation of a weak ontology, which is nothing other than a hermeneutic or an aesthetic of the tragic. If we cast our gaze back at this tragedy, however, it is clear that only an ontology of potentiality or power can save us. We are already suspect: whoever pretends to save him- or herself reaffirms a will, a delirium of subjective will, and thus a metaphysics. Nonetheless, this saving oneself is in the materiality of things; it is not and will not be merely an "idea" of recomposition and reparation. It can be given only as a possibility of possibility, the initial sedimentation of a contingency, of a "remembrance" of time starting from now. It is a memory of the future in which resentment is unthinkable or, in any case, not manifest. Ethics, in this ontology of power, is the extreme possibility of not reaching the end of time, not exhausting the future in the instant. If being occurs, time is constitutively connected to it. Our being is our time and thus our history.

If, however, every history is already finished, then every possible "biography" of being disappears; or, conversely, if what occurs is always waiting to occur, one cannot say anything about anything—except the "direction" of the occurrence, which can be intuited aesthetically. This is why the postmodern chatter, while starting out from a real condition, evolves toward the most facile of solutions. There should be no mystery about the constitutive link that exists between weak thought and postmodern thought. The real question is finally the way in which one interprets the modern. In short, if we limit ourselves to saying that our tragic condition is the specificity of the "disease" of the West, although this is not false, we simply continue to follow that metaphysics that Habermas has rightly considered marred by the myth of the origin. And if we affirm the most obvious conclusion, that this same condition is solidly expressed in its postmodern *specificity*, although this is not false, we take for granted the presumption that modernity has been completed. In truth, all that we have been saying shows exactly the opposite. The modern remains incomplete because no weakness has been able to eliminate its problem: not so much the Promethean myth of the subject, but rather the subjective constitution of the collectivity, a "whatever" being, certainly, if by that we mean the "community" of those "without community."

Translated by Michael Hardt

Notes

1. Some of the primary texts of weak thought in Italy include the following: Gianni Vattimo, *The End of Modernity: Nihilism and Hermeneutics in Postmodern Culture* (Baltimore: Johns Hopkins University Press, 1991); Gianni Vattimo, *The Adventure of Difference: Philosophy after Nietzsche and Heidegger* (Cambridge: Polity Press, 1993); Gianni Vattimo and Pier Aldo Rovatti, eds., *Il pensiero debole* (Milan: Feltrinelli, 1983); and Alessandro Dal Lago, "Il luogo della debolezza," *Aut Aut*, nos. 202–3 (1984). See also Mario Perniola, "Lettera a Gianni Vattimo sul 'peniero debole,'" *Aut Aut*, no. 201 (1984).

2. See Giorgio Agamben, *The Coming Community* (Minneapolis: University of Minnesota Press, 1993).

3. Gilles Deleuze and Félix Guattari, *A Thousand Plateaus*, trans. Brian Massumi (Minneapolis: University of Minnesota Press, 1987). See Toni Negri's interview with Gilles Deleuze, "Control and Becoming," in *Negotiations 1972–1990* (New York: Columbia University Press, 1995), 169–76.

F   I   V   E

Two Hundred Questions for Anyone Who Wants to Be Communist in the 1990s

Rossana Rossanda

This text was written in October 1991 and circulated among the members of the collective that publishes *il manifesto*, an independent communist national daily newspaper founded in the early 1970s.

Why We Cannot Go On as Before

In 1991 the world scene appears radically changed from twenty years ago, when we started the newspaper. The world was then bipolar, and now it is no longer so. The East-West atomic blackmailing that had characterized that world is now gone. Europe was then swept by a strong social conflict that, in five years, pushed half of the continent to the left—Portugal, Spain, Greece, Italy, with the Communist Party in the government majority, and France, with a socialist as president—whereas today we witness the opposite tendency. In Eastern Europe the system was creaking ideologically, but its State structure still appeared to be sound. Now this very system is exploding into political and military conflicts, and the Soviet Union has been radically weakened and divided. We started the newspaper thinking not that the revolution was around the corner, but that the thematics of communism had ripened, and that they had become intrinsic to the needs of masses of people as well as to their struggles and crucial for a new model of development. Today, instead, communism is regarded as a global error.

Everything has changed around us. Few other political groups and no other newspaper have had their original identities put into discussion as much as ours. Even though we have denounced the Italian Communist Party's mistakes since 1966, and although we long ago announced the crisis of "real socialism," their collapse—unsupported by the emergence of any alternative communist and socialist minority—falls also upon us: we were born to ward off this crisis at least partly, and we have failed. We have only been able to exist, politically less strong than in 1971 in the midst of the movements, and editorially less weak than in 1981 in the midst of the repression.

We could choose not to discuss this change, and silently bypass a change of identity for the newspaper, bury our dead, and take care of the still green shoots—even more so because *il manifesto* is today self-propelled, slowed down only by advertising, where we can find no stable support. One could think that, once we solve this and other problems with technical measures and promotional inventiveness, *il manifesto* will live, surviving as the only opposition newspaper in Italy. Yet the choice of proceeding in the direction we have taken is neither prudent nor realistic, as is demonstrated by the collective's unrest. We need to give an answer to our own tensions by verifying the categories according to which we have lived until now. These categories have allowed us to publish a newspaper characterized by the following projects:

> We seek to make visible the contradictions created by American military hegemony and, in minor part, by the capitalist market both in the West and, above all, in the South of the world.

> We work to provide reliable information on Eastern Europe, even though such information has not been accompanied by clear ideas about the ongoing process, generically hailed as democratic.

> We denounce the end of the opposition in Italy in politics (the Democratic Party of the Left that has replaced the Communist Party), in the unions, and in the society at large (see the newly developed reactionary tendency of public opinion), while denouncing too the authoritarian and certainly antiprogressive tendency of the Italian political system today.

> We are resolutely committed to the granting of rights, both political and civil, with some restrictions when the roots of these

freedoms lie in degenerative social forms (such as the Mafia) or in the search for escapism (such as drugs).

We are the only free paper in the midst of the generally unified ownership of the media. The media are all aligned with the interests of capital, and committed openly or covertly to repressing any antagonistic or simply autonomous subject (such as women), as well as the voices of people worried about the degradation of the planet (such as environmentalists) or about the sacrificed, the frustrated, or the marginalized.

We are also listened to by those in the business community who are more democratic, or not monopolistic, or weaker and constrained by the big concentration of capital.

This complex of positions makes us sufficiently different from the rest of the press and unfolds itself in many real "battles." None of them, however, deals with the question of changing the system and the State—the goal for which we were born as a newspaper, and for which it makes sense to call ourselves communists. We are above all a newspaper of democratic, radical, and popular opposition.

The Left Has Not Suffered from Too Much Communism, nor Even Less from Too Much Marxism

Why does our newspaper work? And if it does work, why look for something else? This second question is a commonsense observation, more or less explicit, made by many of us. My opinion is that it has worked because our communism has been, in contrast to the Communist Party after the 1960s, an intelligent updating of the frontist line. I define as the frontist line an ideological tendency bringing together, ever since the 1930s, the *ensemble* of political positions and social figures created in reaction to capital's tendency to develop fascist characteristics, a tendency that found in Nazism its most extreme expression. Frontism survived the two World Wars, particularly in Italy, because the links between the bourgeoisie and authoritarian degeneration were, with good reason, not considered to be eradicated simply with the defeat of the fascist regime. Hence the necessity of mobilizing socialist and democratic forces, so that the political scene would not seize up again. Furthermore, this mobilization would give the subaltern classes the chance for political expression and political rights, as well as the hope for a less unjust social condition. This was the substance of the real culture of the workers' Left in Europe, a culture in which communism has spread, growing ten or twenty times larger after 1935 compared with the late 1920s, and much more so after the Second World War. This cultural arena managed to exercise, especially in Italy, a real hegemony (in the real sense of orientation) over the whole system of democratic forces.

In my view, this line, even with its attention to conflicts and "other" subjects wherever they appear, will not work for twenty more years, and not even for ten. The reason this strategy can no longer work is that we have seen an end of the phase in which the capitalist bloc offered some openings for actions of social change—actions that could solidify into reforms or modernizations, or that could answer social demands. These kinds of actions were possible after World War II and once again when the demand for action in the 1960s assumed a more mature tone and, as such, was able to exercise a more radical pressure. During the 1970s, however, the impulse of this social demand stopped: what we called "repression" developed side by side with a halting of the growth of employment (and the conditions of labor), the level of education, social services, and the decentralization of the administration of welfare. Subjected to a massive pressure on a global scale, capital has restructured itself through a technological transformation of greater dimensions than the modernization it had undergone in the early postwar years. From this position capital poses obstacles, and not only political obstacles, to the struggles (whether led by the unions or not). This explains why in the 1980s the movements as a form of political commitment and therefore as a source of self-identification progressively weakened, so that what is left assumes more and more the symbolic nature of a protest and nothing more.

Today more than twenty years ago, in this sense, either we accept the contemporary model of the reproduction of capital and its restricted base as inevitable, and thus try to operate in selected sectors from within it, or we are forced to confront what are its more and more numerous and by now impassable walls. The question of a radical change of the system thus poses itself again, not in the abstract, but as necessary and inevitable. Once again we need to face the problem of how to carry out such a change, and with the help of what social bloc—as the previous one has been defeated and transformed by the change of the mode of production. I realize that the either/or scenario I have been depicting seems to reproduce the "extremisms" of the 1920s or of the period following 1968. But back then the issue was, if we don't defeat capitalism and the capitalist State, then anything else is useless. Today I tend to think that all the rest is impossible. For a generation like mine, deeply antiextremist, the present situation is almost a cul-de-sac; and yet analysis of the turmoils of the past twenty years has led me to this belief. It is thus impossible to be a newspaper of social opposition without being explicitly anticapitalist; it is not by chance that so few are in the opposition now (the anticapitalists are even fewer) and all sing the same song, which goes, "Let's immediately do something modest, but concrete," which generally, as a program, remains always unfulfilled.

Allow me a few more words on frontism to make things clear. I have said that frontism cannot be defined simply as anticapitalism. Years ago, communist forces did not manage to succeed on this basis because their analysis was more rigid than rigorous, and certainly also because of the elements of immaturity that characterized the Russian Revolution and the failure of the revolutions in Europe — elements that forced communists to assume a defensive stance. The characteristic of frontism is, rather, the multiplicity of the "democratic," "social," or "symbolic" fronts that delay or contrast the sway of capital: this multidirectionality makes frontism effective against capital's most ferocious manifestations.

The birth of the frontist line brought with it a theoretical debate in the Communist International around the time of the VII Congress that led to antifascist resistance. Particularly in Italy, the Communist Party maintained until the VIII Congress a restless conscience, becoming divided between its role as an essentially democratic and reformist force (working toward the reconstruction of the country in the years following 1947–48 and the search for peace at the beginning of the Cold War) and its identity as the representative of a particular class, wanting to be Marxist and Leninist. At the VIII Congress this split was sutured into one univocal will, under the formula that the struggles for democracy and socialism are inseparable.

Also implicit in this position of the VIII Congress, although barely admitted, was the preoccupation with the situation in Eastern Europe as it developed in the period from 1948 to 1956. A thesis was then proposed that "the revolution in the West" must not literally be a dictatorship of the proletariat; this decision was a consequence of the discovery and use of Gramsci's thought, and as such it constituted the initial nucleus of ideas about the complex nature of Western societies. The result of such theories was a practice of actual engagement with the plurality of subjects and planes of struggle (this was the same plurality for which Togliatti was accused of parliamentarism by the sectarians of the 1970s, deeply different from the contemporary sectarians of the Left), moving people and real groups for partial but concrete changes, and feeding into a social bloc that seemed naturally to be grafting itself onto the social bloc of waged labor.

Historically, this has been a direction capable of producing great political and social changes "inside" the system. It has also accelerated the passive revolution that began after 1929, gained ground in the period between 1945 and 1960, and came to an end toward the end of the 1970s with the unrelenting restructuration of capital. In Italy the real novelty of the "second industrial revolution" has become visible with the end of the parallel development of production growth and the growth of the labor force. The workers (and their leaders) came to realize that their opportunity to play a role that could be both "antagonistic" and "favorable" to economic development was over. With it, there also ended the possibility of a passive revolution, through which capital and labor could grow in parallel (as could their political representatives), thus establishing the democratic compromise on a new terrain. Simultaneously, the implosion of socialist countries took place, with which also the so-called progressive alliance with the national bourgeoisie of some Third World countries sank; the bipolarity East-West ended, and the communist parties produced by that phase (1936–89) fell.

Under the force of repression and due to its own weaknesses, the Italian New Left dissolved even more quickly. None of its constituent parts has reflected on the "real material conditions" of the 1970s, and that group that has come closer than others to doing so, Potere Operaio (Workers' Power), has approached this question with a surprisingly contradictory practice. It has fixed its attention exclusively on the "high points," the advanced Western economies and their subjects, as if capital had not become global and found support in the diversified resources offered by the market, and by the labor market in particular, of the entire planet—as if the powers of consumption would not modify the subjects in the advanced economies too, subjects who were granted the opportunity to consume more, as this was less dangerous than their previous practices of "reappropriation."

The rest of the New Left has remained in contemplation of the subjects that produced it, the novelty of the "refusal" they expressed, or the demands that they advanced: "We want everything." Its existence, both strong and brief, confirms how subjectivity is the constituent part of the political-social scenario, and not its mere reflection, as Gramsci said. And yet, as Marx said, this subjectivity quickly yields to material forces (the forces of production and the power of the State) if it is not able to dominate or reduce them. The rapid passage from a powerful subjectivity to active or passive desperation (armed struggle or drugs) and then to resignation (nothing can be changed, or, even more, it's better not to change) has been the living proof of this axiom since 1976.

Il manifesto has been the only one to hold steady, thanks to its culture, which is more complex and less naively extremist, and thanks to its own skepticism and intransigency. The communism of the 1970s, however, has not held, and between frontist inheritances and the difficulty of understanding this changing phase it has started cracking into heterogeneous fragments. For a long time now, the newspaper has lacked an agreed-upon common denominator. What predominates, rather, is the prudent (even though, in comparison with others, it often appears daring) practice of taking shelter under the denunciation and defense of the various rights of the oppressed and the affirmation of political democracy and cultural radicalism, along with the discussion of how to subvert the forms of the imaginary and mass consumption that dominate bourgeois respectability.

Yet Frontism and Progressivism Are Not Dead:

On the Use of Thinking from within History

To say that in the phase we just completed all the Left, including ourselves, was essentially frontist and progressivist does not mean that it was "limited." Frontism and antifascism have not been a mere politics of alliances, of class compromise in the face of an enemy produced by one of these classes and then become common. We need more than a cursory interpretation of two issues. First is the nature and role after 1917 of the workers' and communist movement, and of "real socialism." Although it was not radically anticapitalist, it is not true that the latter, as it has been sometimes affirmed by the extreme Left, did not have a very strong identity and impact. Second is the reason "real socialism" has imploded, both in the form of party and State, because nobody had defeated it from outside, and why it has imploded *now*, by virtue of what foundational shift.

Here we need to reflect carefully on the method of our analysis. It is necessary to intertwine a structural analysis with a historical one. They are not the same thing; the global process has been taking place diachronically, through long periods of time. By looking at the century as a whole, I think we can say that the contradiction represented by the workers' and communist movement, by the October Revolution, and by other revolutions that failed has forced the hegemonic class to produce a different idea of itself, by establishing in the period immediately after the Second World War and since a widespread consciousness, not only of solidarity, but also a class-based consciousness, a consciousness of the exploited and the oppressed. Hence its crucial role in the struggle to end Nazism and fascism, and the powerful influence of this movement on the end of colonialism.

Probably we can identify the end of this movement in the completion, inexorably confronted after 1945, of the "democratization" of the West and in the crisis of colonialism. In the West, the communism of the Third International could not develop further, above all because of an evident lack of expansion of the revolution in the world, particularly in the West. Stalin's famous phrase "Let's gather up the bourgeoisie's flags" was not a mere metaphor. When the revolutionary movements failed, the bourgeoisie inclined toward regressive authoritarianism. The tie between European communism and the French Revolution and its Jacobinism was not fictitious either. Even less fictitious was the very close link (today we have plenty of proof) between, on one hand, the existence of an "exploited, alienated, and oppressed"—that is, politically dissenting—subject and, on the other, the maintenance of a "democratic equilibrium" that denies its own fascist, racist, and ultra-nationalist tendencies.

In short, from the existence of the workers' and communist movement and since the October Revolution, the West has derived a widened notion of the citizen as someone having more "rights" than simply the political ones and a strong conception of the redistributional compromise of the Welfare State. In the 1960s and 1970s, from the acquisition of these rights and from their impact on the model of production and on the State came radical subjects, needs, and cultures, based in the proletarian, working-class sphere (councils and communism as base program), both inside and outside this sphere (in the case of environmentalism), or entirely outside it (in the case of women). All of the above—subjects, needs, and cultures—represented a break, but also a form of continuity (this still needs to be qualified). The analysis of the links between the workers' and communist movement of the first half of the century and these subjects, who cross the boundaries of its culture, is the major historiographic problem of the 1970s in Europe. The prudent acceptance of their self-sufficiency and their declared radicalism (women, environmentalism, pacifism, and national identities) is the major political problem of the contemporary Left. In a world unified under capitalism, by virtue of their self-sufficiency and declared radicalism, they generally refuse any possible totalizing "interpretation" and any centralized struggle. This happens because they are not able to recognize, in their own plurality, any central subject, that is, a subject who—if her or his condition could be resolved—could lead to the resolution of the problems of all other subjects. The complexity of the social scene thus becomes a form of illegibility. With the 1960s came also the end of direct colonial domination in the Third World, the birth of more or less progressive national States, and the impact of Vietnam (linked, in the United States, to the question of civil rights) against the liberal, neocolonialist, and neoimperialist "good conscience."

From this complex growth of movements, above all the peace movement, and not from the fall of the Berlin Wall, came since the late 1960s the end of the Cold War as a destructive effort against the socialist bloc. What followed (and it ceased in 1989) was a maneuver among powers that thought of themselves as bipolar for the control of negotiated areas of influence.

In conclusion, from the struggle of the workers' and communist movement, and from the socialist countries, came a redefinition of the world system of domination, a growth of social subjects, a liberation of national subjects, and a militant consciousness opposing the logic of atomic destruction and, indirectly, contesting the capitalist model of development. How can we explain that in the midst of this global change capitalists of the world have united and the workers are still divided?

Polemics and Melancholias from the Right and the Left

As a preliminary move, it is necessary to confront reactions (from both the Right and the Left) against an opinion that we have always held: that the reason for the defeat of the workers' movement and communism lies in the fact that nowhere in this century have different relations of production been established. "Real socialism" did not change these relations either. After the 1920s, communist parties never tried to follow a line that was more than merely rhetorically revolutionary.

In Italy, the Right is the one to claim that in 1917 there was no real change in the mode of production. Rightists say communism was and could only mean State ownership of the means of production founded on an oppressive system. This was what Marx taught, they say, and the communist parties from the rest of the world have not changed because they are stubbornly preparing for the advent of the oppressive and terroristic Moloch State.

On the Left they say that to study and analyze what communist parties and "real socialism" have been is useless, because that game has been lost forever, and who feels like beginning again? It is better to work on the concrete problems of the present system, looking for the least odious solutions and not "remaining outside the current." (The majority of members of the Democratic Party of the Left and its allied organizations take this line.) Others on the Left claim that "real socialism" and the communist parties were still better than anything else the world scenario has offered. Objectively they were an important support for the liberation movements in colonial and neocolonial countries; they were founded on decent values, even though in practice they contradicted those very values. (The Communist Refoundation Party and its related groups maintain this position.)

The first line (that of the Democratic Party of the Left) relies on the conviction that the only possible mode of production is the capitalist one, because it has demonstrated that it is able to increase wealth and to be transnational:

property and profit propel development. Yet at the moment of its political triumph, the dominant capitalist model ceased to be an agent of development on a global scale, because it no longer needed an expansion of the labor force for the accumulation of capital. Capital itself has thus lost its great capability to unify the world under its model, as happened in the eighteenth century at the time of the so-called second industrial revolution. The "high points," the industrialized economies, stop overflowing into the underdeveloped areas and assimilating them to their standards; rather, they reproduce the split between wealth and poverty, in the South of the globe, the South of each country, the South of each metropolis, and the relationship between East and West.

The second position (that of the Communist Refoundation Party) relies on the refusal to get to the bottom of the crisis of "real socialism." Proponents of this position say it was a real form of socialism, but in the 1920s it became besieged and its power necessarily became oppressive and degenerated; or it was a true socialism but bureaucracy betrayed it; or it was a true socialism but it became the target of an internal plot led by the West. Neither the communist portion of the Democratic Party of the Left nor the Communist Refoundation Party seems to want to discuss the matter in depth; both seem in fact to limit themselves to the contradiction—already expressed by Khrushchev and theorized by Isaac Deutscher—according to which the economic base (the structure) was socialist but the political regime (the superstructure) was not, and the crisis thus resulted from the failure to adjust the latter to the former.

From the Past to the Present: What Happens If Subjects and Objectives Don't Change When Economic Growth Is Separated from Development

To say that today capitalism is capable of "growth" but not "development" implies, for people of our background and the culture we produce, a series of consequences. It implies indeed that the traditional types of struggles for work and education, as well as for the famous rights of citizenship, are only for the select few, the "high points," that is, the privileged layers of the Western capitalist societies. And probably, as the processes of marginalization develop, even these groups may not be able to sustain such conditions.

We are not the only ones to say this. For some time now, economists and sociologists have stopped affirming what they had been preaching since the early 1970s—that different struggles, even though they appeared to be antagonistic ones, functioned in fact as good incentives for development. Today it is maintained that the West cannot avoid closing its frontiers to the demands of immigrant labor and internally it cannot avoid programming the structure of the labor force by reducing its quantity and selecting its quality. The different timing of immigration in France, Germany, and Italy confirms this argument: in the former two countries it took place in the 1960s and 1970s, when the system was still expanding and deploying immigrant labor at low levels of production. Now the economic system is blocked even in France and Germany, while Le Pen and Nazism are advancing. In Italy the immigration from beyond the European Community arrived later and in a much lower proportion (not even a million workers, compared with the more than four million absorbed by the French), and yet it is enough to create tension.

I think it is necessary to reflect on these facts to understand why the movements in the Northern Hemisphere appear not to be building a long-lasting social bloc, but rather to be weak forms of resistance. We need to ask why the student movement never managed to find a real continuity after 1968, without simply limiting our inquiry to cultural or subjective errors. All things considered, the perhaps more serious mistakes made at the beginning of the workers' movement did not entail its end. In its most recent resurgences, the student movement in Italy, both in 1985 and 1989, has seemed to be aware of its own desultory nature and its lack of continuity and solidity. The Panther, as this student movement is called, has looked for residual models through a return to the past, thus managing to avoid the paralyzing question: What need for education is intrinsic to this economic system? In other words, on what real contradiction, capable of grafting itself onto the system and changing some of its aspects, is our movement founded? Why are we so isolated?

The same can be said of the workers' movement of resistance. The system tends to need in its high points "less" labor but it needs "other" labor, which the system itself is still able to reward with money and prestige. (Consider the formation of what Marx calls "general intellect," which, on the other hand, is quickly transformable into "dead labor." Consider also the role of consumption and the consumption that specifically gives a certain status.) In so doing, the system prevents the formation of a social bloc among the different "forms of labor," while the historical absence of a tradition in this kind of alliance makes difficult a proletarian bloc at the global level (as Immanuel Wallerstein wishes). Yet we must ask why capitalist Europe unites while the unions, which have always remained tied to the national State notwithstanding the internationalization of the economic process, prefer to negotiate nationally by region about the labor force that is "still needed."

Furthermore, we must ask why the unions are unable to solve the problem of immigrant labor and are unable to mobilize the immigrants while they are waiting for nonexistent jobs. The unions consider it realistic, by now, to negotiate and protect the labor of already employed workers, perhaps reducing their number for competitiveness, and they accept as a given a growing unemployment or underemployment rate, possibly to be taken care of by welfare structures. This could involve services and relief for the poor or guaranteed subsidies that could substitute, in a more controlled fashion, for the clientelist forms of disability pensions or the escalation of public employment.

The question of democracy is more complex. Its cultural tenets, inherited from the English, French, and American revolutions, are being put into question on two sides. Representation and participation seem to be obstacles to the possibility of governing, as a global intervention in the social and economic process. It is peculiar to Italy that decisionism and the decline of the participatory form of the party have come from the Socialist Party. It is not enough simply to paint the socialists as fascists. It is necessary rather to ask why today Europe tends toward the American model, that is, toward a retrenchment of political expression, nonparticipation, and therefore the transformation of the political class into a technique of power. This is what in fact decisionism and most of the institutional reforms amount to.

Through such a process, after two centuries since 1789, and in contrast to the opinion of the majority, the idea of democracy born from the minds of the men of the Enlightenment truly comes to an end as a political form within which the conflicts of different strata, interests, and classes find expression and create norms. A possible explanation of this fact, also in this case clashing with the dominant opinion from 1990 on, is that democracy is vital as long as conflict really exists and is legitimated by common opinion and as long as the parties do not degenerate from their status as agents of social change to mere political classes. When both conditions no longer exist, democracy necessarily implodes. In this sense, turning the bourgeois formula on its head, we can say that there is democracy where there is capitalism only as long as the latter is established according to its classical formula of formal political compromise (universal suffrage) among the political forms of two or more conflicting classes.

This ought to make us reflect also on our newspaper's limitations—for example, its support for the student movement for what it is and while it lasts, its backing of radical minorities of workers as long as they exist, and its denunciation of the way the Albanian immigrants were treated. On the whole, ours is a role of supportive solidarity, but the newspaper hesitates to "open people's minds" to the actual depth of the problems. Or should we think that the attempt to open them (perhaps by saying to students, "You'll have no place in today's division of labor," or by admitting that it is impossible for Italy to be competitive *and* welcome the immigrants) would soon become unpopular and that it would hardly befit the nature of a newspaper? Could it be that a newspaper with a relatively large circulation cannot tell the truth? Perhaps today we have reached the point when a newspaper must go "beyond" what it is expected to do, by actively hiding the impossibility of finding a solution for everybody, as the mainstream newspapers do; by indicating a possible solution to social problems in a savage competitiveness; or, as we should do, by pointing out the intrinsic limitation of protest. I am clearly for the second option, not in order to preach, as was done in 1968, that everything is to no avail unless the system changes, but rather to dedicate particular attention to the movements or social figures, or to the specific struggles that seem to point to a way out — to figures who are aware of their actual potentialities, who know that it will take a long time, and relentlessly try to connect with each other (an opposite tendency to the current one). We cannot after all end up repeating, even though with more energy, "Proletarians of all trades and of the entire world unite, otherwise they will rip you off."

From the Past to the Present: On the Crisis of the "Real Socialism" Rather Than "Real Progressivism"

From this perspective it is useful to reflect on the crisis of the systems of the Eastern bloc. I have written previously about the nature and formation of State capitalism, and about the persistence of the capitalist relations of production even when the State owns the means of production. This opinion also has provoked extremely tense accusations, without any attempt to verify my argument. The present questions are, Why did the system not hold? Why does its crisis appear so utterly disruptive? Why did it happen now?

In the first place, it is not true that the East entered a crisis essentially because of the untenability of its political regimes. These had been much more rigid in the past, and yet they continued as long as everybody agreed that it was necessary to accept temporary sacrifices (when it was necessary, for example, to drive back the German invasion) and as long as the social compromise lasted (the guarantee of a job for workers and technicians as well as the protection of the peasants' interests in Russia during the 1930s and elsewhere in the years following the Second World War, as well as the guarantee of education and social assistance).

As long as these elements remained priorities, even at a commonsense level, none of the Eastern regimes fell: neither in Poland in 1956 nor Czechoslovakia in 1968 nor Poland again at the outset of the Solidarity movement. Perhaps at every jolt there was some inclination toward "democratic reform," as with the councils in Poland, the "new course" in Prague, and Solidarity's early programs.

The regimes, however, became extremely fragile and began answering popular demands in a classically reactionary manner. Gradually a non-political bureaucratic oppression came to substitute for political oppression. Bureaucracies drew on the economic resources more or less legally and transformed themselves into a dominating class, even in social terms, while the masses remained debilitated, prevented from reflecting on the situation by a still-closed political system and forced into the black market and into taking two jobs—as Marx would say, forced into their own full degradation. At this point the system proceeded at its minimun level of productivity and the transparency that should be proper to any economic or political plan (even the most unfelicitous) was lost.

In the second place, the East entered a crisis once the productive gap between East and West had become so great that any relative parallelism between the two economic models ceased—in other words, when in the West any tendency toward growth or full employment ceased, when the Welfare State contracted, and when the setting of prices as well as the model of accumulation were disrupted. At this stage, during the 1980s, the "common" terrain shared by the two systems (that is, armaments that required the highest level of technology and productivity) made it impossible for the socialist bloc to keep up with the West without drastically cutting State expenses. The East thus reduced the investments necessary to guarantee to its citizens relatively full employment at a low level of productivity and a relatively universal minimum welfare system.

Gorbachev's effort can be interpreted as an attempt to stop the arms race (limiting activities in Eastern Europe, which had become by now an expensive source of trouble) and to revivify domestic production. Why would this attempt be unsuccessful? Perhaps because it is too late; social strata with conflictual and paralyzed interests have already taken shape. The class of the State bureaucracy wants to become a direct entrepreneur. The workers are blackmailed and caught between the global dysfunctionality of the system and the need to resign themselves to losing the rights they had acquired with their work—housing and assistance. Market means competition even among the poor. The situation is exacerbated by the fact that the West cannot implement a plan of development in the East (as it did with the Marshall Plan after the war), because that would be in contradiction with its current model. The West has no time (or, rather, in such a short time it would be too expensive) to set up a relatively healthy capitalist market, well spread and therefore capable of offering a high rate of employment, as had already happened after the Second World War in Europe. In this sense, a good example of this situation is the united Germany, which prefers to create a sort of North-South politics along the lines of the Italian model. In other words, it throws out money in order to take it back immediately, dumping its leftovers on the East while managing to guarantee for the West an economic recovery in the short term. The only choice that the West seems to be making is to demand harshly that the East adjust itself to the West's model: high productivity, reduced employment, and diminished welfare costs—all this without even being able to demonstrate that this will be indeed a period of transition toward a future period of development.

Finally, the crises of the Eastern bloc after 1968 were no longer dealt with through the intervention of the military. In Poland, for example, they looked to Jaruzelski for a solution and gave Solidarity itself power along with the responsibility of cutting welfare costs. This fact shows that the famous "military-industrial complex"—if such definition makes sense, which I doubt—is aware of one thing: that the challenge has changed the terms of the problem. The Western pole has won on a terrain on which the Eastern one cannot stand. It only makes sense to send tanks against internal protests, as China has done, if you are sure that the model you are defending can function; it would be ridiculous to secure your power militarily and at a high political cost over an expensive and unproductive system. The same explanation applies to the Communist Party of the Soviet Union: fourteen million people let the party be dissolved by decree, without organizing even one protest, because they were convinced that there was no other possible solution. It should be noted that in August 1991 the Communist Party of the Soviet Union was still leading both the army and the KGB, and neither did it mobilize them nor did they move by their own will. The coup, or rather a false symbolic coup, was then staged, either provoked by Gorbachev or Yeltsin or simply the bright idea of a few eccentrics.

The Paradoxes of the West at the Fall of the East

We thus find ourselves confronted with a capitalist system defined by several paradoxical conditions. The system has discovered its model for the growth of profit through technological innovation and thus no longer tries to increase labor or to relaunch the geographic extension of advanced production. These strategies had definitely straitjacketed any system of State capitalism based on a social compromise of full employment, and therefore low productivity, and made it unable to compete. This type of victory increases social contradictions, perhaps reaching the limit outlined by Marx between modes of production and growth of general wealth, without any consciousness of the devastating nature of this process on the side of either the masses or any coherent political vanguards.

This may not actually be the case, but if not, I do not see things changing. It is a fact that the supporting base of the dominant system is a portion of the upper-middle-income population of the North. It is also a fact that the alliance with the dominant classes of the countries of the South, interested in maintaining monarchies and military dictatorships, is founded on an increasingly unequal exchange with the center. This process leads to the failure, which even the World Bank admits, of any financing plan for the development of Third World countries or regions whose poverty would be otherwise inexplicable, such as Brazil. It is also a fact that in the East a ruling class proper has not yet come into being—a class, that is, capable of governing and producing, and not only of speculating. At the same time, the bureaucratic ruling class has disappeared and no different social subjects of any type are aggregating, except for the unionization of the Kuzbass miners.

The situation appears therefore highly problematic: What elements could, from the economic point of view, preserve the equilibrium of a system undergoing a "Malthusian development"? In other words, can a mode of production on the threshold of the year 2000 grow off itself if feeding on a relatively reduced base and therefore a relatively limited market? Could this scenario be opposed by a different, nonmonopolistic capitalism moving toward a slower technological development and a broadening of the market, even if there existed in Third World countries the conditions to create it? If not, is it plausible that the current model, concerned about the narrowing of its base and driven by forces that call themselves concretist and reformist, will devote huge investments in order to reproduce itself on a larger scale?

I am not able to answer such crucial questions. The answers could be an alternative to Marx's thesis that capital creates in the form of the proletariat its own grave diggers, which could be acceptable only on the basis of Wallerstein's equation, proletariat = South of the world. The South of the world, however, has not been powerfully transformed into a labor force. And where there is no growth of the labor force, how can a market take shape? This order of problems must be confronted by economists and theorists. It should be the pivot of our reflection, and of all those who insist on the North-South contradiction.

In Conclusion: A Couple of Provocations

Finally, if what I have argued until now is at least partially true, we suddenly have to confront the disconcerting collapse of the concepts that have nourished the Left from 1789 to today, even outside the most immediate political sphere. Let us take only two "scandalous" examples. The first concerns the principle of a people's self-determination that became an international norm after 1945 and was nourished by all the events that took place between the wars, particularly the end of the great Ottoman Empire and its effects, the nature of Nazi expansionism, and the geno-cide of the Jews and the "inferior races," as well as decolonization. However, this principle, which appears obvious, relies on a quite summary idea of "the people." In world institutions, this notion has brazenly functioned as a principle of self-determination for different States. Even going beyond it, however, with the emer-gence of conflicts among ethnic groups, nations, and States, the concept of people appears much more problematic. One can suppose that a people, like a class, really exists only insofar as it becomes a "modern political subject"—with a strong stress on "modern," that is, on its complex nature, a mix of historicity and right. Both make the concept of people politically deployable. Ethnicity instead, understood as a "blood tie" and turned without any mediation into political power, is an archaic and politically unusable concept. By *archaic*, I mean something that has not gone through the experiences of the English, French, and American revolutions, which separated the concepts of ethnicity, religion, and State. Consider, for example, the return of the principle of *cuius regio, eius religio* (one king, one religion) in the States that declared their independence from the Soviet Union. Latvia refuses citizenship to its minorities, although they represent 40 percent of the nation's inhabitants; in Ukraine, the nationalism of the Rukh is at one with the Orthodox hierarchy.

It is quite interesting that the conflict in the former Yugoslavia appears unsolvable, certainly impossible to interpret as a mere rebellion against the State structure of "real socialism." If by *politics* we mean a system of relations con-tracted with some basic sense of universality among the contracting parts, ethnicity remains outside of politics much as Hegel says that the family is outside of the State. If this is true, then suddenly "the State"—that is, the community that one chooses and does not inherit—appears infinitely closer to a communist hypothesis such as ours than the ethnic community coming from our fathers. But of which State would we then be speaking? To what political form should we turn at the moment when the form derived from the national States and from 1789 has entered a crisis?

The second example, which is connected to the first and goes directly against a trend of the 1970s, is the necessary examination of the limits of the culture of differences as self-legitimating. These differences have expressed themselves not only in the various nationalisms, but also in the separatist affirmation of many types of difference — the difference between sexes, or between racial groups, or, moving toward less general categories, between the old and the young, homosexuals and heterosexuals, religions, and so forth. In the 1970s and 1980s the tendency to self-legitimation was accompanied by the refusal of a system of communication that guaranteed any diversity but within a discourse that was not mere coexistence and parallelism.

This is an extraordinarily delicate question, in which there intervenes once again the basic question of the viability of the categories of reason (inherited from the Enlightenment) and the irreducibility of the identity of nature or genealogy or group or custom. In this case, too, I do not think that there should be a return, but I want to stress that the idea of the reduction of each identity to its "partiality" or "alterity" is a victory of silence over political dialogue, and as such it is strictly "reactionary" in the sense that it belongs to a reaction. The question of the rights of citizenship is tainted by this tendency, which, it goes without saying, allows a very reasoning, dominant, and pervasive system to gain legitimation without changing at all.

Translated by Maurizia Boscagli

Note

Rossana Rossanda was a founding member of *il manifesto* and has continually remained one of its leading figures. The newspaper has been at times supportive and at times critical of the social movements and traditions that animate the other essays in this volume. This essay indicates the breadth of the communist tradition outside the realm of the Communist Party in Italy.

PART II

Working in Post-Fordism

S I X

The Anomaly and Exemplariness of the Italian Welfare State

Carlo Vercellone

In many respects, the experiences of the Italian Welfare State represent a particular case. The comparatively late industrial development, the continuity and ferocity of the workers' struggles and social movements, the high levels of Mafia activity and political corruption, and above all the radical division between the northern and southern parts of the country all make Italy an anomaly with respect to the rest of the developed capitalist countries. Precisely because of these anomolous conditions, however, the Italian experience may paradoxically prove to be exemplary for the future of all welfare systems. The need to manage an internal relationship between North and South, for example, has now become a generalized condition for all capitalist economies. Most important, the Italian experiences, especially those emanating from the social movements of the 1970s, show the possibilities of alternative forms of welfare in which systems of aid and socialization are separated from State control and situated instead in autonomous social networks. These alternative experiments may show how systems of social welfare will survive the crisis of the Welfare State.

The Fordist Period: Welfare as Regulation of the Relationship between Development and Underdevelopment

In Italy, as in other developed capitalist countries, the Welfare State was established in the period following World War II, as a central articulation of the Fordist mode of development. With respect to the classical model of Keynes and Beveridge, however, the arrangement of the Welfare State in Italy immediately presented certain important differences that follow from the depth of the geographic division of development between the industrialized North and the underdeveloped South. In fact, in my opinion, the central role played by the dialectic between North and South in the project of Fordist growth in Italy has never been highlighted strongly enough. Before proceeding to analyze the present economic situation, then, I believe it will be helpful to review the elements that are essential for understanding the dynamic that led from the establishment of the Welfare State to its current crisis.

On one hand, thanks to the inexhaustible reservoir of labor power furnished by the underdeveloped South, Italy was the only country in Europe that was not forced to rely on a foreign labor force during the period of Fordist growth. The constitution of the Fordist wage relationship in the large northern factories was established solely on the basis of the internal migration from South to North. On the other hand, the role of the South was not limited simply to that of reservoir of cheap labor for the northern industrial triangle bounded by Milan, Turin, and Genoa. The South also constituted an enormous potential market for the development of mass consumption and, additionally, once the dramatic lack of infrastructure was addressed, it could be a space to accommodate the enlargement of the productive capacities of base sectors of public industries and the redeployment of the large Fordist factories.[1]

The originality of Italy, then, in the theory and practice of the State regulation of Fordist development, consisted in the attempt to define a synthesis of, on one hand, the functions and instruments of the Keynesian State planning characteristic of developed capitalist economies and, on the other, the State development policy typical of underdeveloped countries. In line with the canonical interpretation, Italy experienced a rapid growth in spending for social services during the period from 1954 to 1970, due in part to the country's initial backwardness. This dynamic of compensation, however, demonstrated two essential and original characteristics. In the first place, the welfare system was deprived of one of the central pillars of the canonical model: unemployment compensation. In the logic of Fordist regulation, unemployment insurance corresponds, within the framework of a Keynesian type of unemployment, to a security net guaranteeing the stability of demand in a dynamic of full employment. In Italy, the South was characterized by a backward agricultural sector and an explosive situation of underemployment; it appeared as a pocket of "structural unemployment" that, despite Fordist growth and emigration, could never be absorbed. The demands for the maintenance of buying power and the social control of the labor market in the South led to the replacement of unemployment insurance with direct monetary transfers. This translated into the establishment of a complex system of "complementary allocations," and in particular the so-called socioeconomic disability pensions, based on the recognition of incapacity to earn and not (medically certified) incapacity to work. This was a central institution that characterized at once the backwardness and the modernity of the Italian situation. It defined, in fact, a form of minimum income separated from work, even though its distribution, based on no automatic criterion, was at the base of the logic of a welfare clientelism.

Beside this system of social support we find the second central and original institution of the Italian Welfare State and the regulation of Fordist growth: la Cassa per il Mezzogiorno (the Fund for the South). The role of this fund was to channel additional revenue made available by Fordist growth in the North to the South in order to encourage industrial development. This goal was the central project in the establishment of an explicit Fordist compromise, in which the stabilization of the relationship between wage and productivity was based on a policy of transfers for productive investments. In fact, with the public industries acting as primary motor, the State did manage from the 1960s onward to begin a large process of industrialization in the South. The entire traditional socioeconomic structure of the South was toppled in this attempt to converge with the North.

Certainly, this strategy based on poles of development often ended up merely creating "cathedrals in the desert," and the break with the traditional structure of the agricultural sector served to expand an unproductive public and private service sector, that is, an economy that was largely parasitic and on the dole following a specific and clientelist form of the deployment of the Welfare State. Contrary to common opinion, however, in the zones where public industries were not simply a substitution for the inertia of the large Fordist companies of the North, this strategy did permit the creation of an integrated and differentiated industrial structure that laid the groundwork for self-sustaining development. In effect, the dualism between industrially developed zones and industrially backward zones was displaced so as now to be internal to the South itself. This explains in large part the division that emerged in the period from 1975 to 1990 between the dynamism of the Adriatic South (the eastern provinces of Abruzzo, Puglia, and Molise) and the downward slide of the "deep South" along a Mafia model, which during the 1960s developed only in Sicily.

The Social Crisis of Fordism: Welfare as Transition and
Articulation of an Alternative Mode of Production

Far from being a drag on the Italian model of regulation, the constitution of the Fordist wage relationship solely on the basis of internal migrations proved to be a unifying element that avoided any segmentation of the workforce between national and foreign workers, in terms of both their status on the labor market and their treatment by the unions. In France and Germany this segmentation seriously weakened the political power of the workers. The very mobility of the internal migrations in Italy played a determinant role in the constitution of an actor in the social struggles, favoring the mechanisms of socialization and fostering circulation of struggles, models of life, and political organizations between North and South. This point is essential to an understanding of the social crisis that was opened by the workers' struggles of 1969, the "Hot Autumn," and the precocity with which Italian capital subsequently embarked on the strategies of decentralization that marked a radical rupture with the Fordist system of the large productive concentrations of labor power. There was an enormous social tendency toward the project of an alternative society in which the "refusal of work," a slogan of the workers' movements, was not only a negative expression against the scientific organization of work, but also a positive expression of a need to reappropriate the social mechanisms of production and reproduction. This was the social tie that brought together a plurality of subjects and struggles that, beginning with the large industrial centers, invested the entire set of relations between the factory and society to the point of posing the question of power over the globality of the social conditions of reproduction. The various new forms of social transformation that emerged in Italy in the 1970s — the so-called auto-reduction struggles, the user and consumer strikes, and the radical critiques of the health care system and the total institutions of disciplinary society — all were centered precisely in the attempt to reappropriate the structures of welfare and invert their logic based on the reproduction of the norm of the wage relationship.

From the beginning of the 1970s this new subjectivity, far from passively accepting the terrain of productive flexibility, appropriated the social terrain as a space of struggle and self-valorization. The dramatic increase in small businesses and in the informal economy in the central and northern parts of the country can be understood only in terms of the diffusion across the social terrain of struggles and practices that attempted to make use of this deepening of the social division of labor between the businesses to experiment in alternative forms of productive cooperation. There was a new form of mass entrepreneurship that would in the following years act as the protagonist in the new economic miracle of the so-called diffuse economy.[2]

This new subjectivity that was based on the "refusal of work" and on the high education level of the majority of the population invested all the interstices of the clientelist-Mafia model of regulation of the South along with all the articulations of its integration as dependent participant, realizing finally that class unity between North and South that Gramsci dreamed of in vain in terms of a social bloc between the industrial workers of the North and the peasants of the South. Despite the attempt to reestablish a compromise based on industrialization, the social activism immediately reached the large factories displaced in the South. There was a movement of recomposition that united all the figures of the so-called southern social disaggregation, and its most powerful expression was probably the coordination of the "organized unemployed" in Naples that disrupted the traditional hegemony of the Christian Democratic Party. This social movement broke the clientelist mechanisms of employment in public sector jobs and various aid services along with the myth of the modernization that was supposed to come with "peripheral Fordism." The movement proposed instead the definition of an alternative social model based on the establishment of a universal guaranteed minimum income, which would replace the arbitrary system of disability pensions and other forms of assistance. More important, the Fordist model was opposed by a model based on "cultural" forms of production, such as education and particularly health care, which were drastically inadequate in the South.

Thus, for example, in Naples, when the workers' struggles paralyzed the assembly lines at the Alfa Romeo auto plants in the early 1970s, the "organized unemployed," taking up a form of struggle inherited from the occupation of land of the immediate postwar period, mounted a "reverse" strike against the health care services. Without being hired, they occupied and ran the central hospital of Naples, among other places, showing the social utility and the valorizing character of autonomously organized labor, asking then for the recognition of patients in the form of stable and socially useful employment. In more general terms, the field of mass "illegality" and the so-called criminal economy, which has long been one of the central components of the income of southern families, became during this period a terrain of social experimentation and egalitarianism.

The long period of social struggles, in fact, was also the time when the Mafia experienced a profound crisis of social legitimacy. Thus, as Pino Arlacchi reports, during the long period through the 1970s and into the 1980s when there was no real reconstruction to repair damage caused by an earthquake in Belici in Sicily, the collective force of the social movements had already made possible the emergence of a cultural model in which the traditional attitude of respect for the Mafia had given way to disrespect and even explicit rejection.[3] In short, the relationship between the southern proletariat and the Mafia had been inverted in the same way, we might say, as the relationship between the shop foreman of the large Fordist factories in the Center-North and the immigrant workers. More generally, what was thrown into question was the entire institutional and territorial system of division based on the use of underdevelopment in the South as a resource for Fordist development in the North, as demonstrated by the decline of immigration and the leveling off of wage differences among the various regions. This is why the government attempts beginning in 1975 to break this recomposition strove progressively to dismantle the policies of industrialization and insist instead on a logic of aid and clientelist subsidies. The attempts by the central trade unions to recuperate this dynamic of collective action within a logic of institutional negotiation could not be successful at the beginning without involving at least in part the push of this movement toward the terrain of a relationship between the factory and society or a relationship between North and South. A second front for the struggles was thus open, which involved strikes aimed at reforms that led to a significant extension of guarantees of employment and the social security system, even though this was conducted in an "ultra-Fordist" perspective.[4]

Thus opened the first phase of the fiscal crisis of the State. The public budget took on the responsibility of ensuring the monetarization of the consensus, assuming all the costs of the transformation of the system of social protection. From 1968 to 1975, State spending rose significantly with respect to the gross national product. A system of arbitration that fed inflation was used to make the system of social protection compatible with the general project of capitalist restructuration. According to a logic that culminated in the *scala mobile* system, whereby wages were directly linked to inflation, a modification of tax rates promised to finance the "fiscal drag" through the raising of nominal wages and inversion of the relation between direct and indirect taxes. In fact, from that time on, the increase of the budget deficit, in comparison with the European average, did not result as much from excess spending as from a planned stagnation of receipts. These informal spaces in the budget deficit were part of the attempt to circumvent the rigidity of the working class of the large factories through a maneuver of decentralizing production. Far from arriving at the desired results, however, these articulations of welfare became the new terrain on which the social division of labor was restructured within families and community networks that developed a real synergy of struggles, double employment, small businesses, and informal economy, using these elements as part of experiments in production and syntheses of multiple means of gaining income.

In short, the dynamic of struggles that were set in motion with the Hot Autumn of 1969 defined a process of recomposition and social transformation that shattered the set of institutional and territorial divisions that had served to regulate the Fordist wage relationship and the dependent status of the South. The struggles established a new relationship between North and South based on alternative forms of social and collective cooperation. At the center of this dynamic was the reappropriation of the functions of the Welfare State. The results of the production process, the forms of the socialization of income, and the disposal of the social surplus all appeared as pillars of the constitution of an alternative mode of production at the heart of capitalism, as a first articulation of communism.

The Normalization of the Movements:

Welfare as an Alliance among Producers

The principal vector of the defeat of the movements for social transformation did not consist simply in the maneuver to bypass the "worker strongholds" in production and fiscal relationships. The central elements of this process were the Communist Party's strategy of "historic compromise" to achieve a governing alliance with the Christian Democrats, the neocorporatist strategy of the trade unions, and the recentralization and normalization of the industrial relationship in opposition to the democracy of the councils movements. In the context of the fiscal crisis, this strategy was based on the logic of an "alliance among producers" against the increasingly heavy weight of unproductive labor and rents that burdened the costs of reproduction. In the name of the norm of a wage relationship that was stable and secure, the trade unions opposed the principle of guaranteed income and unemployment compensation, taking up the liberal thesis of its harmful effects on employment: it would encourage businesses to lay off employees.

The perverse effects of the Communist Party strategy of worker sacrifices and historical compromise were felt particularly strongly in the South. This was clear, for example, in Naples, where the Communist Party conducted a struggle against the clientelist welfare system, arguing in terms of administrative efficiency for the establishment of "medical criteria of incapacity to work" that would be necessary for individuals to obtain disability payments. This policy did not take into account the fact that the unproductive employee in the service sector and the payments that employee received, even linked to a clientelist mechanism established by the Christian Democratic Party, represented ineluctable elements of the income of southern families. For the Neapolitans, the question was not posed in economic or moral terms, but rather in terms of the automatic means by which the payments were granted, according to a principle of a minimum guaranteed income for each citizen. In this way, far from eliminating the "wastes" of the clientelist Welfare State, this Communist Party strategy allowed the Christian Democratic Party to win back the consensus it had lost: its traditional management at least appeared to be the guarantee of a secure income.

The policy of national solidarity and compromise between the two major parties thus led to a dramatic rupture of the dynamics of social recomposition that had been active throughout the South. It put a "lead cap" on the possibility of any change through collective action, and thus opened the way in the 1980s for the immense restructuring of the Mafia model. The trade unions and the Communist Party were caught in their own trap. The business owners, once they had won the battle of power on the social terrain, carried the offensive into the factories. The 1980 workers' defeat in the Fiat auto plant in Turin symbolically marked the end of an entire cycle of struggles. The governments of national solidarity between the Communist Party and the Christian Democratic Party in the late 1970s used this strategy, heralding the defense of employment of the central sectors of the working class against the "marginals" of the diffuse economy and the South, to break the process of social recomposition. This resulted in new, even more pernicious forms of dualism between North and South, following a welfare model marked by the degeneration of the entire party structure.

Fiscal Crisis and the Violence of Money:

Dismantling the Welfare State

The beginning of the 1980s marked the explosion of the relationship between North and South into two models of welfare. The shift that gave rise to this rupture was itself the result of a monetarist strategy of financing the public deficit. On one hand, during the 1980s in the Center-North and in the Adriatic regions of the South, the economy dominated by large industries, with the victory of the neo-Taylorist model of the Fiat plant and the "new *condottieri*" (the new captains of industry), was able to bring the diffuse economy under its control progressively by subjugating it through the classical relations of subcontracting. These regions experienced a new miracle, a new period of economic growth. The decline of industrial jobs went hand in hand with the rise of independent jobs in small businesses and the "underground" economy. Welfare State, tax evasion, and tax exemptions all contributed to keeping the economic miracle alive.

On the other hand, in the South, notably in the southwestern regions of Compania, Calabria, and Sicily, the economic changes translated into a growth of subsidies to support incomes and consumption according to a logic that was increasingly captive to clientelist and "Mafia" structures. With unemployment rates rising to more than 20 percent in the 1980s, the pensions for "incapacity to work" largely outnumbered retirement pensions and continued to rise. This is the context in which we have to understand the increasing entrepreneurship of the Mafia, which, thanks to the drug "boom" and the deregulation of the financial markets, was able to reverse its traditional dependence on the political and public structures. The "Mafia business" of the 1950s and 1960s was transformed into the "Mafia financial holding company." In the entire South, the Mafia constructed a new economic model, linking strictly together legal and illegal dealings, the formal and the informal economy, and financial activity and directly productive business. It created an integrated and self-sustaining circuit. The considerable wealth that was accumulated through drug and arms trafficking was reinvested in the "political market," influencing public policy over the entire range of the formal and informal economy.

The Mafia by this point controlled the majority of businesses in Sicily, Calabria, and Compania, and it had introduced violent methods of regulating the labor market and competition, erecting rigid controls on hiring. This model explains why, despite the economic crisis and high unemployment, the disposable income of the South remained at levels comparable to that in the northern regions. Furthermore, the contribution of the criminal economy to the gross national product was estimated at about 10 percent, and this indication of the dynamism of the Mafia economy does not even take into account the importance of the penetration of the Mafia into the circuits of the formal economy in the Center-North and in Europe more generally. In fact, the Mafia was the principal beneficiary of the politics of the public deficit, along with the large corporations, finance capital, and the politicians. Capital could only respond to the deficit with high interest rates, which allowed it, in a parasitical way, to reexert control over the movement of "productive cooperation" and guarantee, from the perspective of both macroeconomic regulation and social and political positions, the complementarity of the relationship between the neo-Taylorist model in the North and the Mafia-clientelist model in the South.

The regime of accumulation and the forms of regulation of this post-Fordist mode of development itself entered into crisis progressively during the later half of the 1980s under the pressure of these two structural tendencies and linked to the decline of the regime's internal and external conditions of possibility. The dialectical play between internal factors and international pressures helps explain certain fundamental reasons why the crisis of the Italian model of the Welfare State implied both the risk of a dissolution of national unity and the risk of a more general threat to European unity and its processes of integration.

The growing financial globalization of the world economy has progressively destabilized the self-centered circuit of Fordism in Italy as elsewhere. Threatening this structural condition that had been at the base of the Keynesian policies of national regulation also drew into question the macroeconomic policy that made the development of the South, albeit in a subordinate position, an indispensable condition for the expansion of production in the Center-North. This process at the base of the crisis of the policies of Fordist and Keynesian regulation was the very same process that led all the European economies during the 1970s toward a monetarist shift and policies of competitive deflation. This is why the constitution of a coherent supranational space is the only possible response to the loss of national autonomy over regulation. As Alain Lipietz has argued, however, the modalities of the process of the constitution of a United Europe have reproduced the perverse logic of the internationalization of capital according to a neoliberal model, constructing a single market without establishing the bases of a common regulation, while limiting the adjustment capacities of each country. Faced with external pressure and the threat of not being at the center of the new European monetary system, for example, the Socialist government in France had to abandon the attempt it launched in 1983 to establish a policy of Keynesianism in one country for a policy of competitive deflation and fiscal austerity.

In Italy, too, there was a passage in the early 1980s from a period of inflationist regulation with negative interest rates to a second phase marked by deflation and policies in line with the European monetary system. Italy, however, was able to maintain a policy of expanding domestic demand at a higher level than were the other European countries. It set up a model of growth on credit that in several respects could be compared to the Reagan policies in the United States, particularly with respect to the monetary policy of high interest rates feeding a budget deficit based largely on informal tax exemptions. The Italian model differed, however, in that it also maintained a high level of spending on welfare programs, raising the budget deficit even higher. Public spending was crucial to maintaining a consensus, and the national and local politicians profited from the State finances. All this, however, led to a vicious circle: raising the interest rates and overvaluing the currency sent the public deficit into an increasing spiral. These economic policies aimed at circumventing the pressures of European monetary convergence began to reach their limits near the end of the 1980s.

The spiraling deficit had even stronger effects on the domestic structural crisis, in which the large corporations had followed the Fiat model and met the crisis of Fordism with a purely technological response. Precisely the heart of the network of industrial areas and small firms encountered the greatest difficulties. The neo-Taylorist project ran up against the qualitative decline of the reserve of the labor force, despite the government's attempts to encourage immigration and the passage of legislation favoring the employment of young people. It was essentially an intellectual unemployment, composed primarily of a well-educated labor force whose members preferred to remain unemployed or chose only certain kinds of employment rather than accept jobs for which they were overqualified. This new subjectivity made impossible any simple reorganization of the neo-Taylorist model.

With the joint pressure of the external demands and the decline of domestic socioeconomic structures, all the supports of the social organization of labor that had been put in place during the period of normalization at the beginning of the 1980s were now, at the end of the decade, collapsing. One one hand, the explosion of the deficit had undermined the credibility of the monetary authorities and the Italian government, making inevitable a policy of fiscal readjustment. The survival of both the neo-Taylorist model of the large industries and the political class that was corrupt and linked to the Mafia implied at this point a frontal attack against the very model of welfare that, despite the defeat of the movements for social transformation in the 1970s, had reestablished a consensus based on the uninterrupted rise of the level of consumption. Furthermore, recourse to that welfare model risked putting Italy outside of a United Europe at a point when Italy had no possibility of conducting an expansive policy on its own. In any case, the politicians could only hope to give themselves a semblance of legitimacy in the name of Europe and its criteria for monetary convergence.

In this context, then, it is only an apparent paradox that the policies of the Amato government in the early 1990s, following a neoliberal logic to dismantle the Welfare State, were given their first and fundamental impetus with the 1990 decision to integrate the lira into the strict margins of fluctuation of the European union monetary policies. This decision was designed in part to demonstrate to European governments and markets the Italian will to respect the criteria for entry in the European economic and monetary union. It was also and primarily, however, a message aimed at an internal audience: the politicians and the large industries wanted to make the dismantling of the welfare system appear to be a structural adjustment required by an objective rationality beyond their control. "The violence of money" thus became the essential means of blackmail, transforming the management of the deficit from a fragile and unstable enterprise into a political and social compromise, an instrument wielded over the economy to maintain the command of a regressive and purely parasitic capital over the field of productive and social cooperation.

The trade unions responded to this message once again as an "attentive and conscientious" partner in facing the emergency, which posed the "necessity" of dealing with the deficit. The unions played a role that increasingly resembled that of a State apparatus, adopting, within the constraints of global macroeconomic structures, a corporatist defense of the working class that corresponded in effect to reproposing the old "compromise among producers" against the ineffectiveness of public services and public administration. The central point of the conception of welfare reform that was subsequently defended by the institutional Left consisted in denouncing the injustice of financing the welfare system essentially on the basis of the taxes of a dependent industrial labor force; the continually diminishing industrial labor force was called upon to bear the costs of reproduction of an expanding population and to support the privileges of the autonomous workers and small businesses of the diffuse economy that engaged in tax evasion. The policies of the unions, then, far from guaranteeing the interests of the central segments of the working class, favored the fragmentation of the different components of the social labor force. In particular, this strategy seemed to ignore the social structures that had supported the miracle of the diffuse economy in the 1980s, in which family income structure and the division of labor were not opposed to but actually articulated through mixtures of guaranteed employment and independent work, family subsidies and tax evasion, and unemployment benefits and participation in the informal economy. The overall management logic of the unions appeared as a support for the survival of a politically corrupt system that had for years enriched itself through this kind of informal taxation, which in the North and the South had characterized the political system's control over public expenditures and projects.

The Italian Debacle

The so-called northern question was born in the early 1990s in the midst of the dismantling of the Welfare State. The federalism of self-management that the social movements had created in the 1970s was now inverted in a particularist localism in the form of political parties known as the Northern Leagues. The emergence of this political force was part of the initial phase of the collapse of the party system that had long dominated Italian politics. The Leagues' electoral success and their power to topple the established political institutions was due in large part to their ability to offer a space for the recomposition of different actors of the diffuse economy in the Center-North in the form of a fiscal protest against the bureaucratic State and the unproductive South. The leaders of the Leagues belonged to a popular and conservative Right that took part in a more general revival of nationalism and racism. The electoral consensus that acted as the real catalyst for the crisis of the party system, however, can be attributed only in very small part to ethnic and racial questions. The Northern Leagues threatened, in effect, to secede from the rest of the country, and this appeared to be a real and effective form of blackmail, when there was no plausible hypothesis about how to save the welfare system and secure a certain standard of living and consumption. If the new Europe was going to have two speeds or two economic levels, then this would allow northern Italy to approach the European center of gravity, represented by Germany, whereas the South would be relegated toward the most distant periphery.

The South was confronted by this threat of secession by the northern regions, and whereas previously it had been the electoral pillar of the traditional parties, now it was the terrain of a new Mafia offensive aimed at the State magistrates, which included the assassination of two of the principal anti-Mafia judges. This offensive could be interpreted as analogous to the Leagues' strategy in the North, renewing the Mafia's tradition of Sicilian separatism and trying to make Sicily into a kind of Switzerland of the criminal economy. The autonomy and power of the economic and financial circuits the Mafia had already developed indeed made the region less dependent on State subsidies. The role of the subsidies in the Mafia economy were already secondary with respect to the guarantee of the institutional mechanisms of recycling the flow of capital in the criminal economy and the possibility of removing the legal obstacles that restricted the Mafia model of accumulation. This dynamic led gradually to a reversal of the Mafia's dependence on government politicians as the Mafia became more capable of controlling voting and gained increased financial and economic power. This changing relationship of force served to destroy the long-standing alliance between the Christian Democratic Party and the Mafia.[5]

The neoliberal strategy of the Amato government in the early 1990s, then, trying to reconcile a program to dismantle the structures of the Welfare State with the survival of the old party system, was inevitably plagued by several insurmountable obstacles: not only the inability to reform an ossified institutional system and the difficulty of winning the confidence of international financial markets, but also the incapacity to manage the volatile relationship between the central State and the regions. The two enormous investigations conducted by the magistrature, the one against the Mafia and the so-called clean-hands investigation of political corruption, marked the definitive end of both Italy's First Republic, which had lasted since the end of World War II, and the economic model that Italy had pursued through the 1980s, bringing out into the open its ugly underside. The investigations literally blew away the common ground that held together the culturally and economically developed Center-North and the parasitic, subsidized, and Mafia-infested South.

As the magistrature's investigations of Mafia and political leaders revealed how broad the system of corruption and illegal accumulation had been in political and macroeconomic terms, it became clear that the South should not be singled out as a backward region; rather, all the economic, political, and cultural centers of Italy were equally invested by the moral question — Lombardy just like Calabria, Milan just like Palermo. Certainly, there remains a difference between the industries of the North and the underdevelopment of the South, and there is a kind of corruption involved in northern political and business circles that is different from that in the Mafia, but nonetheless the arrangement of political exchanges between the business world and the political administration is equally systematic in both cases. The political and industrial establishment, in fact, operated along the lines of a Mafia-style model of corruption based on a partnership between, on one hand, business leaders who were close to a particular party or system of parties and, on the other, a new generation of political entrepreneurs who acted as mediators, "broker capitalists," living off the control and diversion of public resources. In short, already in the mid-1980s there had been institutionalized on a national scale a situation of high corruption, that is, an economic formation in which illegal political practices and exchanges were no longer marginal phenomena but rather infested the entire set of networks of civil society and the institutions of the central and peripheral State administration.

The economic crisis opened as one of its central dimensions the crisis of the political and institutional spheres. The protagonists of this revolution, however, were no longer the subjectivities characterized by the "refusal of work" and "mass intellectuality" that animated the movements in the 1970s; now the protagonists were the magistrates, along with a caricature of a resurgence of civil society in the form of the Northern Leagues. The Leagues took up from the movements of the 1970s a distorted version of the "localist" aspects of the demand for a radical democracy and combined that with a call for separatism, which was often merely a cover for racist and antisouthern sentiments. The only real content of the Leagues' demands was the idea of financial and fiscal federalism linked to the hope of escaping the burden of an expensive welfare system and thus entering into the first row of the United Europe and the international markets as a highly competitive region.

Faced with the challenge of the Leagues and the collapse of the traditional party system, the institutional Left has been unable to construct an alternative that does not take recourse to either a logic of corporatist localism (which is indistinguishable from the Leagues) or the logic of global capital. The approach of the Democratic Party of the Left, which is the primary heir of the disbanded Communist Party, consists for the most part of the attempt to reconcile the Leagues' demands for a localist-secessionist corporativism with a new national economic compromise between capital and labor under the hegemony of big capital and the "socialliberal" logic of dismantling the Welfare State to prepare for entry into the United Europe. It is not hard to recognize in this strategy a continuation of the old Communist Party project of historical compromise and national solidarity, aimed at creating an agreement between big capital and the Catholic heirs of the Christian Democratic Party, that would create a governable system assuring a transition toward a new constitutional form and permitting de facto the survival of the old political class and the logic of the Fordist constitution dressed up, perhaps, in new clothes.

It should be clear, however, that the crisis of the Welfare State represents the demise of the social-democratic Fordist conception of welfare, in which the development of the indirect wage remained anchored to the principles of a proportional relationship between benefits and wage contributions, on the basis of an almost full level of employment in which each person earned his or her living working for a wage. That model of financing welfare has proved untenable. Although the level of social productivity has allowed for a drastic reduction in the number of hours dedicated to work, and precisely because of this fact, full employment has been shown to be an impossible goal, capital has imposed the absurd survival of the wage relationship, creating a perverse dualism in society. In short, the fiscal crisis of the Welfare State is only the crisis of the Fordist mechanism of financing centered on the norm of a wage relationship and full employment; the rising levels of unemployment and more generally of a second society of nonwork only translate, in a distorted way, the generalized reduction of "necessary" labor time linked to the increasingly social character of the productivity of post-Fordist labor.

We can clearly identify today the terms of a social productivity that for more than ten years has allowed Italy to guarantee, with a progressive reduction of the active population, a continual increase of the income and the well-being of the society of "nonwork." The movements for social transformation of the 1970s conceived of this social surplus as the basis for a welfare system of the universal income of all citizens. This system would be founded on a nonnegotiable set of use values, cultural products, and techniques of self-management, a solidarity between rich regions and poor regions that goes together with a decentralized management of services in function of local needs. The logic of this new form of welfare would destroy the common notion that State and socialization must be intimately linked.

On the remains of the defeated movements of the 1970s that attempted social transformation from below, however, the conservative revolution of the 1990s is constructing its power from above. The "Forza Italia" party, with Silvio Berlusconi, the media magnate, at its head, combines an ultraconservative discourse typical of the Thatcher government with the nationalist and populist rhetoric of the traditional Italian Right, forging links with the former fascists. This conservative revolution claims it will maintain the Welfare State and bring about an economic upturn that will lead to the reestablishment of almost full levels of employment. Despite the fears of many, however, the omnipotence of Berlusconi's mass media form of rule is not yet, happily, an exact science of government and social control. There exists also, inherited from years of social struggles, the potential for an alternative form of welfare based on autonomous self-management and social solidarity outside of State control. The history of the Second Italian Republic will perhaps be written between these two poles.

Translated by Michael Hardt

Notes

1. See Alain Lipietz, *Sur les fordismes peripheriques de l'Europe du Sud* (Paris: CEPREMAP, 1983).

2. The notion of a new mass entrepreneurship refers to a new social and productive stratum of society that was consolidated both in terms of socioeconomic and class structure and in terms of political organization. This new stratum contributed to a radical change of the old equilibria that characterized the Italian society of the Fordist compromise and the First Republic. In part, this group has formed the social bases of the Northern Leagues.

3. See Pino Arlacchi, *La Mafia imprenditrice: l'etica mafiosa e lo spirito del capitalismo* (Bologna: Il Mulino, 1983).

4. See Robert Boyer, *La theorie de la regulation: une analyse critique* (Paris: La Decouverte, 1986).

5. The hypothesis of an effective synergy between the separatist project of the Northern Leagues and that of the Sicilian Mafia seemed to be confirmed in part when Gianfranco Miglio, the principal theoretician of the Northern Leagues, who broke with their leader Umberto Bossi in order to rally behind Silvio Berlusconi, proposed a federalist reform of the constitution that would give Sicily complete autonomy with respect to the maintenance of public order.

S E V E N

Women and Welfare: Where Is Jocasta?

Alisa Del Re

In the Oedipus myth, Oedipus's body and his desires significantly contribute to the making of the individual's free will, his autonomy as well as the relationship between knowledge and will. Yet the other body at stake, that of his mother, Jocasta, is hardly visible. We know nothing about her, neither her desires, nor her guilt, nor whether she is self-aware.[1] She is the Mother, unself-conscious and loving, and nothing is said about her concerns, her aspirations, and her needs. She has no desire: in Oedipus's drama she endures and disappears. Not even Freud is interested in Jocasta, and in his interpretation of the Oedipus myth he disingenuously disregards the mother, who must have certainly suffered, as well as felt emotions and desires. The relationship between mother and son is so asymmetrical, and the interpretation of their desires so incommensurable, that in both the myth and contemporary psychoanalytic interpretations of it, we are presented with a mutilated reading of the situation. The Oedipus myth thus stands as the most blatant emblem of the phallocentric bias of an interpretation that claims to be "scientific." This type of reading denies the question of sexual difference as it is inscribed in the story and refuses to acknowledge Jocasta as a constitutive element of both reality and the formation of thought.

As of today, things have not really changed. In a recent issue of the French journal *Sciences Humaines*, a long series of articles proposed that the human sciences are founded on a few constantly reformulated themes, questions, and myths that continue to fuel research in the humanities.[2] The articles do not take into account, as a crucial fact, the question of sexual difference. None of the pieces in the collection acknowledges that the object of analysis, the human being, is gendered, that gender is instrumental for the human being's social constitution, or that gender concerns and informs the categories of race, class, and ethnicity. The fact that sexual difference does not invest only one minority, to which fundamental issues can be referred, but rather is per se a fundamental issue is never mentioned at all. The question of sexual difference is thus emptied of meaning in the name of a subject who, in the symbolic order of the researcher, is imagined as masculine and in the name of a society whose power and organizational structures are founded on this subject. To think the difference between man and woman as incommensurable and asymmetrical implies an interpretation of reality and of the production of discourse that acknowledges sexual difference as the foundation of social reality. This difference constitutes a necessary value, capable of producing change; as such, it represents a tool of analysis superior to the current paradigms of research. It is worth stressing that we are not dealing with the mere task of "adding" women here and there in our studies; such a move would only have the effect of assimilating a new element within an unchanging symbolic order. Feminist discourse in the social sciences has already offered suggestions and pointed to new directions for an analysis that could confer meaning and human value upon the real.[3]

The inclusion of sexual difference in the scientific analysis of social phenomena dramatically brings to the fore an often forgotten question, that of the social and private, material, and psychological reproduction of individuals. For women, the continual alternation between reproduction and productive labor, between emancipation and traditional female roles, implies a change in their interpretation of reality as well as in their way of organizing their lives. The unilateralism of traditional parameters of interpretation (such as the exploitation of waged labor, State control, and capitalist crisis and development) clashes with more complex visions of transformation. If we accept (1) that to see oneself as gendered implies the notion of a "social construction" founded on the relationship between gendered subjects, (2) that such a relationship continually and inevitably changes through time, and (3) that even a crystallized notion of biological difference carries within itself the promise of at least a spark of social change,[4] then the theoretical production of the feminist movement becomes a cultural tool to show how scientific paradigms, particularly in the social sciences, are an inadequate basis for an understanding of reality.

ALISA DEL RE

It is crucial, therefore, that women's lives—their existence, their nature, as well as their activities—become an integral part of philosophical and intellectual discourse, so that the acknowledgment of female subjectivity, constructed as it is in multiple symbolic and material loci, can reveal the partiality of a vision of the world that even today is considered universal.

Welfare, Women, and the State

After the wave of economic liberalism that during the 1980s brought to power in the United States two Republican administrations (now substituted by Clinton's Democratic one), the phrase *Welfare State*, often uttered in a derogatory tone, came to signify all public expenditures (for instance, public education and transportation, public administration salaries, and public health and pensions).[5] It should be clear that the State produces a series of goods and services (such as public transportation) that have nothing to do with the Welfare State; furthermore, public education was not born within the sphere of the Welfare State, but as the necessary means for the secular formation of the emerging industrial bourgeoisie of the capitalist State.[6] Several other public expenses (such as those for defense, public order, and justice) concern the State in general, and not the Welfare State. Since the 1930s, management techniques perfunctorily defined as "Keynesian policies" have found wider and wider application: they have been deployed because of the inadequacy of laissez-faire theory to provide tools for the management of complex industrial economies. This is not the Welfare State either. The Welfare State is established once the secular principle of solidarity is substituted for the religious principle of charity. The idea is that all citizens have the right to live decently, even when the events of their lives, starting from unfavorable initial chances, would not allow it.[7] Assistance, social security, and public health thus pertain to the Welfare State, and as such represent a form of income and social services distribution.[8] Helga Maria Hernes talks about two waves of welfare: the first is mainly concerned with the labor market, and the second involves the sphere of reproduction.[9] More clearly stated, there is a shift from the sphere of the production of goods, where the producers and the owners of the means of production are guaranteed that they will be able to continue producing, to the sphere of reproduction, where what is guaranteed and controlled (without direct links to production but nonetheless aimed at it) is the reproduction of individuals.

Historically, the reproduction of individuals has been the task of women. In the Welfare State, the labor of reproduction became the basis of a specific relation between women and the State. The State is the institution that historically has regulated the adjustment between the process of accumulation and the process of social reproduction of the population. Modern States control the conflicts inherent to the distribution of waged labor, the specific distribution of labor, and the resources that it entails. In the systems founded on waged labor, the work of reproduction consists mostly of unpaid domestic labor. Through it the system can, by taking advantage of the social authority indirectly assured it by the endemic insecurity of salaries, affirm its control over the perpetuation of the processes of production and reproduction. The "right" balance between the two processes represents the condition for the continuity of the process of capitalist accumulation.[10] Many institutions and several administrative practices intervene in the social relations between the sexes, which, in turn, are directly influenced by the interventions of the Welfare State: for example, the sexual division of labor (which includes the organization of the work of care and those who perform it), the access to waged labor (as the access to a central form of regulation in our societies and a means of survival), marriage, and family relations.

The insecurity of access to the means of survival for citizens has led the State to assume some direct responsibilities toward the population, particularly in the case of wage workers, the unemployed, and those who cannot directly count on salaries.[11] The State, however, which has never been neutral toward social classes, is certainly not neutral in the case of gender. In fact, the State's control over women allows it to control the population, a key element in a world of production in which labor is the most basic commodity. With the welfare system, the State tolerates that women work more, and that they are poorer and less protected from the point of view of social security than are men. Although the State has assumed direct responsibility in relation to the issue of reproduction, its interventions in this sphere have never meant to substitute but rather only to integrate the family. In the formulation of any social policy, women are always implicitly expected to do their domestic duties. The entire welfare system is principally addressed to male waged workers: in fact, women receive a significantly inferior percentage of its financial resources, so that the discriminations actually existing in the spheres of waged labor and domestic labor are perpetuated.[12] Even in those countries where the rates of women's working for wages are high and public services are widespread — as, for instance, in the Scandinavian countries — the relation between women and the State, centered on the domestic labor of reproduction, remains unresolved. The case of Sweden, exactly because it is an advanced country, shows how difficult it is, in the family, in the labor market, and in public institutions, to dislodge the conviction that women are the primary means of social reproduction.[13] This said, it is, however, necessary to add that the terrain of the relationship with the State has, to all effects, created for women a few possibilities of emancipation from the private relationship of dependency on male waged labor.

The State has not always been considered an enemy in the strategy of women's struggles. Feminism's "long march" through the institutions is historically visible in all the European countries: it suffices to mention the long battle for equal opportunity, which entailed not only the demand for nondiscrimination in the workplace and in salaries, but also affirmative action (*azioni positive*), a system that allowed for consideration of the compatibility of a given job with the work of reproduction.[14] The limit of these battles lies in their being the *conditio sine qua non* for obtaining a waged job, and therefore in their aiding women, whose chief task is the work of reproduction, to adapt to the conditions of waged labor.

The feminist critique of the liberal State and the empty formalism of the notion of juridical equality, however, has never turned into a full endorsement of the Welfare State. To its patronizing attitudes feminists have always counterposed specific demands for raises in income or in the quantity and quality of social services. In Europe, within the system of social security, these demands have been accompanied by a pressing general proposal for a substantial system of welfare, which few understand correctly: women have stopped having children in the quantities required by demographic plans, thus imposing a life model for themselves and for the entire society in which they live, so that to the reduced workload of reproduction corresponds also an improved standard of life.[15]

An alternative project of welfare was drafted in Italy in 1990, with a bill supported by popular demand, called "the bill on time."[16] The aim of this bill was to overcome the sexual division of labor by redistributing equally productive and domestic labor (not only between the two sexes, but also between society and the individual subject) and allowing the individual to self-manage her or his time. This would be an alternative model of development for the entire society: by taking as its point of departure the question of time and scheduling, it would also involve the structure of the city, because it would negotiate the functioning of the spaces where we live. The model has actually been applied as an experiment in several places.[17] The interweaving of production and reproduction in women's lives has provoked, in the social sphere of reproduction, the demand for a reduction of work time.[18] In this initiative, which has attracted much interest among women of all European countries, besides having been proposed by women (and perhaps for this reason it has been little debated by political parties and not yet discussed in the Italian Parliament), the most significant element is represented by the lack of any separation of labor time for the production of goods and services from the time of reproductive labor. In other words, the entire time of living is taken into account, and not simply partial temporalities. What is taken into consideration is time to be managed concretely in the spaces of the everyday. The centrality of the reproduction of individuals, and therefore the subordination of the workplace and the market to it, is the founding element of this "universality" proposed by women.

What is needed is more political and theoretical attention to the situation of women, not only in socioeconomic terms (even though the economic factor is an important element in the attempt to win autonomy), but also as the principle of a critique that can help us fight and overcome the bourgeois State and its mechanisms of exploitation, as well as the limitations of a distributive logic of justice reproducing the same oppressive and exploitative relationship between men and women. Explicit reference to women's problematics could therefore provide new ideas and new impulses for the analysis and the overcoming of the Welfare State.

Waged Labor, Women, and Welfare

In the film *The Fountainhead*, Gary Cooper, as an extremely upright architect, cries out: "A man working for free for other men is a slave." And what about women? Women have always supplied their reproductive work to others for free, yet we do not realize, or we do not want to realize, even when part of this labor is paid, how much it would cost at full price to the national budget.

The socialization of reproduction operated by the Welfare State is indeed one way of transforming traditional domestic tasks (such as health care, hygiene, motherhood, and education). Instead of being organized in the private sphere, these are now organized by State institutions or are controlled by the State (aside from the general control of domestic labor within the family). In connection with this socialization, the transformation of reproduction into a wage-earning activity is realized with waged jobs concerning the control of the reproduction of individuals, and explicitly created for women, such as social workers and nurses. This "professionalization" of reproduction marks a deep transformation of the labor of reproduction, as well as the entry into the labor market of the specific forms of women's work, that is, jobs historically assigned to women.

In all the European Community countries, the sectors of health, teaching, and what are modestly referred to as "other services," together with distribution and food service jobs, in 1991 constituted more than half of the total female employment (against 28 percent of male employment). In the same year, 94–100 percent of preschool teachers were women; this percentage decreases once we move toward secondary school teaching, where only 25 percent of teachers were women in most countries.[19] Even though education is not strictly part of the welfare system (preschool teaching, however, can be considered a social service), we can see that this system has deepened the sexual division of labor, both vertically (among different sectors) and horizontally (among different career levels). Yet we must consider that the service sector was for a long time the only one to have shown a significant development in terms of numbers of jobs offered to women: it has helped women to become part of the waged working population. This sexual division of labor on the one hand has protected women,[20] but on the other it has exploited them, tapping their unacknowledged and therefore underpaid laboring qualities, expertise, and capabilities.

State intervention in the institution of the family has partially transferred into the public sphere some of the family's traditional tasks, such as the socialization of children, education, health care, and the care of the elderly. As a result, there has been a professionalization and expansion of these types of work, which had formerly been organized by the extended family, the church, and the local communities and performed by women in these social groups. Now women become customers and employees of the welfare system, and, for free, compensate its disfunctions both with their unpaid work of care and by feeding into it with competences and needs that exceed strictly waged labor relations. This creates a reciprocal dependence between women and the State.

Andre Gorz critiques, but only in a gender-blind perspective, the formation of a wage society that perpetuates itself by continually monetizing, professionalizing, and turning into waged labor even the everyday and most elemental activities of life.[21] Gorz forgets, like many other analysts of a welfare system of the future, that it is not particularly pleasant to perform for oneself and for others these everyday and elemental activities, for free and often side by side with a paid job. I must thus propose a gendered reading of the "full employment" society that he analyzes in order to clarify what the division of labor would be and to whom the different tasks would be assigned; otherwise, the utopia of a more equal society, with the least degree of exploitation possible, would not be realized in the same measure for the two sexes. On the contrary, such a utopia would be founded on the exploitation of women and their unpaid labor of reproduction.

With the loss of jobs produced by economic crisis (in industry, and above all in the service sectors), women do not necessarily become unemployed. They exit the labor market and increase the numbers of the inactive, nonworking population. This process—obligatory layoffs of the female labor force—has never been considered scandalous. Perhaps some foolish sociologist will say that it is an individual choice, even though nobody believes so anymore. The other result of the reduction of female employment manifests itself more explicitly in terms of unemployment. The situation is difficult, because it does not seem to be likely that there will be a large development of the services tied to the welfare system, services that in general absorb this component of the labor force.

The conflict between provisions (the goods and services produced) and entitlements (the attribution of the rights of access to their use)[22] is now at the core of a debate on the transformations of the welfare system, because it is clear that to a larger and larger supply of goods corresponds a more and more evident restriction of the rights of access (entitlements). One of the most recent and most limited interpretations of the welfare system is the concept of "workfare," imported from the United States and now very fashionable in Europe also. Workfare establishes a correspondence between social rights and assistance and the recipients' availability to work.[23] This method would exclude from the market all the weak subjects, or those depending on others' wages; last but not least, it would impose the entire cost of this "reform" on the unpaid labor of reproduction.

Welfare, Women, and Social Rights

The history of the women's movement has demonstrated an institutional effect of the thesis used by feminism to try to make visible the exploitation of women: the private is public. If this is the case, the legislative and administrative sphere can invade the sphere of reproduction, the so-called private sphere, through State intervention. Such intervention has very often assumed the eminent character of social and cultural policy; that is to say, it has functioned to assimilate and appropriate forms of experience that have been autonomously produced by the women's movement. The act of asking the State to intervene by legislating and administrating in the sphere of reproduction, the family, and the protection of women as weak subjects in labor relations has certainly assumed a character of bureaucratization and control.[24]

The welfare policies that seem to favor women most are those concerning the protection of maternity. These have a long and complex history and include the regulation of labor (reduced schedules, leaves of absence, and prohibition of night work and hard jobs), the constitution of services (nursing rooms, maternity clinics, institutions for the protection of mother and child), and the redistribution of income (welfare subsidies).[25] In fact, these policies do not constitute specific social rights. Elizabeth Wolgast defines them as "false rights"; in the case of the protection of maternity, for instance, it is the child or the fetus that is actually to be protected.[26] The foremost right of protection for women should be their ability to decide autonomously whether or not to become mothers without risking their lives — that is, the right to make decisions about their own bodies.[27] In this context, it is perhaps useful to remember that at the beginning of this century the broadening of the laws for the protection of maternity was accompanied by the persistence of laws against abortion and contraception.

Protesting by using the language of rights obviously means asking the State's permission for protection. "Rights" are invoked, contested, distributed, and protected, but also limited and appointed by the law. Sexual difference is thus reduced to the social roles protected by the State. Furthermore, even though social rights are established within the sphere of reproduction, and as such concern women in particular, it is not for this reason that such rights can be considered favorable to women, because women paradoxically consume fewer social rights than they produce. Their labor of reproduction (controlled by the State) functions as a substitute for the welfare system.[28]

It is important, moreover, to study how differences among women are articulated through the constitution and realization of social policies: these are differences of representation, identity, social status, and political choice, both in practice and in theory. In the book *Il genere delle politiche sociali in Europa* (The gender of social policies in Europe), by the research group État et rapports sociaux de sexe, we see how the consumers and the employees of Gautier's welfare, Spensky's "average mothers" and "unmarried mothers," the assisting and the assisted ones, and those taken care of according to their different ethnicity, as well as Jenson's "radical," "unionist," or "revolutionary" feminists, represent different models, groups, and variables of aggregation and relationships among women.[29] They all contribute to establishing the terms of a political discourse in which the expression of interests is the fruit of a mediation, when indeed there is a mediation or when a mediation is possible. In the majority of cases, however, when they do not even represent an obstacle, social policies merely tend to make waged labor and reproductive labor compatible.[30] Furthermore, they do not even cover entirely the costs of the adjustment of the female labor force to the model of labor performance demanded by the market (which calculates a full-time housewife for each male worker). These costs are therefore passed on to the "private" resources of the concerned subjects (substantially, the other women in the family, the younger and older ones). When this happens, a process of redistribution of global social labor takes place, which, founded as it is on strong differentiations within the female population, becomes particularly discriminatory.

A Different Welfare System: Finding Jocasta

Acknowledgment of the gendered character of the Welfare State and its social policies could represent an important corrective for the analytic literature on this topic, which is too often blind in its general definitions of the concepts of class and citizenship.[31] In the many existing studies on welfare, each analysis calls up various interpretive conceptions that are at times in conflict with each other: the commutative conception, according to which the right to security is linked to the exercise of waged labor, is juxtaposed to the distributive approach, according to which the same right is founded on the individual's needs; the functionalist approach, in which the social policies would be functional to capitalist development, is counterposed to the conflictualist approach, which defines the welfare system as the result of the workers' social gains and their struggles.[32] The primary subjects of all these analyses are in the first place the poor, the workers, and finally the citizens in general. Even one of the most recent and substantially correct analyses of welfare, according to which the Welfare State subjects the dynamics of reproduction to that of production (thus establishing an extraordinary mechanism of control over the entire life of individuals), disregards the subjects of reproduction as well as the mechanisms through which women's reproductive labor has contributed to the development of the welfare system.[33] In so doing, this analysis conceals its internal contradictions, tied as they are to different proposed and practiced models. Yet, within the welfare system women are paid workers, privileged customers, and disciplined individuals, who not only have transferred their knowledge and expertise from the private into the social sphere without retribution, but have also transformed and standardized their own lives. The welfare system has imposed limitations on the quality of life: women have always rebelled and struggled against such limitations, asking for a better quality of social services and a higher level of income.

The welfare system has reproduced and socialized the capitalist sexual division of labor: male = production, female = reproduction. It has also, however, introduced internal mechanisms of adjustment (the work of care has been transformed into a wage-earning activity, for instance), thus liberating the labor of reproduction from its dependence on another person's salary. Within the work of reproduction there have been established many divisions among women: between those who depend on welfare and those who administer it, and between those who do the work of care (paid or unpaid) and those who, thanks to these, can work in other areas. Another characteristic of the work of care performed as part of the welfare system is that it has reproduced, even in typically "feminine" work, a gender hierarchy: in the pyramidal structure of this work, the greater the distance from the actual taking care of others, the more the work is connoted as masculine and therefore more valorized and prestigious.

Now, with the European economic crisis, we also witness a recessionary and repressive reorganization in both production and reproduction processes. This move represents an attack on the material conditions of women's lives, and as such diminishes their social and political power. The mere defense of the system of welfare in the way it is practiced by the unions and the traditional Left in general reduces these agencies to mere means of preservation. They cannot be considered a privileged political channel for women to make visible a conflict that should call into question the deep structure of the system. In Italy, the confused program of the Northern Leagues and what they call "the new advances"—that is, the proposal to pay less in taxes, send women back into the home, and return to a nonsocialized reproduction—has encountered strong resistance. For instance, faced with the privatization and/or increase of day-care fees, women have reacted by organizing and developing a system of baby-sitting. A defensive, intergenerational network of women is coming into being; combined with the demographic decrease, or the postponing of the birth of the first child, this network allows women to resist the cuts imposed on the welfare system.[34]

Does this mean that women must struggle to preserve the current system of welfare? There is a fundamental misunderstanding about the Welfare State: even in its heyday it was not particularly satisfying—not because it was too costly (as they want us to believe now), but because it was too meager in the sense that the State spent too little to guarantee the quality and the quantity of the services necessary for the reproduction of individuals. In fact, the welfare system, even at the moment of its progressive birth, was founded on the labor of women, without ever questioning it or including it among the costs of social reproduction. With the crisis, these costs, which are not calculated but which weigh more heavily on women's shoulders, will increase.

There are a few things, however, that have become irreversible: on the one hand, some services can no longer be substituted for by domestic labor; on the other, men and women of our generation cannot afford to ignore the cost of the work of care. For the first time in history, care is perceived as a right, and it is evident to all those who work in this field (paid or unpaid) that it has become extremely valuable. The women whose job is the professional care of people (in the health care system as well as in social, psychological, and educational services) have only recently discovered how valuable their work is. This discovery gives a new sense and a new quality to the struggles in this field, and can produce innovations in ways of managing the work itself and its future development. (I am thinking particularly of the struggles of nurses and social workers in France.)[35]

The socialization of reproduction operated by the welfare system can therefore be considered a perverse process, because part of the unpaid work of women has been socialized as specifically "feminine." At the same time, the models of the centrality of the reproduction of goods and accumulation have remained unchanged, while reproduction has not been made central for society. Welfare is not part of a project of change exactly because it has always accepted, and even worked to ensure, that reproduction would be compatible with the productive system and its changes. One of the constitutive elements of welfare as a system is its way of considering reproduction a social fact and the labor of reproduction by women as controllable and capable of being disciplined. This means controlling and disciplining socially women's lives through a general standardizing and flattening of the quality of those lives.

The problem today is thus to confront the radical question of the conflict over social reproduction, without thinking that one can cut out for oneself a niche of personal self-defense, and without accepting any compatibility with the centrality of the current mode of production as well as with the market. Yet the radical models of change experimented with until now (such as seizure of the State, war, and even revolution) do not appear particularly useful. Confronted by a system founded on the concealment of the actual costs of reproduction—which women have paid for until now, and calculable in terms of money and labor, but also in terms of quality of individual and social life—women must find a way to present their bill. First of all, we must keep trying to make visible the labor of reproduction in its totality and not only in the part made public by the welfare system; at the same time, we must try to underline its centrality with respect to production and the market. For this reason, women must become capable of intervening in the crucial questions of our society and strongly imposing the new parameters for change. These parameters, such as the proposal to go beyond welfare by taking as our goal the improvement of the quality of life, starting from the reorganization of the time of our lives, must be worked out and designed through a political mediation among women.

Translated by Maurizia Boscagli

Notes

1. See Christiane Olivier, *Les enfants de Jocaste* (Paris: Denoël/Gonthier, 1980).

2. "Les défis des sciences humaines" (special issue), *Sciences Humaines*, no. 25 (February 1993).

3. See, for example, Cristina Marcuzzo and Anna Rossi Doria, eds., *La ricerca delle donne* (Turin: Rosemberg and Sellier, 1987); Marina Addis Saba, *Storia delle donne, una scienza possibile* (Rome: Felina, 1986); Ginevra Conti Odorisio, ed., *Gli studi sulle donne nelle Universita: ricerca e trasformazione del sapere* (Naples: Edizioni Scientifiche Italiane, 1988); "Savoir et différence des sexes" (special issue), *Les Cahiers du Grif,* no. 45 (Autumn 1990).

4. See Marie J. Dhavernas, "Bioetica: progressi scientifici e arretramenti politici," *Antigone,* no. 1 (1991); and Anne Marie Daune-Richard, Marie-Claude Hurtig, and Marie-France Pichevin, *Catégorisation de sexe et constructions scientifiques* (Aix-en-Provence: Université de Provence, CEFUP, 1989).

5. See Alessandra Nannei, "Stato sociale: l'acqua sporca e il bambino," *Via Dogana,* nos. 10/11 (1993): 3–5.

6. Christopher Hill, in *The Intellectual Origins of the English Revolution* (Oxford: Clarendon, 1965), describes the process through which scientists and the professional class, through spontaneous initiatives, spread the new secular culture and technological knowledge in seventeenth-century England. In so doing, they prompted the formation of a large class of technicians, inventors, and specialized craftsmen, which sowed the seed of the industrial revolution. Instead, we can ascribe mass education and a free and widely spread level of literacy to the welfare system. However, we often forget how much effort is demanded at home by elementary and secondary education. Some scholars consider the whole education system to be part of Welfare State policies; see, for instance, P. Flora and A. Heidenheimer, eds., *The Development of Welfare States in Europe and America* (New Brunswick, N.J.: Transaction, 1981).

7. François Ewald, in *L'Etat providence* (Paris: Grasset, 1986), also confirms that there has been a shift from the notion of risk — used by insurance companies — to the idea of solidarity. The social security system establishes a solidarity on the basis of the classic social contract to cover the worker against the temporary and accidental loss of her or his source of sustenance. For Ewald, with the advent of social security — that is, the formalization of the insurance coverage of the worker, the centralization of the State, and the mass propagation of social policies — the questions of income and need come to the fore.

8. Ann Orloff's definition of Welfare State is much looser: she describes it as any State intervention into civil society that is capable of modifying social and market relations. See Ann S. Orloff, "Gender and Social Rights of Citizenship," *American Sociological Review* 58 (June 1993).

9. See Helga Maria Hernes, "Women and the Welfare State: The Transition from Private to Public Dependence," in *Women and the State,* ed. Anne Showstack Sassoon (London: Hutchinson, 1987).

10. Here I am following Antonella Picchio's thesis in "Il lavoro di riproduzione, questione centrale nelle analisi del mercato del lavoro," *Politiche del lavoro,* no. 19 (December 1992). See also Antonella Picchio, *Social Reproduction: The Political Economy of the Labor Market* (Cambridge: Cambridge University Press, 1992).

11. See Mariarosa Dalla Costa, "Stato, lavoro, rapporti di sesso nel femminismo marxista," in *Stato e rapporti sociali di sesso,* ed. Alisa Del Re (Milan: Franco Angeli, 1989).

12. See Antonella Picchio, "Il lavoro domestico: Reale meccanismo di aggiustamento fra riproduzione sociale e accumulazione capitalistica," in *Primo rapporto: Il lavoro femminile in Italia tra produzione e riproduzione,* ed. Anna Maria Nassisi (Rome: Fondazione Gramsci, 1990).

13. See Laura Balbo, "Crazy Quilts: Rethinking the Welfare State Debate from a Woman's Point of View," in *Women and the State,* ed. Anne Showstack Sassoon (London: Hutchinson, 1987).

14. The affirmative action system works both at the level of individual States and at the European Community level, with a series of specific programs and ad hoc institutions.

15. *Population et sociétés,* no. 282 (August-September 1993) reproduces the *World Population Data Sheet,* which the Population Reference Bureau assembles by using the most precise information on world population available. In Europe, the synthetic fertility rate (number of children per woman) is 1.8 for France (one of the highest), 1.3 for Italy, 1.4 for Portugal, and 1.4 for Spain, with an average for Europe (Russia excluded) of 1.6. The United States has a rate of 2.0. In connection with these data we can notice that, once again in Europe, the employment rate of women who have no children or one child does not change, whereas the same rate is reduced for those who have more than one child. It is evident, almost banal, but worth saying: having or not having children does not change men's employment rate. See Commission des Communautes Europeennes, *L'Emploi en Europe* (Luxembourg: Office des Publications Officielles des Communautes Europeennes, 1993).

16. In October 1990 a bill prompted by popular demand (300,000 signatures of women) was presented to the Parliament by the president of the Senate, Nilde Iotti, on the initiative of the women's section of what was then the Italian Communist Party and is now the Democratic Party of the Left.

17. Bill 142 on local governments has offered the administrators of several municipalities the chance to determine, thanks to a plan regulating their schedules, the timetable of city services and the power to decree by law how citizens should take part in the operation. The city of Modena, whose mayor, Alfonsina Rinaldi, was a woman, was the first to try this in 1988. The experiment has spread to other Italian cities (Reggio Emilia, Terni, Siena, Venice, and Catania) thanks to the presence of large numbers of women in the local administrations. Clearly, the experiment does not cover all the different parts of the bill (which is a framework for legislation). A rationalization of the schedules of social and administrative services, of shops and transportation, implies not only a process of reorganization, but also the agreement of all social parties: the demands of the citizens must be measured in relation to the needs of the women working in public and private services, with those of the tradespeople, and so forth. Experiments have also been made with the reduction and flexibility of working time, in both public and private sectors.

18. The idea of reducing working time is not new. Paul Lafargue, in the famous *Le Droit à la paresse* (1879, 1890), and Bertrand Russell, in *In Praise of Idleness* (1935), have argued in favor of a possible reduction in working time. For Tommaso Campanella, four hours of work per day were enough; six hours for Thomas Moore; five hours for Claude Gilbert; three hours for Lenin; and, in our days, two hours for Andre Gorz. Yet none of these authors explicitly affirms that one is entitled to a free period of time for reproducing oneself and others—a period of time that is unpaid work for women.

19. These data are taken from Commission des Communautes Europeennes, *L'Emploi en Europe*. For Italy see also *Dossier ambiente*, no. 9 (March 1990); and L. Aburra, *L'occupazione femminile dal declino alla crescita* (Turin: Rosemberg and Sellier, 1989).

20. I am thinking of the ideology and legislative practice widespread in European countries during the 1930s. In response to the world crisis and growing unemployment, this ideology tended to send back into the home women who "stole" jobs. In the same period, without any scandal, many socially "feminine" jobs were created in Italy, including the formation of fascist job lists for women.

21. Andre Gorz, *Capitalism, Socialism, Ecology* (London: Verso, 1994).

22. See Ralf Dahrendorf, *Reflections on the Revolution in Europe* (London: Chatto, 1990).

23. See Lawrence Mead, *Beyond Entitlements: The Social Obligations of Citizenship* (New York: Free Press, 1991).

24. See Laura Boella, "Distinguere pubblico e privato," in *Cultura e politica delle donne in Italia*, Atti del Seminario Nazionale di Roma, May 4–5 1992, ed. Anna Maria Crispino and Francesca Izzo (Rome: Fondazione Instituto Gramsci, 1992).

25. Alisa Del Re, "Transformations de l'Etat capitaliste et constitution d'un sujet politique: les femmes (Europe Occidentale)," in *Genèse de l'Etat moderne en Méditerranée*, ed. C. Veauvy and H. Bresc (Rome: Ecole française de Rome, 1993).

26. See Elizabeth Wolgast, *The Grammar of Justice* (Ithaca, N.Y.: Cornell University Press, 1987).

27. The 1993 report of the Population Action International affirms that every year, 200,000 women die in the world during illegal abortions (cited by Vittorio Zucconi in *Espresso*, no. 38 [1993]).

28. See Givanna Zincone, *Da sudditi a cittadini* (Bologna: Il Mulino, 1992).

29. Alisa Del Re, ed., *Il genere delle politiche sociali in Europa* (Padua: CEDAM, 1993).

30. Because of the legislation "protecting" women's work, many women in Italy and Germany have been forced to sign work contracts that obligate them to quit their jobs if they become pregnant. In this regard, there has been a notable increase in cases of female sterilization in the former East Germany; women are having themselves sterilized in order to avoid unwanted pregnancies while they are searching for jobs.

31. Important ongoing feminist research on the welfare system (particularly Anglophone) already exists. I will mention only a few works, besides the books already cited: État et rapports sociaux de sexe, *I rapporti sociali di sesso in Europa (1930–1960): L'impatto delle politiche sociali* (Padua: CEDAM, 1989) and *Il genere delle politiche sociali in Europa (1960–1990)* (Padua: CEDAM, 1993); L. Gordon, ed., *Women, the State and Welfare* (Madison: University of Wisconsin Press, 1990); H. Hernes, *Welfare State and Woman Power* (Oslo: Norwegian University Press, 1987); B. Hobson, "No Exit, No Voice: Women's Economic Dependency and the Welfare State," *Acta Sociologica* 33, no. 3 (1990); J. Jenson, "Gender and Reproduction: Or, Babies and the State," *Studies in Political Economy* (Summer 1986); C. McKinnon, *Toward a Feminist Theory of the State* (Cambridge: Harvard University Press, 1989); C. Pateman, *The Disorder of Women: Democracy, Feminism and Political Theory* (Stanford, Calif.: Stanford University Press, 1989); B. Siim, "Toward a Feminist Rethinking of the Welfare State," in *The Political Interests of Gender*, ed. K. Jones and A. Jonasdottir (Newbury Park, Calif.: Sage, 1990); T. Skocpol, *Protecting Soldiers and Mothers* (Cambridge: Harvard University Press, 1992); M. Weir, A. Orloff, and T. Skocpol, eds., *Women and the Welfare State* (London: Tavistock, 1977).

32. There is an interesting feminist functionalist current. Particularly worth mentioning is Mimi Abramowitz, *Regulating the Lives of Women: Social Welfare Policy from Colonial Times to the Present* (Boston: South End, 1988). Abramowitz uses a method of analysis very similar to the Marxist functionalist approach, except that Marxists do not take gender into account. A typical example is Klaus Offe, *The Contradictions of the Welfare State* (Cambridge: MIT Press, 1984).

33. Giuseppe Cocco and Maurizio Lazzarato, "Au-delà du Welfare State," *Futur antérieur*, no. 15 (1993).

34. See L. Aburra, *L'occupazione femminile dal declino alla crescita* (Turin: Rosenberg and Sellier, 1989).

35. See D. Kergoat, F. Imbert, H. Le Doare, and D. Senotier, *Les Infirmières et leur coordination (1988–89)* (Paris: Lamane, 1992).

E I G H T

Worker Identity in the Factory Desert

Marco Revelli

If we review the political developments of the past quarter century in the light of concepts of "rootedness" and "movement," it is easy to reach conclusions that are disconcerting, or, if you prefer, counterintuitive. What appears to have happened is that the central subject of transformation seems, over this period, to have become a motor that is immobile. The working class—the factor par excellence for contestation of the existing order of things—seems to have adopted as its principal weapon practices of preservation of the status quo, staticness, rigidity, and *resistance*, while, on the other hand, change, proteiformity, and speed—the grand myths of modernity—have to all intents and purposes become the attributes of capital, or, if you like, the forms of class struggle on the employers' side. In short, the essence of the "movement" seems in fact to have been *immobility*, whereas the essence of conservatism seems to have been *movement*. This paradox is precisely what we find in the meager (in fact very meager) sociological literature in Italy dedicated to the overall social cycle spanning the period from the 1960s to the 1980s, the literature, in other words, that does not limit itself purely to the initial moment of mass autonomy or the mid-period phase of trade unionization and normalization, but that considers the entire trajectory—from economic liftoff to crisis, from the 1960s to the 1980s—and thus enables us to make judgments based on "perspective."

A brief review of some of this literature will clarify the terms of this paradox. Consider, for example, the book *L'Altra faccia della FIAT* (The other face of Fiat).[1] This is a historical overview of the "Mirafiori" Fiat auto plant in Turin produced by the members of the Laid-Off Workers Group (Coordinamento Cassintegrati), who examine their own personal histories. Here we have twenty-two "autobiographies" of working-class militants who after the "35 Days of Fiat" (the massive and unsuccessful strike in 1979) carried on for years an organized resistance against being uprooted, and who produced this publication as a further way of preserving a unified group identity. These twenty-two stories are very different from one another — in their language and in the geographic origins, ages, and political and trade-union perspectives of their protagonists — but they all concur on one point: the absolute centrality of the factory as a privileged space for the grounding and developing of their collective identity (through conflict). They all share a stubborn determination to defend that *sense of belonging*, a determination to "last" through to the other side of the technological-industrial changes taking place. There is a particularly striking aspect to this collective document, beyond its immediately political nature, namely, the extraordinary interplay of movement and rootedness that characterizes each of the case studies: *movement as one's destiny and rootedness as an ideal.*

It is as if all these people were being continually driven by a force that stood over them and dragged them from one place to another. We see this from the titles of some of the accounts — "From Puglia to Fiat," "From Calabria to Fiat," "From the Puglia Countryside to the Mirafiori Foundries," "From Lingotto to Mirafiori," "From the Mirafiori Body Plant to Forestale," "From the Mirafiori Presses to Layoffs," "To Borgaretto and Back," and so forth. At the same time, all these accounts contain a marked sense of regret for that moment in which, during their history of "social nomadism," they finally found (and then lost again) a place in which they could "settle," a "country" into which they could set down the roots of their own "being togetherness." It is as if the fact of emerging from individual solitude in order to accede to a stronger collective dimension presupposed the stopping of that movement, an entering into a slower and more cumulative rhythm of becoming.

Of course, you might say, but this is Turin, this is Fiat. And, as we know, Turin is a city characterized by historical depth and viscosity. Fiat is an anomalous situation in Italy as a whole. But then we might take a look at the book *Gli anni difficili* (The difficult years), by Gianfranco Porta and Carlo Simoni, a very interesting study of FIOM metalworker shop stewards in Brescia.[2] This is the kind of study that, if it were extended to other Italian cities, would finally give us the social history of the First Italian Republic that we so badly need. Here we find the same thing we found at Fiat. The fifty long interviews that provide the raw material for this book, containing various people's personal accounts of their lives, describe a situation completely analogous to that of Turin.

Here too we have a wide-ranging series of life experiences, coming from the most diverse social origins, and all flowing together into one single point: the factory of the early 1970s, the place that gave meaning and substance to all these individual existences — the place that laid the basis not only for political meaning, but also for underlying motivations, shared values, and the ability to read society and orient one's life. At the moment the workers entered the factory, the Babel of languages and different ways of experiencing life became somehow composed, taking on a choral dimension, and becoming to all intents and purposes a collective culture. You get this feeling even from the names and acronyms of the places in which they worked: Pietra, OM, Atfb, Idra, and so forth. It is also present in the evocations of particularly significant periods of time: 1968–69 as "a new beginning," the early 1970s as a realm of consolidation, and 1974 and the Brescia bombing as the dramatic peak of political mobilization. Finally, what emerges is a culture that has shared assumptions. In the Brescia accounts too we find a unanimous opinion that the onset of crisis came at the start of the 1980s, when the process of restructuring initiated by events at Fiat began to make its mark on the factory. It "unfroze" the factory, so to speak, getting things moving again and opening a process of mobility that neutralized the factory as a place of belonging and aggregation, and sent individuals back to a state of atomization and isolation. In the same way as happened at Fiat, the labor mobility and forced layoffs in Brescia, along with the demands of technology and the market (the characteristic forms of modern uprooting), had a devastating effect on the collective entity of the working class. They forced it irretrievably onto the defensive, and disaggregated it, with consequences that were not merely political but also existential and, in some respects, pathological.

There had already been a study of the Turin working class published in the early 1980s, *Cooperativa Matraia: Caratteristiche e comportamenti degli operai FIAT in mobilità* (Matraia Cooperative: characteristics and attitudes of Fiat workers in a period of labor mobility).[3] This study had documented the intransigence of the Fiat workers, their rootedness in the territory of the factory, and their unwillingness (not only political but also psychological and existential) to accept any form of "mobility." One might call this a refusal that was directly proportional to the intensity of their conflictual protagonism and the strength of the collective identity that had been established in the factory. More than 60 percent of those interviewed (62.2 percent, to be precise) declared themselves totally hostile to any notion of a "transfer" from their jobs to any job outside of the Fiat empire. Of the remaining 37.8 percent, only 3.2 percent could be said to have been truly "available for mobility," as defined in the 1980 Fiat agreement—in other words, ready to be moved to equivalent factory jobs in other productive units. (The fact that only twenty-nine out of the sixty-five hundred workers placed on the "mobility" lists eventually found jobs in other factories, through the crazy procedures that had been invented at the time, provides a grotesque justification for this intransigence.) A further 11.2 percent—labeled in the study as "Pioneers"—saw the fact of being made redundant as a new opening, a possible means of freeing themselves from their condition as workers, and another 19.2 percent—the "Migrants"—saw it as an opportunity for territorial mobility, for leaving the city.

Perhaps the most interesting statistics, however, come in the figures relating to the ages of the interviewees and the period of their entry into Fiat. A large majority of the Pioneers (64 percent) and the Migrants (58.4 percent) were under the age of twenty-five. Almost all of them had been hired post-1975. Very few of them belonged to the generation that had been engaged in conflict in the period of the "great transformation." On the other hand, virtually all of those who made up the army of refuseniks—particularly the "Exiles" (those who still see the factory as a "country" to which they hope to return) and the "Militants" (the trade-union members and activists)—were aged between thirty and forty-five, and had come into the factory between the end of the 1950s and the mid-1970s. In other words, they were the central protagonists of the cycle of struggles: those who had most intensely "fixed" their identities through that collective experience. And they were the ones who suffered most devastatingly from the collapse of that "identificational space."

There has recently been a further study, sponsored by the health authorities for the Piedmont region and carried out by a group of sociologists under the direction of Filippo Barbano, titled *Cassintegrati e disagio psichico* (Laid-off workers and their psychological problems).[4] This book documents the psychiatric aspects, the human and social costs, of the employers' unilateral imposition of "mobility." From 1981 onward, a large number of laid-off workers sought help from the Turin mental health authorities for various kinds of psychological problems, ranging from simple depression to suicidal behavior. The vast majority (65.4 percent) came from the thirty to fifty age group, were originally from the South or the Islands (67.5

percent), had limited secondary school education, and were categorized as factory workers (90.3 percent). In other words, in certain respects they were an exact sociological match to the protagonists of the cycle of struggles of the 1960s and the early 1970s. These were the people who had most contributed to changing the factory, and who, in turn, had been hardest hit by the transformations of that factory. This fact provides a clear rebuff to the "sociology of industrial consensus," which has for some time been suggesting that the condition of the factory working class has become less dramatic. It is also a useful tool for attempting to unravel our initial problem: the nature of the interplay between movement and rootedness, identity and transformation.

Pietro Ingrao is right, in his fine introduction to *L'Altra faccia della FIAT*, in stressing the importance of the "work group." He speaks of a "collective entity that has a material corporeality and that seems to stand over and transform the irreducible specificity of individual experience." He also highlights the dramatic nature of the challenge that the big factory presents to the individual dimension and speaks of a "need for creating forms of acting together that will be capable of facing up to a trial of strength that seems likely to be long and hard."[5] The construction of collective action was probably the principal point of the working-class program of the 1970s. It was a "physiological" form of self-defense against the alienating aspects of the factory. It also, however, constituted the revolutionary character of that working class—in other words, its specific way of expressing its own refusal of the commodity form and denying its own existence as variable capital by affirming the only way in which individuals can retain their humanity. They resisted the "uprooting" brought about by technology through joint action, in a communitarian context.

This inevitably involved a "rootedness," the identification of a "place" in which their "being togetherness" could be developed, with its ethical codes, its unwritten laws, and its criteria of justice. Movement, in order to become effective change (transformation of reality and not simply a shifting from one place to another), always presupposes a fixed horizon, a territory that is defined in its geographic and technological coordinates. This project was defeated—precisely—by a process that was equal and contrary; it was defeated by a radical metamorphosis of capital, which belied its nature as concrete and "static" (as an ensemble of means of production) and reproposed itself as money and abstract knowledge.

A few years ago, in a fascinating book titled *Exodus and Revolution*, Michael Walzer proposed a striking image of the Exodus as the archetype of every idea of revolution.[6] His intention with this notion was to highlight the related character of movement, process, and liberation, along with the resonances with the metaphor of travel, proceeding, and becoming. However, while accepting all this, I have to say that the motivating force of the sticking together and the unity—the "being together"—of that group that was on its way ("in movement") toward the Promised Land, toward the collective dimension of its own emancipation, was probably more the unidimensionality of the desert, its immobility and immutability, than any hopes for the approach of some eventual future goal.

Perhaps this was precisely what was happening in the 1970s, namely, that a mass minority was trying to take the "desert" of the factory and turn it into a place where they could implant their own working-class identity, their own class belonging. Perhaps they built their identities on that, and from there initiated a resistance against everything—against objective processes of technological innovation and against the subjective dynamics of postmaterialist society, in explicit countertendency to the majority who were "in movement" toward consumerism and, if they could manage it, out of their condition as working-class. This mass minority was defeated by the mobility of capital, by its speed, by the metamorphosis and transformation of that desert. This does nothing, however, to diminish the grandeur of a project that was perhaps the last bastion of resistance to the structurally nihilistic realities of latter-day modernity.

Translated by Ed Emory

Notes

1. Coordinamento Cassintegrati, *L'Altra faccia della FIAT* (Rome: Erre emme, 1990).

2. Gianfranco Porta and Carlo Simoni, *Gli anni difficili* (Milan: Angeli 1990).

3. *Cooperativa Matraia: Caratteristiche e comportamenti degli operai FIAT in mobilità* (Quaderni di Formazione, ISFOL, no. 3) (1983).

4. E. Bruzzone, ed., *Cassintegrati e disagio psichico* (Genoa: Sagep, 1990).

5. Pietro Ingrao, "Introduzione," in Coordinamento Cassintegrati, *L'Altra faccia della FIAT* (Rome: Erre emme, 1990), 8–9.

6. Michael Walzer, *Exodus and Revolution* (New York: Basic Books, 1985).

N   I   N   E

Technological Innovation and Sentimental Education

Franco Piperno

Marx and Turing

If, just for fun, in order to shake off the tedium of defeat, we were to choose Marx's "Fragment on Machines" from the *Grundrisse* as a biblical passage, a place where the word resounds prophetically, then the appropriate commentary on that text would be a concise exposition of the theory of automatons, that is to say, a broad description of Turing's machine. Conceiving production in terms of cybernetic machines gives production the character of a natural science, a scientifically reproduced natural process. At the same time, it reduces the work of the human body, living labor, to a simple element of this process: the conscious organ, the observing eye that serves to avoid interruption. In the "Fragment on Machines," Marx advances the thesis that the systematic application of technico-scientific knowledge to production would achieve the outcome of freeing the worker from the factory, thus making the measurement of wealth in terms of human labor time completely impossible.

Things did not exactly turn out that way. Working hours continue to govern industrial relations and the distribution of income. The paradoxical result of this is that a great variety of human activity is thrown into the abyss of nonwork. For economics, for the economic *mentality*, the time of human work remains the meager basis on which social wealth rests. Nevertheless, if the concepts and definitions of the economic mentality are preserved, the liberation of human labor from factory production, a condition that was intuited by Marx and that today is becoming real before our very eyes, seems to bring about a mutation of common affects and sentiments, a different deployment of common sense, a *semantic alteration* of key words for daily life — words such as *time*, *truth*, and *memory*.

The Extinction of Time

The computer is characterized by a notion of time that ends up being unrepresentable for the human condition, anthropologically understood. The characteristic time of the computer is the shortest temporal interval, that is, the highest speed iteratively attributable to the physical processes of the machine. The characteristic time of the computer is close to optic time, to the time measured by the speed of light. The second has, for this machine, a duration that is virtually boundless. The day, the temporal unity that is proper to the gravitational movement of Earth, becomes an almost infinite time, magically long.

If we look back at the history of the relationship between human time and machine time in the course of technological development, we easily ascertain the vast distance that separates the computer from both the simple tool and the clock. As long as the machine is a tool of human labor, an instrument produced by the manual workmanship of humans, it follows the rhythm of the human body; body and instrument proceed in synchrony, there is no autonomous movement of the machine whatsoever, so that the realm of the artificial conforms with the time that is conferred on it by humans. When the tool is replaced by the clock, with its characteristic mechanical time, the human body has the bewildering experience of being synchronized with the rhythm of the machine; the time of the machine builds a nest in the body of the worker — think, for instance, of Charlie Chaplin's film *Modern Times*. The advent of the computer, finally, introduces a time that escapes the very possibility of experience. The machine can carry out and write out calculations in a time so short that it cannot even be captured in thought. The computer reduces work to calculation and executes it with such vertiginous speed that it renders possible in a few hours what once required a few centuries.

This gigantic dilation of the present unhinges the modern temporal mentality, the psychic machine that is structured on the triad of past, present, and future. Time unveils itself to be a linguistic convention, a verbal construction, not a fixed quality of reality. This disenchantment authorizes a new social freedom: the freedom to redefine time, to change the meaning of the word *time*. On the other hand, from an epistemological point of view, the computer realizes the spirit of modernity, and thus exhausts modern time. The specifically human faculty of producing and reproducing mathematical languages belongs at this point also to the machine, insofar as the limits of mathematical knowledge coincide with the limits of the computer. The mathematicization of the world is thus actually accomplished. What may be said in mathematical form coincides with all that the machine can actually or potentially state.

This definitive completion of an era certainly does not signal the end of technology, but rather the reorganization of an ideology of technology: the mathematical myth of technology, mathematics as a guarantee of the truth of technology. Corresponding to this final completion, to this touching of the limit, is a leap of human awareness, a different way of conceiving the relation between the human and the natural. For example, precisely because doing mathematics is an attribute of the machine, in the representation of nature we can abandon mathematics to oblivion, we can *forget mathematics*.

Speaking, Writing, Searching for Meaning

The computer, like writing, is an intellectual technology. Its advent may be compared to the very passage from oral culture to writing. It is worth remembering that the thinking we call *logical* corresponds to a relatively recent mentality, molded by alphabetic writing and by the canon of learning that it involves. Anthropological research shows, with considerable evidence, how the speakers of written culture think by means of categories, whereas those of oral culture think instead by means of situations. The alphabet and phonetic writing were the conditions of possibility that permitted the development of rational thought. By passing from ideography to the alphabet and then from calligraphy to print, the mnemotechnic obsession of oral culture lost its meaning and narration ceased to hold hegemony over transmittable knowledge. In Hesiod, justice is a person who acts, who is moved, and who suffers; in Plato, it is a concept. The characters and heroes of oral culture, subjects of mythical adventures, are translated by writing into ideas and principles.

It goes without saying that the appearance of the alphabet and the development of the written word did not drive out the sonorous word; they merely changed its constitution. Primary orality defers to the centrality of the sonorous word before the community can adopt writing; secondary orality reduces the sonorous word to the object of what is written. Thus, for example, poetry and song certainly survive in written cultures. They nonetheless have their mnemonic and encyclopedic functions mutilated, and become, in the strictest sense of the word, aesthetic values.

In the West, the process of the expansion of written culture reached a paradoxical situation by investing the realm of sound itself, the realm of music. Written music was a real innovation. It developed in a dizzying succession of styles, completely extraneous to the music of the oral tradition. This dynamic was inseparable from the comparison of the link between writing and sound inasmuch as the musical work was identified with the score, a structure of abstract signs fixed once and for all on paper. And is it not perhaps paradoxical that the sound is called a "note," that is, a sign of writing? The note refers to a conventional system of the visual representation of sounds. On an epistemological plane, it would be wrong to confuse music with written music, just as it would to reduce thinking to the syntactic rules of writing.

Written prose, of course, is not a simple expressive vehicle of philosophical or juridical or scientific thought, as these cultural spheres do not exist before writing. In fact, without writing, there is no dating, or lists of observation, or tables of figures, or legislative codes, or philosophical systems—and even fewer critiques of these systems. With the advent of writing memory detaches itself from the individual as it does from the community. Knowledge is congealed in written words: it is there, available, consultable, and comparable. This sort of objective memory disjoins knowledge from the individual or collective corporeity. Knowledge is no longer what nurtures the human being, what forms it as part of a given linguistic community. It has become an analyzable, criticizable, and verifiable object. The need for truth, in the modern and critical sense of the term, is a collateral effect of the partial necrosis of corporeal memory, which takes place when knowledge is captured by the web of signs woven by writing.

And it is again writing that assures the diffusion of those two modes of knowledge—theory and hermeneutics—that have become the very "commonplaces" of Western culture. *Theory*, as its etymology attests, means vision, contemplation. It comes into being as a metaphor of seeing, knowledge acquired through the sense of sight, the sense through which one reaches the written text. Theory is also procession, that long series of signs aligned one beside the other that form the text. Thus in mathematical literature, in Euclid's *Elements*, for instance, a long series of theorems follows a few axioms, like the Greeks who went to the solemn feasts of Olympia and who were lined up behind their priests and idols. The other mode of knowledge, the hermeneutical one, which seeks meaning, comes into being as a metaphor of deciphering signs, by analogy with the activity of divination. The search for meaning achieves its apogee in all civilizations of writing by means of the interpretation of sacred texts, a task to which generations of clerics have dedicated themselves with a furor itself also sacred. There is no doubt, moreover, that theory as much as interpretation is a mode of knowledge known to primary orality, but only with the development of writing does it acquire a privileged gnoseological constitution and become a major genre.

Consider, for example, the book. In classical Greece, it had to be read out loud either in public or in private, because only by way of resonance was the text fulfilled. In the modern era the book is precisely no longer mnemonic for the reader; rather, as Schiller has noted, the body and the human voice provide characters for mute thoughts. For the moderns, writing directly realizes a mute thought that acquires body and voice through the one who writes.

The computer diffuses a third mode of knowledge that is distinct from both theory and hermeneutics: information knowledge. Even in this case one must avoid the naïveté of believing in the absolutely new, thinking that information knowledge was born today, and fearing that in one fell swoop it could drive out the classical modes of knowledge. What is taking place is instead a different combination of forms of knowledge, a different hierarchical order of forms, such that cybernetics now holds the status of a major form of knowledge, relegating theory and interpretation to a subordinate, if not completely marginal, role. They have been displaced from the dominant position just as in a previous era poetry, song, and tale were dethroned from their classification as major genres of knowledge by theoretical prose and interpretive commentary.

Information knowledge distinguishes itself from the other modes of knowledge by way of its operative nature. Clearly, it has a double nature. The first is due to the fact that cybernetics involves the manipulation of a discrete number of signs according to well-defined operative rules. The second derives from the computer's characteristic of storing information for operative ends. The central aim of information knowledge is not the completeness and coherence of facts and judgments on the world, but rather the optimization of procedures, be they for decisions, diagnosis, management, or planning. Information knowledge incessantly transforms procedures so that the action may be more effective and, above all, faster.

The primacy of operative culture over theory and interpretation affirms itself through a devaluing redefinition of the latter on the part of the former. Even the formulation of mathematical theories is beginning to be seen by the scientific community as an activity of aesthetic decoration. The ordinary practice of scientific research and development is limited at this point, not without some satisfaction, to simulation, numeric models, "open systems," and complete, up-to-date databases. Theories degenerate into mnemonic tricks used to facilitate calculation—tricks one can free oneself from even without providing any explanation whenever a clever algorithm is constructed to allow for prediction and action. The paradigm of calculation that has now invaded biology, psychology, and even the social sciences redefines theory as an unsuccessful computation, just as the knowledge of savage societies was redefined by anthropologists of the last century as false or incoherent theory, although it was in no way theory.

Memory

The introduction of computer technology into production and service industries powerfully contributes to the semantic slippage of another key word: *memory*. At first, one could think that the disproportionate multiplication of computer memories, in the form of databases, continues the task of the accumulation and conservation of knowledge undertaken previously by writing. This is a mistaken notion. In the majority of cases, databases do not gather all of the truths on a given question, but only the whole of the knowledge usable for a certain paying client. Almost two-thirds of information accumulated in the world deals with ultraspecialized strategic, economic, commercial, or financial data. The reason for the use of databases is first of all operative: to obtain the most trustworthy information as soon as possible, to make the most effective decision. Obsolete data are systematically eliminated, so that a database is much less memory than it is a mirror, as faithful as possible in a given instant of a market or a specialized activity.

The "expert systems," which can be considered the most complex databases, capable of autonomously arriving at new conclusions by using the available information as a point of departure, accentuate this loss of meaning of the word *memory*. These systems are not in fact conceived in order to preserve the know-how of an expert, but rather to evolve without rest, starting from the nucleus of knowledge borrowed from the expert. The program of the "expert system" is not rewritten every time it reaches an original conclusion; the declarative language permits the enrichment and modification of the system without having to begin again from the top. In a certain way, the "expert system" autonomously improves its functioning as it gains experience. Here knowledge is no longer congealed in writing; on the contrary, it is possessed by an incessant movement, changing continuously so as always to be current and ready for use. Here memory is so entrusted to automatic devices, so much object of manipulation and elaboration, so extraneous to the bodies of individuals and collective habits as to merit another name, another meaning.

In oral culture the community and memory are united as one, and knowledge is dedicated to the conservation of the identical, the transformation immutable in itself. The semiobjectification of memory, which characterizes the civilization of writing, has made possible the search for truth that is modern science. Information knowledge is thus free from the human activity of "remembering," or, if you will, information memory is such an attribute of the machine that truth can cease to be the fundamental aim of knowledge, in favor of operativeness and speed.

The Collective Freedom to Evoke Meanings

By transforming the persons and the adventurous heroes of orality into concepts, the civilization of writing made possible the unfolding of the thought of being. By pulverizing in its programs the concepts conceived by writing and by using logic as a motor, the computer reabsorbs the thought of being into pure acceleration. We collectively perceive the waning of a culture and the obscuring of modes of knowledge that we have learned to love by way of a long education. We equally recognize the uselessness of resistance. The information technologies are here to stay, and we are only at the beginning of a transformation of the mode of communication and thinking.

The transformation taking place is comparable to the invention of a certain type of "rational discourse" among the ancient Greeks. We are dealing with an alteration of mentality analogous to the one that took place in the succession between orality and writing. The comparison should also be understood as a reminder of the historicity of our modes of knowledge: what is born can die. Our culture has withstood the disappearance of the living mythologies of the oral world and the appearance of writing; we today will withstand with intimate anguish the advent of our intellectual universe of technological information.

To close without concluding, I should note that it is worthwhile to remember that the characteristics of the computer play a role of conditions of possibility and not of determination: a new machine is always compatible with old nonsense. Transformations of mentality are correlated with, not caused by, technological innovations. The computer authorizes us to recognize the collective human freedom to change the meanings of words that seemed to be certain forever and to change what words mean to change the feelings and affects that they evoke. This is a freedom that would be difficult to put to good use in the case of an emergency. Thus, even if it is true that information technology produces unemployment because it makes repetitive human labor absolutely superfluous, it is doubtful that the machine is the cause of the poverty of the unemployed; of that loss of communication that follows being excluded from socially recognized work, as painful and as degrading as it may be; of that temporality that is so private as to brush up dangerously against the chaotic and asocial time of the dream. The poverty of the unemployed, the true one, the suffering of the freedom to determine one's own time, originates in desire or, better, in the absence of desire, in the self-interdiction of daring to stipulate a new meaning for the word *labor*, another calendar, a different collective time.

Translated by Paul Colilli

T   E   N

Immaterial Labor

Maurizio Lazzarato

A significant amount of empirical research has been conducted concerning the new forms of the organization of work. This, combined with a corresponding wealth of theoretical reflection, has made possible the identification of a new conception of what work is nowadays and what new power relations it implies.

An initial synthesis of these results—framed in terms of an attempt to define the technical and subjective-political composition of the working class—can be expressed in the concept of *immaterial labor*, which is defined as the labor that produces the informational and cultural content of the commodity. The concept of immaterial labor refers to *two different aspects* of labor. On the one hand, as regards the "informational content" of the commodity, it refers directly to the changes taking place in workers' labor processes in big companies in the industrial and tertiary sectors, where the skills involved in direct labor are increasingly skills involving cybernetics and computer control (and horizontal and vertical communication). On the other hand, as regards the activity that produces the "cultural content" of the commodity, immaterial labor involves a series of activities that are not normally recognized as "work"—in other words, the kinds of activities involved in defining and fixing cultural and artistic standards, fashions, tastes, consumer norms, and, more strategically, public opinion. Once the privileged domain of the bourgeoisie and its children, these activities have since the end of the 1970s become the domain of what we have come to define as "mass intellectuality." The profound changes in these strategic sectors have radically modified not only the composition, management, and regulation of the workforce—the organization of production—but also, and more deeply, the role and function of intellectuals and their activities within society.

The "great transformation" that began at the start of the 1970s has changed the very terms in which the question is posed. Manual labor is increasingly coming to involve procedures that could be defined as "intellectual," and the new communications technologies increasingly require subjectivities that are rich in knowledge. It is not simply that intellectual labor has become subjected to the norms of capitalist production. What has happened is that a new "mass intellectuality" has come into being, created out of a combination of the demands of capitalist production and the forms of "self-valorization" that the struggle against work has produced. The old dichotomy between "mental and manual labor," or between "material labor and immaterial labor," risks failing to grasp the new nature of productive activity, which takes this separation on board and transforms it. The split between conception and execution, between labor and creativity, between author and audience, is simultaneously transcended within the "labor process" and reimposed as political command within the "process of valorization."

The Restructured Worker

Twenty years of restructuring of the big factories has led to a curious paradox. The various different post-Fordist models have been constructed both on the defeat of the Fordist worker and on the recognition of the centrality of (an ever increasingly intellectualized) living labor within production. In today's large restructured company, a worker's work increasingly involves, at various levels, an ability to choose among different alternatives and thus a degree of responsibility regarding decision making. The concept of "interface" used by communications sociologists provides a fair definition of the activities of this kind of worker—as an interface between different functions, between different work teams, between different levels of the hierarchy, and so forth. What modern management techniques are looking for is for "the worker's soul to become part of the factory." The worker's personality and subjectivity have to be made susceptible to organization and command. It is around immateriality that the quality and quantity of labor are organized. This transformation of working-class labor into a labor of control, of handling information, into a decision-making capacity that involves the investment of subjectivity, affects workers in varying ways according to their positions within the factory hierarchy, but it is nevertheless present as an irreversible process. Work can thus be defined as the capacity to activate and manage productive cooperation. In this phase, workers are expected to become "active subjects" in the coordination of the various functions of production, instead of being subjected to it as simple command. We arrive at a point where a collective learning process becomes the heart of productivity, because it is no longer a matter of finding different ways of composing or organizing already existing job functions, but of looking for new ones.

The problem, however, of subjectivity and its collective form, its constitution and its development, has immediately expressed itself as a clash between social classes within the organization of work. I should point out that what I am describing is not some utopian vision of recomposition, but the very real terrain and conditions of the conflict between social classes.

The capitalist needs to find an unmediated way of establishing command over subjectivity itself; the prescription and definition of tasks transforms into a prescription of subjectivities. The new slogan of Western societies is that we should all "become subjects." Participative management is a technology of power, a technology for creating and controlling the "subjective processes." As it is no longer possible to confine subjectivity merely to tasks of execution, it becomes necessary for the subject's competence in the areas of management, communication, and creativity to be made compatible with the conditions of "production for production's sake." Thus the slogan "become subjects," far from eliminating the antagonism between hierarchy and cooperation, between autonomy and command, actually re-poses the antagonism at a higher level, because it both mobilizes and clashes with the very personality of the individual worker. First and foremost, we have here a discourse that is authoritarian: one *has to* express oneself, one *has to* speak, communicate, cooperate, and so forth. The "tone" is that of the people who were in executive command under Taylorization; all that has changed is the content. Second, if it is no longer possible to lay down and specify jobs and responsibilities rigidly (in the way that was once done with "scientific" studies of work), but if, on the contrary, jobs now require cooperation and collective coordination, then the subjects of that production must be capable of communication — they must be active participants within a work team. The communicational relationship (both vertically and horizontally) is thus completely predetermined in both form and content; it is subordinated to the "circulation of information" and is not expected to be anything other. The subject becomes a simple relayer of codification and decodification, whose transmitted messages must be "clear and free of ambiguity," within a communications context that has been completely normalized by management. The necessity of imposing command and the violence that goes along with it here take on a normative communicative form.

The management mandate to "become subjects of communication" threatens to be even more totalitarian than the earlier rigid division between mental and manual labor (ideas and execution), because capitalism seeks to involve even the worker's personality and subjectivity within the production of value. Capital wants a situation where command resides within the subject him- or herself, and within the communicative process. The worker is to be responsible for his or her own control and motivation within the work group without a foreman needing to intervene, and the foreman's role is redefined into that of a facilitator. In fact, employers are extremely worried by the double problem this creates: on one hand, they are forced to recognize the autonomy and freedom of labor as the only possible form of cooperation in production, but on the other hand, at the same time, they are obliged (a life-and-death necessity for the capitalist) not to "redistribute" the power that the new quality of labor and its organization imply. Today's management thinking takes workers' subjectivity into consideration only in order to codify it in line with the requirements of production. And once again this phase of transformation succeeds in concealing the fact that the individual and collective interests of workers and those of the company are not identical.

I have defined working-class labor as an abstract activity that nowadays involves the application of subjectivity. In order to avoid misunderstandings, however, I should add that this form of productive activity is not limited only to highly skilled workers; it refers to a use value of labor power today, and, more generally, to the form of activity of every productive subject within postindustrial society. One could say that in the highly skilled, qualified worker, the "communicational model" is already given, already constituted, and that its potentialities are already defined. In the young worker, however, the "precarious" worker, and the unemployed youth, we are dealing with a pure virtuality, a capacity that is as yet undetermined but that already shares all the characteristics of postindustrial productive subjectivity. The virtuality of this capacity is neither empty nor ahistoric; it is, rather, an opening and a potentiality that have as their historical origins and antecedents the "struggle against work" of the Fordist worker and, in more recent times, the processes of socialization, educational formation, and cultural self-valorization.

This transformation of the world of work appears even more evident when one studies the social cycle of production: the "diffuse factory" and decentralization of production on the one hand and the various forms of tertiarization on the other. Here one can measure the extent to which the cycle of immaterial labor has come to assume a strategic role within the global organization of production. The various activities of research, conceptualization, management of human resources, and so forth, together with all the various tertiary activities, are organized within computerized and multimedia networks. These are the terms in which we have to understand the cycle of production and the organization of labor. The integration of scientific labor into industrial and tertiary labor has become one of the principal sources of productivity, and it is becoming a growing factor in the cycles of production that organize it.

"Immaterial Labor" in the Classic Definition

All the characteristics of the postindustrial economy (both in industry and society as a whole) are highly present within the classic forms of "immaterial" production: audiovisual production, advertising, fashion, the production of software, photography, cultural activities, and so forth. The activities of this kind of immaterial labor force us to question the classic definitions of *work* and *workforce*, because they combine the results of various different types of work skill: intellectual skills, as regards the cultural-informational content; manual skills for the ability to combine creativity, imagination, and technical and manual labor; and entrepreneurial skills in the management of social relations and the structuring of that social cooperation of which they are a part. This immaterial labor constitutes itself in forms that are immediately collective, and we might say that it exists only in the form of networks and flows. The organization of the cycle of production of immaterial labor (because this is exactly what it is, once we abandon our factoryist prejudices—a cycle of production) is not obviously apparent to the eye, because it is not defined by the four walls of a factory. The location in which it operates is outside in the society at large, at a territorial level that we could call "the basin of immaterial labor." Small and sometimes very small "productive units" (often consisting of only one individual) are organized for specific ad hoc projects, and may exist only for the duration of those particular jobs. The cycle of production comes into operation only when it is required by the capitalist; once the job has been done, the cycle dissolves back into the networks and flows that make possible the reproduction and enrichment of its productive capacities. Precariousness, hyperexploitation, mobility, and hierarchy are the most obvious characteristics of metropolitan immaterial labor. Behind the label of the independent "self-employed" worker, what we actually find is an intellectual proletarian, but who is recognized as such only by the employers who exploit him or her. It is worth noting that in this kind of working existence it becomes increasingly difficult to distinguish leisure time from work time. In a sense, life becomes inseparable from work.

This labor form is also characterized by real managerial functions that consist in (1) a certain ability to manage its social relations and (2) the eliciting of social cooperation within the structures of the basin of immaterial labor. The quality of this kind of labor power is thus defined not only by its professional capacities (which make possible the construction of the cultural-informational content of the commodity), but also by its ability to "manage" its own activity and act as the coordinator of the immaterial labor of others (production and management of the cycle). This immaterial labor appears as a real mutation of "living labor." Here we are quite far from the Taylorist model of organization.

Immaterial labor finds itself at the crossroads (or rather, it is the interface) of a new relationship between production and consumption. The activation of both productive cooperation and the social relationship with the consumer is materialized within and by the process of communication. The role of immaterial labor is to promote continual innovation in the forms and conditions of communication (and thus in work and consumption). It gives form to and materializes needs, the imaginary, consumer tastes, and so forth, and these products in turn become powerful producers of needs, images, and tastes. The particularity of the commodity produced through immaterial labor (its essential use value being given by its value as informational and cultural content) consists in the fact that it is not destroyed in the act of consumption, but rather it enlarges, transforms, and creates the "ideological" and cultural environment of the consumer. This commodity does not produce the physical capacity of labor power; instead, it transforms the person who uses it. Immaterial labor produces first and foremost a "social relationship" (a relationship of innovation, production, and consumption). Only if it succeeds in this production does its activity have an economic value. This activity makes immediately apparent something that material production had "hidden," namely, that labor produces not only commodities, but first and foremost it produces the capital relation.

The Autonomy of the Productive Synergies of Immaterial Labor

My working hypothesis, then, is that the cycle of immaterial labor takes as its starting point a social labor power that is independent and able to organize both its own work and its relations with business entities. Industry does not form or create this new labor power, but simply takes it on board and adapts it. Industry's control over this new labor power presupposes the independent organization and "free entrepreneurial activity" of the labor power. Advancing further on this terrain brings us into the debate on the nature of work in the post-Fordist phase of the organization of labor. Among economists, the predominant view of this problematic can be expressed in a single statement: immaterial labor operates within the forms of organization that the centralization of industry allows. Moving from this common basis, there are two differing schools of thought: one is the extension of neoclassical analysis; the other is that of systems theory.

In the former, the attempt to solve the problem comes through a redefinition of the problematic of the market. It is suggested that in order to explain the phenomena of communication and the new dimensions of organization one should introduce not only cooperation and intensity of labor, but also other analytic variables (anthropological variables? immaterial variables?) and that on this basis one might introduce other objectives of optimization and so forth. In fact, the neoclassical model has considerable difficulty in freeing itself from the coherence constraints imposed by the theory of general equilibrium. The new phenomenologies of labor, the new dimensions of organization, communication, the potentiality of spontaneous synergies, the autonomy of the subjects involved, and the independence of the networks were neither foreseen nor foreseeable by a general theory that believed that material labor and an industrial economy were indispensable. Today, with the new data available, we find the microeconomy in revolt against the macroeconomy, and the classical model is corroded by a new and irreducible anthropological reality.

Systems theory, by eliminating the constraint of the market and giving pride of place to organization, is more open to the new phenomenology of labor and in particular to the emergence of immaterial labor. In more developed systemic theories, organization is conceived as an ensemble of factors, both material and immaterial, both individual and collective, that can permit a given group to reach objectives. The success of this organizational process requires instruments of regulation, either voluntary or automatic. It becomes possible to look at things from the point of view of social synergies, and immaterial labor can be taken on board by virtue of its global efficacy. These viewpoints, however, are still tied to an image of the organization of work and its social territory within which effective activity from an economic viewpoint (in other words, the activity conforming to the objective) must inevitably be considered as a surplus in relation to collective cognitive mechanisms. Sociology and labor economics, being systemic disciplines, are both incapable of detaching themselves from this position.

I believe that an analysis of immaterial labor and a description of its organization can lead us beyond the presuppositions of business theory — whether in its neoclassical school or its systems theory school. It can lead us to define, at a territorial level, a space for a radical autonomy of the productive synergies of immaterial labor. We can thus move against the old schools of thought to establish, decisively, the viewpoint of an "anthropo-sociology" that is constitutive.

Once this viewpoint comes to dominate within social production, we find that we have an interruption in the continuity of models of production. By this I mean that, unlike the position held by many theoreticians of post-Fordism, I do not believe that this new labor power is merely functional to a new historical phase of capitalism and its processes of accumulation and reproduction. This labor power is the product of a "silent revolution" taking place within the anthropological realities of work and within the reconfiguration of its meanings. Waged labor and direct subjugation (to organization) no longer constitute the principal form of the contractual relationship between capitalist and worker. A polymorphous self-employed autonomous work has emerged as the dominant form, a kind of "intellectual worker" who is him- or herself an entrepreneur, inserted within a market that is constantly shifting and within networks that are changeable in time and space.

The Cycle of Immaterial Production

Up to this point I have been analyzing and constructing the concept of immaterial labor from a point of view that could be defined, so to speak, as "microeconomic." If now we consider immaterial labor within the globality of the production cycle, of which it is the strategic stage, we will be able to see a series of characteristics of post-Taylorist production that have not yet been taken into consideration.

I want to demonstrate in particular how the process of valorization tends to be identified with the process of the production of social communication and how the two stages (valorization and communication) immediately have a social and territorial dimension. The concept of immaterial labor presupposes and results in an enlargement of productive cooperation that even includes the production and reproduction of communication and hence of its most important contents: subjectivity. If Fordism integrated consumption into the cycle of the reproduction of capital, post-Fordism integrates communication into it. From a strictly economic point of view, the cycle of reproduction of immaterial labor dislocates the production-consumption relationship as it is defined as much by the "virtuous Keynesian circle" as by the Marxist reproduction schemes of the second volume of

Capital. Now, rather than speaking of the toppling of "supply and demand," we should speak about a redefinition of the production-consumption relationship. As we saw earlier, the consumer is inscribed in the manufacturing of the product from its conception. The consumer is no longer limited to consuming commodities (destroying them in the act of consumption). On the contrary, his or her consumption should be productive in accordance to the necessary conditions and the new products. Consumption is then first of all a consumption of information. Consumption is no longer only the "realization" of a product, but a real and proper social process that for the moment is defined with the term *communication.*

Large-Scale Industry and Services

To recognize the new characteristics of the production cycle of immaterial labor, we should compare it with the production of large-scale industry and services. If the cycle of immaterial production immediately demonstrates to us the secret of post-Taylorist production (that is to say, that social communication and the social relationship that constitutes it become productive), then it would be interesting to examine how these new social relationships innervate even industry and services, and how they oblige us to reformulate and reorganize even the classical forms of "production."

Large-Scale Industry

The postindustrial enterprise and economy are founded on the manipulation of information. Rather than ensuring (as nineteenth-century enterprises did) the surveillance of the inner workings of the production process and the supervision of the markets of raw materials (labor included), business is focused on the terrain outside of the production process: sales and the relationship with the consumer. It always leans more toward commercialization and financing than toward production. Prior to being manufactured, a product must be sold, even in "heavy" industries such as automobile manufacturing; a car is put into production only after the sales network orders it. This strategy is based on the production and consumption of information. It mobilizes important communication and marketing strategies in order to gather information (recognizing the tendencies of the market) and circulate it (constructing a market). In the Taylorist and Fordist systems of production, by introducing the mass consumption of standardized commodities, Ford could still say that the consumer has the choice between one black model T5 and another black model T5. "Today the standard commodity is no longer the recipe to success, and the automobile industry itself, which used to be the champion of the great 'low price' series, would want to boast about having become a neoindustry of singularization"—and quality.[1] For the majority of businesses, survival involves the permanent search for new commercial openings that lead to the identification of always more ample or differentiated product lines. Innovation is no longer subordinated only to the rationalization of labor, but also to commercial imperatives. It seems, then, that the postindustrial commodity is the result of a creative process that involves both the producer and the consumer.

Services

If from industry proper we move on to the "services" sector (large banking services, insurance, and so forth), the characteristics of the process I have described appear even more clearly. We are witnessing today not really a growth of services, but rather a development of the "relations of service." The move beyond the Taylorist organization of services is characterized by the integration of the relationship between production and consumption, where in fact the consumer intervenes in an active way in the composition of the product. The product "service" becomes a social construction and a social process of "conception" and innovation. In service industries, the "back-office" tasks (the classic work of services) have diminished and the tasks of the "front office" (the relationship with clients) have grown. There has been thus a shift of human resources toward the outer part of business. As recent sociological analyses tell us, the more a product handled by the service sector is characterized as an immaterial product, the more it distances itself from the model of industrial organization of the relationship between production and consumption. The change in this relationship between production and consumption has direct consequences for the organization of the Taylorist labor of production of services, because it draws into question both the contents of labor and the division of labor (and thus the relationship between conception and execution loses its unilateral character). If the product is defined through the intervention of the consumer, and is therefore in permanent evolution, it becomes always more difficult to define the norms of the production of services and establish an "objective" measure of productivity.

Immaterial Labor

All of these characteristics of postindustrial economics (present both in large-scale industry and the tertiary sector) are accentuated in the form of properly "immaterial" production. Audiovisual production, advertising, fashion, software, the management of territory, and so forth are all defined by means of the particular relationship between production and its market or consumers. Here we are at the furthest point from the Taylorist model. Immaterial labor continually creates and modifies the forms and conditions of communication, which in turn acts as the interface that negotiates the relationship between production and consumption. As I noted earlier, immaterial labor produces first and foremost a social relation — it produces not only commodities, but also the capital relation.

If production today is directly the production of a social relation, then the "raw material" of immaterial labor is subjectivity and the "ideological" environment in which this subjectivity lives and reproduces. The production of subjectivity ceases to be only an instrument of social control (for the reproduction of mercantile relationships) and becomes directly productive, because the goal of our postindustrial society is to construct the consumer/communicator — and to construct it as "active." Immaterial workers (those who work in advertising, fashion, marketing, television, cybernetics, and so forth) satisfy a demand by the consumer and at the same time establish that demand. The fact that immaterial labor produces subjectivity and economic value at the same time demonstrates how capitalist production has invaded our lives and has broken down all the oppositions among economy, power, and knowledge. The process of social communication (and its principal content, the production of subjectivity) becomes here directly productive because in a certain way it "produces" production. The process by which the "social" (and what is even more social, that is, language, communication, and so forth) becomes "economic" has not yet been sufficiently studied. In effect, on the one hand, we are familiar with an analysis of the production of subjectivity defined as the constitutive "process" specific to a "relation to the self" with respect to the forms of production particular to knowledge and power (as in a certain vein of poststructuralist French philosophy), but this analysis never intersects sufficiently with the forms of capitalist valorization. On the other hand, in the 1980s a network of economists and sociologists (and before them the Italian postworkerist tradition) developed an extensive analysis of the "social form of production," but that analysis does not integrate sufficiently the production of subjectivity as the content of valorization. Now, the post-Taylorist mode of production is defined precisely by putting subjectivity to work both in the activation of productive cooperation and in the production of the "cultural" contents of commodities.

The Aesthetic Model

But how is the production process of social communication formed? How does the production of subjectivity take place within this process? How does the production of subjectivity become the production of the consumer/communicator and its capacities to consume and communicate? What role does immaterial labor have in this process? As I have already said, my hypothesis is this: *the process of the production of communication tends to become immediately the process of valorization.* If in the past communication was organized fundamentally by means of language and the institutions of ideological and literary/artistic production, today, because it is invested with industrial production, communication is reproduced by means of specific technological schemes (knowledge, thought, image, sound, and language reproduction technologies) and by means of forms of organization and "management" that are bearers of a new mode of production.

It is more useful, in attempting to grasp the process of the formation of social communication and its subsumption within the "economic," to use, rather than the "material" model of production, the "aesthetic" model that involves author, reproduction, and reception. This model reveals aspects that traditional economic categories tend to obscure and that, as I will show, constitute the "specific differences" of the post-Taylorist means of production.[2] The "aesthetic/ideological" model of production will be transformed into a small-scale sociological model with all the limits and difficulties that such a sociological transformation brings. The model of author, reproduction, and reception requires a double transformation: in the first place, the three stages of this creation process must be immediately characterized by their social form; in the second place, the three stages must be understood as the articulations of an actual productive cycle.[3]

The "author" must lose its individual dimension and be transformed into an industrially organized production process (with a division of labor, investments, orders, and so forth), "reproduction" becomes a mass reproduction organized according to the imperatives of profitability, and the audience ("reception") tends to become the consumer/communicator. In this process of socialization and subsumption within the economy of intellectual activity the "ideological" product tends to assume the form of a commodity. I should emphasize, however, that the subsumption of this process under capitalist logic and the transformation of its products into commodities does not abolish the specificity of aesthetic production, that is to say, the creative relationship between author and audience.

The Specific Differences of the Immaterial Labor Cycle

Allow me to underline briefly the *specific differences* of the "stages" that make up the production cycle of immaterial labor (immaterial labor itself, its "ideological/ commodity products," and the "public/consumer") in relation to the classical forms of the reproduction of "capital."

As far as immaterial labor being an "author" is concerned, it is necessary to emphasize *the radical autonomy of its productive synergies*. As we have seen, immaterial labor forces us to question the classical definitions of *work* and *workforce*, because it results from a synthesis of different types of know-how: intellectual skills, manual skills, and entrepreneurial skills. Immaterial labor constitutes itself in immediately collective forms that exist as networks and flows. The subjugation of this form of cooperation and the "use value" of these skills to capitalist logic does not take away the autonomy of the constitution and meaning of immaterial labor. On the contrary, it opens up antagonisms and contradictions that, to use once again a Marxist formula, demand at least a "new form of exposition."

The "ideological product" becomes in every respect a commodity. The term *ideological* does not characterize the product as a "reflection" of reality, as false or true consciousness of reality. Ideological products produce, on the contrary, new stratifications of reality; they are the intersection where human power, knowledge, and action meet. New modes of seeing and knowing demand new technologies, and new technologies demand new forms of seeing and knowing. These ideological products are completely internal to the processes of the formation of social communication; that is, they are at once the results and the prerequisites of these processes. The ensemble of ideological products constitutes the human ideological environment. Ideological products are transformed into commodities without ever losing their specificity; that is, *they are always addressed to someone, they are "ideally signifying,"* and thus they pose the problem of "meaning."

The general public tends to become the model for the consumer (audience/client). The public (in the sense of the user—the reader, the music listener, the television audience) whom the author addresses has as such a double productive function. In the first place, as the addressee of the ideological product, the public is a constitutive element of the production process. In the second place, the public is productive by means of the reception that gives the product "a place in life" (in other words, integrates it into social communication) and allows it to live and evolve. *Reception is thus, from this point of view, a creative act* and an integrative part of the product. The transformation of the product into a commodity cannot abolish this double process of "creativity"; it must rather assume it as it is, and attempt to control it and subordinate it to its own values.

What the transformation of the product into a commodity cannot remove, then, is the *character of event*, the open process of creation that is established between immaterial labor and the public and organized by communication. If the innovation in immaterial production is introduced by this open process of

creation, the entrepreneur, in order to further consumption and its perpetual renewal, will be constrained to draw from the "values" that the public/consumer produces. These values presuppose the modes of being, modes of existing, and forms
of life that support them. From these considerations there emerge two principal
consequences. First, values are "put to work." The transformation of the ideological
product into a commodity distorts or deflects the social imaginary that is produced
in the forms of life, but at the same time, commodity production must recognize
itself as powerless as far as its own production is concerned. The second consequence is that the forms of life (in their collective and cooperative forms) are now
the source of innovation.

The analysis of the different "stages" of the cycle of immaterial
labor permits me to advance the hypothesis that what is "productive" is the whole
of the social relation (here represented by the author-work-audience relationship)
according to modalities that directly bring into play the "meaning." The specificity
of this type of production not only leaves its imprint on the "form" of the process
of production by establishing a new relationship between production and consumption, but it also poses a problem of legitimacy for the capitalist appropriation of this
process. This cooperation can in no case be predetermined by economics, because
it deals with the very life of society. "Economics" can only appropriate the forms
and products of this cooperation, normalizing and standardizing them. The creative
and innovative elements are tightly linked to the values that only the forms of life
produce. Creativity and productivity in postindustrial societies reside, on the one
hand, in the dialectic between the forms of life and values they produce and, on the
other, in the activities of subjects that constitute them. The legitimation that the
(Schumpeterian) entrepreneur found in his or her capacity for innovation has lost
its foundation. Because the capitalist entrepreneur does not produce the forms and
contents of immaterial labor, he or she does not even produce innovation. For economics there remains only the possibility of managing and regulating the activity
of immaterial labor and creating some devices for the control and creation of the
public/consumer by means of the control of communication and information technologies and their organizational processes.

Creation and Intellectual Labor

These brief considerations permit us to begin questioning the model of creation
and diffusion specific to intellectual labor and to get beyond the concept of creativity as an expression of "individuality" or as the patrimony of the "superior" classes.
The works of Simmel and Bakhtin, conceived in a time when immaterial production

had just begun to become "productive," present us with two completely different ways of posing the relationship between immaterial labor and society. The first, Simmel's, remain completely invested in the division between manual labor and intellectual labor and give us a theory of the creativity of intellectual labor. The second, Bakhtin's, in refusing to accept the capitalist division of labor as a given, elaborate a theory of social creativity. Simmel, in effect, explains the function of "fashion" by means of the phenomenon of imitation or distinction as regulated and commanded by class relationships. Thus the superior levels of the middle classes are the ones that create fashion, and the lower classes attempt to imitate them. Fashion here functions like a barrier that incessantly comes up because it is incessantly battered down. What is interesting for this discussion is that, according to this conception, the immaterial labor of creation is limited to a specific social group and is not diffused except through imitation. At a deeper level, this model accepts the division of labor founded on the opposition between manual and intellectual labor that has as its end the regulation and "mystification" of the social process of creation and innovation. If this model had some probability of corresponding to the dynamics of the market of immaterial labor at the moment of the birth of mass consumption (whose effects Simmel very intelligently anticipates), it could not be utilized to account for the relationship between immaterial labor and consumer-public in postindustrial society. Bakhtin, on the contrary, defines immaterial labor as the superseding of the division between "material labor and intellectual labor" and demonstrates how creativity is a social process. In fact, the work on "aesthetic production" of Bakhtin and the rest of the Leningrad circle has this same social focus. This is the line of investigation that seems most promising for developing a theory of the social cycle of immaterial production.

Translated by Paul Colilli and Ed Emory

Notes

1. Yves Clot, "Renouveau de l'industrialisme et activité philosophique," *Futur antérieur*, no. 10 (1992): 22.

2. Both the creative and the social elements of this production encourage me to venture the use of the "aesthetic model." It is interesting to see how one could arrive at this new concept of labor by starting either from artistic activity (following the situationists) or from the traditional activity of the factory (following Italian

workerist theories), both relying on the very Marxist concept of "living labor."

3. Walter Benjamin has already analyzed how since the end of the nineteenth century both artistic production and reproduction, along with its perception, have assumed collective forms. I cannot pause here to consider his works, but they are certainly fundamental for any genealogy of immaterial labor and its forms of reproduction.

III

Concepts for a Potential Politics

ELEVEN

Form-of-Life

Giorgio Agamben

The ancient Greeks did not have only one term to express what we mean by the word *life*. They used two semantically and morphologically distinct terms: *zoé*, which expressed the simple fact of living common to all living beings (animals, humans, or gods), and *bios*, which signified the form or manner of living peculiar to a single individual or group. In modern languages this opposition has gradually disappeared from the lexicon (and where it is retained, as in *biology* and *zoology*, it no longer indicates any substantial difference); one term only — the opacity of which increases in proportion to the sacralization of its referent — designates that naked presupposed common element that it is always possible to isolate in each of the numerous forms of life.

By the term *form-of-life*, on the other hand, I mean a life that can never be separated from its form, a life in which it is never possible to isolate something such as naked life.

A life that cannot be separated from its form is a life for which what is at stake in its way of living is living itself. What does this formulation mean? It defines a life — human life — in which the single ways, acts, and processes of living are never simply *facts* but always and above all *possibilities* of life, always and above all power (*potenza*).[1] Each behavior and each form of human living is never prescribed by a specific biological vocation, nor is it assigned by whatever necessity; instead, no matter how customary, repeated, and socially compulsory, it always retains the character of a possibility; that is, it always puts at stake living itself. That is why human beings—as beings of power who can do or not do, succeed or fail, lose themselves or find themselves—are the only beings for whom happiness is always at stake in their living, the only beings whose lives are irremediably and painfully assigned to happiness. But this immediately constitutes the form-of-life as political life. "Civitatem . . . communitatem esse institutam propter vivere et bene vivere hominum in ea [The State is a community instituted for the sake of the living and the well living of men in it]."[2]

Political power (*potere*) as we know it, on the other hand, always founds itself—in the last instance—on the separation of a sphere of naked life from the context of the forms of life.[3] In Roman law, *vita* (life) is not a juridical concept, but rather indicates the simple fact of living or a particular way of life. There is only one case in which the term *life* acquires a juridical meaning that transforms it into a veritable *terminus technicus*, and that is in the expression *vitae necisque potestas*, which designates the *pater*'s power of life and death over the male son. J. Thomas has shown that, in this formula, *que* does not have disjunctive function and *vita* is nothing but a corollary of *nex*, the power to kill.

Life, thus, originally appears in law only as the counterpart of a power that threatens death. But what is valid for the *pater*'s right of life and death is even more valid for sovereign power (*imperium*), of which the former constitutes the originary cell. Thus, in the Hobbesian foundation of sovereignty, life in the state of nature is defined only by its being unconditionally exposed to a death threat (the limitless right of everybody over everything) and political life—that is, the life that unfolds under the protection of the Leviathan—is nothing but this very same life always exposed to a threat that now rests exclusively in the hands of the sovereign. The *puissance absolue et perpetuelle*, which defines State power, is not founded—in the last instance—on a political will but rather on naked life, which is kept safe and protected only to the degree to which it submits itself to the sovereign's (or the law's) right of life and death. (This is precisely the originary meaning of the adjective *sacer* [sacred] when used to refer to human life.) The state of exception, which is what the sovereign each and every time decides, takes place precisely when naked life—which normally appears rejoined to the multifarious forms of social life—is explicitly put into question and revoked as the ultimate foundation of political power. The ultimate subject that needs to be at once turned into the exception and included in the city is always naked life.

"The tradition of the oppressed teaches us that the 'state of emergency' in which we live is not the exception but the rule. We must attain to a conception of history that is in keeping with this insight."[4] Walter Benjamin's diagnosis, which by now is more than fifty years old, has lost none of its relevance. And that is so not really or not only because power (*potere*) no longer has today any form of legitimation other than emergency, and because power everywhere and continuously refers and appeals to emergency as well as laboring secretly to produce it. (How could we not think that a system that can no longer function at all but on the basis of emergency would not also be interested in preserving such an emergency at any price?) This is the case also and above all because naked life, which was the hidden foundation of sovereignty, has become, in the meanwhile, the dominant form of life everywhere. Life—in its state of exception that has now become the norm—is the naked life that in every context separates the forms of life from their cohering into a form-of-life. The Marxian division between man and citizen is thus superseded by the division between naked life (ultimate and opaque bearer of sovereignty) and the multifarious forms of life abstractly recodified as social-juridical identities (the voter, the worker, the journalist, the student, but also the HIV-positive, the transvestite, the porno star, the elderly, the parent, the woman) that all rest on naked life. (To have mistaken such a naked life separate from its form, in its abjection, for a superior principle—sovereignty or the sacred—is the limit of Bataille's thought, which makes it useless to us.)

Foucault's thesis—according to which "what is at stake today is life" and hence politics has become biopolitics—is, in this sense, substantially correct. What is decisive, however, is the way in which one understands the sense of this transformation. What is left unquestioned in the contemporary debates on bioethics and biopolitics, in fact, is precisely what would deserve to be questioned before anything else, that is, the very biological concept of life. Paul Rabinow conceives of two models of life as symmetrical opposites: on the one hand, the experimental life of the scientist who is ill with leukemia and who turns his very life into a laboratory for unlimited research and experimentation, and, on the other hand, the one who, in the name of life's sacredness, exasperates the antinomy between individual ethics and techno-science. Both models, however, participate without being aware in the same concept of naked life. This concept—which today presents itself under the guises of a scientific notion—is actually a secularized political concept. (From a strictly scientific point of view, the concept of life makes no sense. Peter and Jean Medawar tell us that in biology, discussions about the real meaning of the words *life* and *death* are an index of a low level of conversation. Such words have no intrinsic meaning and such a meaning, hence, cannot be clarified by deeper and more careful studies.)[5]

Such is the provenance of the (often unperceived and yet decisive) function of medical-scientific ideology within the system of power and the increasing use of pseudoscientific concepts for ends of political control. That same withdrawal of naked life that, in certain circumstances, the sovereign used to be able to exact from the forms of life is now massively and daily exacted by the pseudoscientific representations of the body, illness, and health, and by the "medicalization" of ever-widening spheres of life and individual imagination.[6] Biological life, which is the secularized form of naked life and which shares its unutterability and impenetrability, thus constitutes the real forms of life literally as forms of survival: biological life remains inviolate in such forms as that obscure threat that can suddenly actualize itself in violence, in extraneity, in illnesses, in accidents. It is the invisible sovereign that stares at us behind the dull-witted masks of the powerful, who, whether or not they realize it, govern us in its name.

A political life, that is, a life directed toward the idea of happiness and cohesive with a form-of-life, is thinkable only starting with the emancipation from such a division, with the irrevocable exodus from any sovereignty. The question about the possibility of a non-Statist politics necessarily takes this form: Is today something like a form-of-life, a life for which living itself would be at stake in its own living, possible? Is today a life of power (*potenza*) available?[7]

I call thought the nexus that constitutes the forms of life in an inseparable context as form-of-life. I do not mean by this the individual exercise of an organ or a psychic faculty, but rather an experience, an *experimentum* that has as its object the potential character of life and human intelligence. To think does not mean merely to be affected by this or that thing, by this or that content of enacted thought, but rather at once to be affected by one's own receptiveness and experience in each and every thing that is thought a pure power of thinking. ("When thought has become each thing in the way in which a man who actually knows is said to do so...its condition is still one of potentiality...and thought is then able to think of itself.")[8]

Only if I am not always already and solely enacted, but rather delivered to a possibility and a power, only if living and intending and apprehending themselves are at stake each time in what I live and intend and apprehend—only if, in other words, there is thought—only then a form of life can become, in its own factness and thingness, form-of-life, in which it is never possible to isolate something like naked life.

The experience of thought that is here in question is always the experience of a common power. Community and power identify one with the other completely, without residue, because the inherence of a communitarian principle to any power is a function of the necessarily potential character of any community. Among beings who would always already be enacted, who would always already be this or that thing, this or that identity, and who would have entirely exhausted their power in these things and identities—among such beings there could not be any community but only coincidences and factual partitions. We can communicate with others only through what in us—as much as in others—has remained potential, and any communication (as Benjamin perceives for language) is first of all communication not of something in common but of communicability itself. After all, if there existed one and only one being, it would be absolutely impotent. (That is why theologians affirm that God created the world *ex nihilo*, in other words, absolutely without power.) Where I have power, we are always already many (just like when, if there is a language, that is, a power of speech, there cannot be then one and only one being who speaks it).

That is why modern political philosophy does not begin with classical thought, which had made of contemplation, of the *bios theoreticos*, a separate and solitary activity ("exile of the alone to the alone"), but rather only with Averroism, that is, with the thought of the one and only possible intellect common to all human beings, and, crucially, with Dante's affirmation—in *De Monarchia*—of the inherence of a multitude to the very power of thought:

It is clear that man's basic capacity is to have a potentiality or power for being intellectual. And since this power cannot be completely actualized in a single man or in any of the particular communities of men above mentioned, there must be a multitude in mankind through whom this whole power can be actualized.... the proper work of mankind taken as a whole is to exercise continually its entire capacity for intellectual growth, first, in theoretical matters, and, secondarily, as an extension of theory, in practice. [9]

The diffuse intellectuality I am talking about and the Marxian notion of a "general intellect" acquire their meaning only within the perspective of this experience. They name the multitude that inheres to the power of thought as such. Intellectuality and thought are not a form of life among others in which life and social production articulate themselves, but they are rather the unitary power that constitutes the multiple forms of life as form-of-life. In the face of State sovereignty, which can affirm itself only by separating in every context naked life from its form, they are the power that incessantly reunites life to its form or prevents it from being dissociated from its form. The act of distinguishing between the mere, massive inscription of social knowledge into the productive processes (an inscription that characterizes the contemporary phase of capitalism, the society of the spectacle) and intellectuality as antagonistic power and form-of-life—such an act passes through the experience of this cohesion and this inseparability. Thought is form-of-life, life that cannot be segregated from its form; and anywhere the intimacy of this inseparable life appears, in the materiality of corporeal processes and habitual ways of life no less than in theory, there and only there is there thought. And it is this thought, this form-of-life, that, abandoning naked life to "Man" and to the "Citizen" who clothe it temporarily and represent it with their "rights," must become the guiding concept and the unitary center of the coming politics.

Translated by Cesare Casarino

Notes

1. The English term *power* corresponds to two distinct terms in Italian, *potenza* and *potere*. See the entry for "Power" in the glossary at the end of this volume. In this essay I will use the original Italian term when there may be some confusion between these two notions of power. The subsequent instance where *power* appears in this paragraph also refers to *potenza*.

2. Marsilius of Padua, *The Defensor of Peace*, trans. Alan Gewirth (New York: Harper & Row, 1956), 15. I have modified Gewirth's translation.

3. All subsequent uses of the word *power* in this section refer to *potere*.

4. Walter Benjamin, "Theses on the Philosophy of History," in *Illuminations*, trans. Harry Zohn (New York: Schocken, 1989), 257. [In the Italian translation of Benjamin's passage, "state of emergency" is translated as

"state of exception," which is the phrase Agamben uses in the preceding section of this essay. Trans.]

5. See, for example, Peter Medawar and Jean Medawar, *Aristotle to Zoos* (Oxford: Oxford University Press, 1983), 66–67.

6. [The terminology in the original is the same as that used for bank transactions (and thus "naked life" becomes here the cash reserve contained in accounts such as the "forms of life"). Trans.]

7. All uses of the word *power* in the remainder of the essay refer to *potenza*.

8. Aristotle, *On the Soul*, in *The Complete Works of Aristotle*, vol. 1, ed. Jonathan Barnes (Princeton, N.J.: Princeton University Press, 1984), 682–83.

9. Dante Alighieri, *On World Government*, trans. Herbert W. Schneider (Indianapolis: Liberal Arts, 1957), 6–7.

T W E L V E

Beyond Human Rights

Giorgio Agamben

In 1943, Hannah Arendt published in a small English-language Jewish publication, the *Menorah Journal*, an article titled "We Refugees." At the end of this brief but significant piece of writing, after having polemically sketched the portrait of Mr. Cohn, the assimilated Jew who, after having been 150 percent German, 150 percent Viennese, and 150 percent French, must bitterly realize in the end that "on ne parvient pas deux fois, " she turns the condition of countryless refugee — a condition she herself was living — upside down in order to present it as paradigm of a new historical consciousness. The refugees who have lost all rights and who, however, no longer want to be assimilated at all costs in a new national identity, but want instead to contemplate lucidly their condition, receive in exchange for assured unpopularity a priceless advantage: "History is no longer a closed book to them and politics is no longer the privilege of Gentiles. They know that the outlawing of the Jewish people in Europe has been followed closely by the outlawing of most European nations. Refugees driven from country to country represent the vanguard of their peoples."[1]

One ought to reflect on the meaning of this analysis, which after fifty years has lost none of its relevance. It is not only the case that the problem presents itself inside and outside of Europe with just as much urgency now as then. It is also the case that, given the by now unstoppable decline of the Nation-State and the general corrosion of traditional political-juridical categories, the refugee is perhaps the only thinkable figure for the people of our time and the only category in which one may see today—at least until the process of dissolution of the Nation-State and its sovereignty has achieved full completion—the forms and limits of a coming political community. It is even possible that, if we want to be equal to the absolutely new tasks ahead, we will have to abandon decidedly, without reserve, the fundamental concepts through which we have so far represented the subjects of the political (Man, the Citizen and its rights, but also the sovereign people, the worker, and so forth) and build our political philosophy anew starting from the one and only figure of the refugee.

The first appearance of refugees as a mass phenomenon took place at the end of World War I, when the fall of the Russian, Austro-Hungarian, and Ottoman empires, along with the new order created by the peace treaties, upset profoundly the demographic and territorial constitution of Central Eastern Europe. In a short period, 1.5 million White Russians, seven hundred thousand Armenians, five hundred thousand Bulgarians, a million Greeks, and hundreds of thousands of Germans, Hungarians, and Rumanians left their countries. To these moving masses, one needs to add the explosive situation determined by the fact that about 30 percent of the population in the new states created by the peace treaties on the model of the Nation-State (Yugoslavia and Czechoslovakia, for example) was constituted by minorities that had to be safeguarded by a series of international treaties—the so-called Minority Treaties—which very often were never enforced. A few years later, the racial laws in Germany and the civil war in Spain disseminated throughout Europe a new and significant contingent of refugees.

We are used to distinguishing between refugees and stateless people, but this distinction was not then as simple as it may seem at first glance, nor is it even today. From the beginning, many refugees, who were not technically stateless, preferred to become such rather than return to their countries. (This was the case with the Polish and Rumanian Jews who were in France or Germany at the end of the war, and today it is the case with those who are politically persecuted or for whom return to their countries would mean putting their own survival at risk.) On the other hand, Russian, Armenian, and Hungarian refugees were promptly denationalized by the new Turkish amd Soviet governments. It is important to note how, starting with World War I, many European States began to pass laws allowing the denaturalization and denationalization of their own citizens: France was first in 1915 with regard to naturalized citizens of "enemy origin"; in 1922, Belgium followed this example by revoking the naturalization of those citizens who had committed "antinational" acts during the war; in 1926, the Italian Fascist regime passed an analogous law with regard to citizens who had showed themselves "undeserving of Italian citizenship"; in 1933, it was Austria's turn; and so on, until in 1935 the Nuremberg laws divided German citizens into citizens with full rights and citizens without political rights. Such laws—and the mass statelessness resulting from them—mark a decisive turn in the life of the modern Nation-State as well as its definitive emancipation from naive notions of the citizen and a people.

This is not the place to retrace the history of the various international organizations through which single States, the Society of Nations, and later the United Nations have tried to face the refugee problem, from the Nansen Bureau for the Russian and Armenian refugees (1921) to the High Commission for Refugees from Germany (1936) to the Intergovernmental Committee for Refugees (1938) to the U.N.'s International Refugee Organization (1951), whose activity, according to its statute, does not have a political character but rather only a "social and humanitarian" one. What is essential is that each and every time refugees no longer represent individual cases but rather a mass phenomenon (as was the case between the two World Wars and is now once again), these organizations as well as the single States—all the solemn evocations of the inalienable rights of human beings notwithstanding—have proved to be absolutely incapable not only of solving the problem but also of facing it in an adequate manner. The whole question, thus, was handed over to humanitarian organizations and to the police.

The reasons for such impotence lie not only in the selfishness and blindness of bureacratic apparatuses, but also in the very ambiguity of the fundamental notions regulating the inscription of the *native* (that is, of life) in the juridical order of the Nation-State. Hannah Arendt titled the chapter of her book *Imperialism* that concerns the refugee problem, "The Decline of the Nation-State and the End of the Rights of Man."[2] One should try to take seriously this formulation, which links indissolubly the fate of human rights with the fate of the modern Nation-State in such a way that the waning of the latter necessarily implies the obsolescence of the former. Here the paradox is that precisely the figure that should have embodied human rights more than any other—namely, the refugee—marked instead the radical crisis of the concept. The conception of human rights based on the supposed existence of a human being as such, Arendt tells us, proves to be untenable as soon as those who profess it find themselves confronted for the first time with people who have really lost every quality and every specific relation except for the pure fact of being human.[3] In the system of the Nation-State, the so-called sacred and inalienable human rights are revealed to be without any protection precisely when it is no longer possible to conceive of them as rights of the citizens of a State. This is implicit, after all, in the ambiguity of the very title of the 1789 *Déclaration des droits de l'homme et du citoyen*, in which it is unclear whether the two terms are to name two distinct realities or whether they are to form, instead, a hendiadys in which the first term is actually always already contained in the second.

That there is no autonomous space in the political order of the Nation-State for something like the pure human in itself is evident at the very least from the fact that, even in the best of cases, the status of refugee has always been considered a temporary condition that ought to lead either to naturalization or repatriation. A stable statute for the human in itself is inconceivable in the law of the Nation-State.

It is time to stop looking at all the declarations of rights from 1789 to the present day as proclamations of eternal metajuridical values aimed at binding the legislator to the respect of such values; it is time, rather, to understand them according to their real function in the modern State. Human rights, in fact, represent first of all the originary figure for the inscription of natural naked life in the political-juridical order of the Nation-State. Naked life (the human being), which in antiquity belonged to God and in the classical world was clearly distinct (as *zoé*) from political life (*biós*), comes to the forefront in the management of the State and becomes, so to speak, its earthly foundation. *Nation-State* means a State that makes nativity or birth (*nascita*) (that is, naked human life) the foundation of its own sovereignty. This is the meaning (which is not really hidden) of the first three articles of the 1789 Declaration: it is only because this declaration inscribed (in articles 1 and 2) the native element in the heart of any political organization that it can firmly bind (in article 3) the principle of sovereignty to the nation (in conformity with its etymon, native [*natío*] originally meant simply "birth" [*nascita*]). The fiction that is implicit here is that birth (*nascita*) comes into being immediately as nation, so that there may not be any difference between the two moments. Rights, in other words, are attributed to the human being only to the degree in which they are the immediately vanishing presupposition (and, in fact, the presupposition that must never come to light as such) of the citizen.

If the refugee represents such a disquieting element in the order of the Nation-State, that is so primarily because, by breaking the identity between the human and the citizen and that between nativity and nationality, it brings the originary fiction of sovereignty to crisis. Single exceptions to such a principle, of course, have always existed. What is new in our time is that growing sections of humankind are no longer representable inside the Nation-State — and this novelty threatens the very foundations of the latter. Inasmuch as the refugee, an apparently marginal figure, unhinges the old trinity of State-nation-territory, it deserves instead to be regarded as the central figure of our political history. We should not forget that the first camps were built in Europe as spaces for controlling refugees, and that the succession of internment camps-concentration camps-extermination camps represents a perfectly real filiation. One of the few rules the Nazis constantly obeyed throughout the course of the "final solution" was that Jews and Gypsies could be sent to extermination camps only after having been fully denationalized (that is, after they had been stripped of even that second-class citizenship to which they had been relegated after the Nuremberg laws). When their rights are no longer the rights of the citizen, that is when humans are truly sacred, in the sense that this term used to have in ancient Roman law: doomed to death.

The concept of refugee must be resolutely separated from the concept of "human rights," and the right of asylum (which in any case is by now in the process of being drastically restricted in the legislation of the European States) must no longer be considered as the conceptual category in which to inscribe the phenomenon of refugees. The refugee should be considered for what it is, namely, nothing less than a limit-concept that at once brings a radical crisis to the principles of the Nation-State and clears the way for a renewal of categories that can no longer be delayed.

       In the meanwhile, in fact, the phenomenon of so-called illegal immigration into the countries of the European Union has reached (and shall increasingly reach in the coming years, given the estimated twenty million immigrants from Central European countries) characteristics and proportions such that this reversal of perspective is fully justified. What industrialized countries face today is a *permanently resident mass of noncitizens* who do not want to and cannot be either naturalized or repatriated. These noncitizens often have nationalities of origin, but, inasmuch as they prefer not to benefit from their own States' protection, they find themselves, as refugees, in a condition of de facto Statelessness. Tomas Hammar has created the neologism of "denizens" for these noncitizen residents, a neologism that has the merit of showing how the concept of "citizen" is no longer adequate for describing the social-political reality of modern States.[4] On the other hand, the citizens of advanced industrial States (in the United States as well as Europe) demonstrate, through an increasing desertion of the codified instances of political participation, an evident propensity to turn into denizens, into noncitizen permanent residents, so that citizens and denizens—at least in certain social strata—are entering an area of potential indistinction. In a parallel way, xenophobic reactions and defensive mobilizations are growing, in conformity with the well-known principle according to which substantial assimilation in the presence of formal differences exacerbates hatred and intolerance.

Before extermination camps are reopened in Europe (something that is already starting to happen), it is necessary that the Nation-States find the courage to question the very principle of the inscription of nativity as well as the trinity of State-nation-territory that is founded in that principle. It is not easy to indicate right now the ways in which all this may concretely happen. One of the options taken into consideration for solving the problem of Jerusalem is that it become—simultaneously and without any territorial partition—the capital of two different States. The paradoxical condition of reciprocal extraterritoriality (or, better yet, aterritoriality) that would thus be implied could be generalized as a model of new international relations. Instead of two national States separated by uncertain and threatening boundaries, it might be possible to imagine two political communities insisting on the same region and in a condition of exodus from each other—communities that would articulate each other through a series of reciprocal extraterritorialities in which the guiding concept would no longer be the *ius* (right) of the citizen but rather the *refugium* (refuge) of the singular. In an analogous way, we could conceive of Europe not as an impossible "Europe of the nations," whose catastrophe one can already foresee in the short run, but rather as an aterritorial or extraterritorial space in which all the (citizen and noncitizen) residents of the European States would be in a position of exodus or refuge; the status of European would then mean the being-in-exodus of the citizen (a condition that obviously could also be one of immobility). European space would thus mark an irreducible difference between birth (*nascita*) and nation in which the old concept of people (which, as is well known, is always a minority) could find again a political meaning, thus decidedly opposing itself to the concept of nation (which has so far unduly usurped it).

      This space would coincide neither with any of the homogeneous national territories nor with their *topographical* sum, but would rather act on them by articulating and perforating them *topologically* as in the Leida bottle or the Möbius strip, where exterior and interior in-determine each other. In this new space, European cities would rediscover their ancient vocation as cities of the world by entering into relations of reciprocal extraterritoriality.

As I write this essay, 425 Palestinians expelled by the State of Israel find themselves in a sort of no-man's-land. These men certainly constitute, following Hanna Arendt's suggestion, "the vanguard of their people." But that is so not necessarily or not merely in the sense that they might form the originary nucleus of a future national State, or in the sense that they might solve the Palestinian question in a way just as insufficient as the way in which Israel has solved the Jewish question. Rather, the no-man's-land in which they are refugees has already started from this very moment to act back onto the territory of the State of Israel by perforating it and altering it in such a way that the image of that snowy mountain has become more internal to it than any other region of Heretz Israel. Only in a world in which the spaces of State have been thus perforated and topologically deformed and in which the citizen has been able to recognize the refugee that he or she is — only in such a world is the political survival of humankind today thinkable.

Translated by Cesare Casarino

Notes

1. Hanna Arendt, "We Refugees," *Menorah Journal*, no. 1 (1943): 77.

2. Hanna Arendt, *Imperialism*, pt. 2 of *The Origins of Totalitarianism* (New York: Harcourt, Brace, 1951), 266–98.

3. Ibid., 290–95.

4. Tomas Hammar, *Democracy and the Nation State: Aliens, Denizens, and Citizens in a World of International Migration* (Brookfield, Vt.: Gower, 1990).

THIRTEEN

Unrepresentable Citizenship

Augusto Illuminati

The human is a social animal, and the social is evil. We cannot do anything about it, and

yet we cannot accept it if we do not want to lose our souls. Life can thus be nothing but

laceration. This world is uninhabitable. And therefore we must escape to the other. But the

door is closed. How long we must knock before it opens! In order truly to enter, not to

remain on the threshold, one must stop being a social being.

Simone Weil, Cahiers, 1974

In our modern apolitical condition politics has spread out into spheres from which it has traditionally been excluded and where, hence, it has to be reinterpreted, just as an image reflected in a cylindrical surface has to be straightened anamorphically.[1] In this way we should single out the practices, tactics, strategies, objectives, and organizational apparatuses of a movement that articulates itself through either limited and provisory issues or permanent differences, such as sexual difference or the difference of ethnic or cultural minorities. The politicization of uncustomary spheres goes hand in hand with the desertion of ossified institutions.

A reactive practice responding to this situation might involve a process of integration into the representative structures with new lobbies or demands of quotas for minorities. Such a process would trace faithfully the passage from the bourgeoisie's secretly organized apolitical nature to the synthesis of publicity and rule—even though it has not yet been realized with a visible institutional rearrangement or even with a more flexible redefinition of subjectivity. The other side of the same phenomenon consists instead in the abandonment of the modern notion of political practice, modeled on work and domination, in favor of a more originary notion of action. This more utopic and unforeseeable side would involve a refusal of representation. The two sides, however, come together, as much in the revolt against the abstractness and obsoleteness of the current political system as in an inclination toward the reflexivity of praxis. In the "letting be" that is set against institutional arrogance, there live together both the not-yet-represented (which searches in lobbyist fashion for representation) and the radical refusal of representation.

The Modern Observer

In a suggestive passage, Maurice Blanchot, borrowing a term from Jean-Luc Nancy, writes that the inoperative community is "a bastardized surrogate of the people of God (quite similar to what the gathering of the Children of Israel at the time of the Exodus could have been like, if they had reunited and at the same time forgotten to leave)."[2] In this aggregation there live together dreamers and opportunists, cynical pluralists and subversives, representable differences and ascetics of an unrepresentable subjectivity. All have given up on the Promised Land or have silently dismissed it, although their interests remain diversified and conflicting. The refusal or the elusion of ethical-judicial coercion (which in other times was expressed in the utopia of the abolition of the State) can be for some the practical beginnings of communism and for others a liberalism of the market and egotistical drives. This ambiguity inheres in the modern paradox according to which the center is the periphery, if *modern* is to mean the unceasing revolution of one's own assumptions, displacement to the edge of yesterday's essentials, the accession to the center of what was at first perceived as eccentric. The movement of this vortex is the fluctuation that looks out to the limit.

Remaining at the margins of politics and history is the place of the observer, a position that has a long history but takes on specific characteristics as the paradigmatic figure of modernity. It is not by chance that Hannah Arendt underlines Kant's position as "spectator" of the French Revolution, reevaluating the communicative flexibility of reflective judgment, the interface between *active life* and *contemplative life*.[3] Only the spectator, and never the actor, is capable of recognizing and understanding what is offered to the gaze as a spectacle. We are thus far from Rousseau's identification of actor and spectator in the popular festival, of subject and ruler in the "common self" of the social contract, that is, the coinciding of will and freedom in the shadow of a controlled and immediate relationship. In our case, the spectator has the key to the meaning of human affairs because he or she maintains a distance from the scene of action and from the rest of the audience, that is, the public. The spectator guarantees the plurality of interpretations discussed by the public, but does not identify him- or herself individually in them. In such a way, the spectator escapes the antinomies of good and sociability in the collective representations of will, and thus escapes also the threatening dilemma that Simone Weil announces in the epigraph that opens this essay.

The geometric and symbolic city is the site of analytic and moral judgments, precisely delimiting or witnessing the universal. Social structure and political obligation mirror each other in it and thus draw rational certainty. This is as true for utopias and also for philosophical metaphors — certainly for Descartes, but also for Leibniz, who, in a famous April 1669 letter to J. Thomasius, wrote:

Essence differs from its own qualities only because of its relation with sensibility, just as a city offers its outline in a different way if you look at it from the height of a tower situated in its center, which corresponds to the intuition of essence itself, and if instead you approach it from the exterior, which corresponds to the perception of corporeal qualities. And just as the external aspects of the city vary, if you approach it from the Eastern part or the Western one, so too similarly qualities vary because of the variety of organs.[4]

The spectator here is faced with a preestablished visual scene, a categorical specification of what is possible governed by the principle of harmony, which gives complete advantage to the stability of power and hierarchies.[5] Not by chance, again, in the nineteenth-century utopias of progress — as, for example, in the last dream of Vera Pavlovna in Nikolai Chernyshevsky's *What Is to Be Done?*, which was vehemently criticized by Dostoyevsky — the place of realized ideality and transparent joy is situated outside of the city, which is used solely for the exchange of commodities. The modern city, variegated and unforeseeable, is instead subjected to the variable reorganization of reflective judgment, the lord of taste and political evaluation. Its exemplary figure is the *flâneur*, in which the observer has been transcribed from the realm of the philosophy of history into that of the social phenomenology of consumption. The *flâneur* maintains the same capacity of judgment and critical detachment with respect to commodities and history; he or she travels the entire breadth of the city with the ubiquitous freedom of one who is not an actor of a specific part and at the same time knows how to evaluate not by means of statistics or ultimate ends but on the basis of significant cases, which rely on common sense to be persuasive. The singular fact is preserved in its exemplary contingency. The observer and the *flâneur* love to reorder the fragments; they know how to save phenomena. Their marginality with respect to history and consumption does not negate them; rather, they expose the profound meaning of marginality by flaunting a participating nonsubordination.

The importance of the marginal observer is thus precisely circumscribed, so as not to make him or her a pathetic equivalent of the victors. Any loss is an anticipation of revenge, as it is in a good novel; the loser, in Stephen King style, is a substantial winner. The reflective role of the spectator in Hannah Arendt is inseparable from the characteristic of the historical actor: the actor reveals its subjectivity by means of a rupture of the context, a process of initiation that introduces the new in the world. The agent is not the author of history, because his or her intentions are included with those of a plurality of other agents, but the agent's initiative is what precedes and complements the reflexivity that reconstructs the meaning of what happened, and permits the formulation of further interventions. The power that is constituted with the action and that at times suspends itself in the reflection is inseparable from the plurality of the agents and the reflective public. Hence "the apolitical" is a relation that is internal to politics: a collectively conditioned gesture more than a refolding into the interiority of thought or will, in the silence of the intellectual or individual labor, in the transcendence of nonworldly human experience. Moreover, reflexivity constrains the singularities, which in themselves are unrelated in the action, to communicate, thus avoiding any slippage into the idiocy of pure difference. Observation is not only an attribute or a phase of the mind, but a resource for circumventing the latent mysticism of action, its surrender to a "private language" outside of the context of an interactive public.

The conservative management of the apolitical is an everyday affair that appeals not so much to the call to contemplation as to the tendency to leave alone the mundane things that go along with the privacy of work and consumption. The movement of exodus is ambiguously marked both by the opposition to dominant ideas and classes and by their profound establishment and molecular renewal. This mixture of individual and collective nature, of quietism and rebellion, is significant. Without indulging in the evocation of an "elsewhere," the guarantor of passivity and separateness, the exodus is of interest if it implies refusal of domination—if, in short, it comes to terms with the capitalist mode of production and the regime of waged labor. If it does not attack and break this barrier, it risks instead falling back into the ordinary internal mobility of bourgeois civil society, and thus betrays the promise of community implicit in its gesture of uprooting, establishing new consolatory forms of belonging and new insoluble conflicts between ghettoized and resentful minorities. Even "differences" like to wrap themselves in parodistic halos, collapse into the incommunicable privacy of the mystical and work, and adorn themselves with showy and terrifying tribal tattoos—the poorest of the self-representations.

Community

Frenesi dreamed of a mysterious people's oneness, drawing together toward the best chances of light, achieved once or twice that she'd seen in the street, in short, timeless bursts, all paths, human and projectile, true, the people in a single presence, the police likewise simple as a moving blade.... But DL admitted she was a little less saintly—"Is the asskicking part's usually what I'm lookin' for," watching Frenesi, waiting for disapproval. "But somebody told me it don't mean much unless I make what they call the correct analysis? and then act on it? Ever hear of that one?"

Thomas Pynchon, *Vineland,* 1990

Blanchot's "unavowable" community hinges on a relationship of love, whose paradoxical affectivity turns out to be similar to our late-modern apolitical condition.[6] Allow me to cite a few passages:

Passion escapes possibility, escaping (for those who are taken by it) their very powers, their decision-making, and even their "desire," and thus strangeness itself, which regards neither what they can do nor what they want, but attracts them in what is strange, in which they become strangers to themselves, in an intimacy that also makes them strangers to one another.... Not separated, nor divided: they are inaccessible, and being inaccessibe, they are in infinite relation. (72)

The community of lovers, whether they want it or not, whether they enjoy it or not ... has as its essential goal the destruction of society. Wherever there is formed an episodic community between two beings who are or are not made for each other, a war machine is formed, or better yet, a possibility of disaster that carries with it, even in infinitesimal doses, the threat of universal annihilation. (80)

Is something like a community *formed despite... the* lie *of this union that always is accomplished by not being accomplished? It is rather because of this that a community is formed.* (82)

By analogy, mass movements in the process of formation ignore the structures that could make them both stable and threatening to the possessors of a power that does not recognize them. They constitute both "the dissolution of the social pact" and the obstinate insistence on reinventing it "in a sovereignty that the law cannot circumscribe, because [they] refuse the law even though they hold themselves as its foundation" (56). This suspended spontaneity of the community is instantaneous, because this community is loath to make institutional and juridically unsayable arrangements. This spontaneity itself is the basis of every organized cohabitation, the reason of life prior to every constituted order. The community of lovers contains an essential element of every cohabitation that cannot be transvalued politically; at the same time, however, it pushes to re-create nostalgically past collective formations. There is a risk, then, that the demagogy and mysticism of power will take the place of the fragile ineffability of love, and that the flight from society will be inverted into a perverse identification with the hyperrepresented masses in a leader or an organization.

Jean-Luc Nancy's notion of an "inoperative community" is meant to elude this ambiguity.[7] The communion of lovers (if the community slips into fusion) takes as its model the State formation, the Hegelian attribution to the State of the truth of the singular, hence a humanism that realizes itself completely in the sign of death, an infinite immanentism. The ecstatic sovereignty of lovers or artists risks reconstituting, in forms quite different from the fascist orgiastic, a doubtful privilege—an *Erlebnis*, as Benjamin might say, that substitutes for and devalues a degraded *Erfahrung*.

The principle of community distributes singular beings, that is, finite beings, like others among themselves. Politics in a strong sense is the trace of the ecstatic communication of singularities, wherein their being-common manifests itself in an appearing together, in reciprocal exposition. The community is not the collective sum or preliminary essence of individuals, but the communication of singular separated beings that only by means of the community exist as such; it is a being *in* common and not a *common being*. This is Hannah Arendt's space of appearing, where the political actor appears to the others and the others explicitly appear to the actor, not limiting him- or herself to exist as do the other living or inanimate things. Power is thus formed and conditioned by the plurality of agents.

Community is a community of others, their being-together more than relating to each other: "being-together is alterity," the arrival of the new, the heterogeneous in time and space. Finiteness consists in this arrival of alterity. If tyranny does not expose anything or if it presents in a totalitarian way an essence of being, democracy limits itself to exposing that such an essence is inexposable. The implicit defect of representation (Carl Schmitt's "neutralization") constitutes the lesser evil, and certainly cannot be criticized with arguments inspired by illusions of ethical-social communion. The limit of democracy is rather that of not being able to succeed in exposing the in-common, of articulating the in-common of the population whose name it programmatically carries.[8]

If freedom cannot be reduced to any definition of representation, then revolution, which is the opening of decision, does not have institutions to knock down, reform, or refound; it is a constituent power that disintegrates every constituted power. This approach does not merely withdraw into the social; rather, it dissolves the opposition between State and society, instituting a paradoxical community founded on absolute contingency, on the encounter with the other in the common exposition for freedom and death.[9] Its context is impoverished experience, reduced to the nakedness of the rules and confronted by the powers of the abstract, while its conflictual articulation requires a structure that is nonrepresentative and does not homologize citizenship. The singular structure of action—what Arendt calls a second birth, which brings forth the naked reality of the originary physical apparition—requires a plurality of distinct unities, agents, and reflections, and discards both the solipsism of "private" languages and the internal dialectic of the will, along with the tendency of a social or institutional representation to fuse subjectivities together.

The fact that pluralism is to be understood in a strong sense—which invests, that is, the very constitution of singularity—could be exemplified with reference to the fundamental role in modern culture played by the migration of the Marrano population (of converted Jews) to escape persecution from Spain to Portugal to Holland from the fifteenth to the seventeenth centuries. Here we find together the themes of the ghetto, exodus, and abjuration, the theme of the persecution of what is different and the productivity of defection, as well as the unsustainable and fertile ambiguity of badly serving one or the other god to the point of dissipating its transcendence into libertinism and immanentism—at the risk of being burned at the stake or suffering a tragic breakdown. The intellectuals who betrayed their own god were watched with suspicion by the followers of the god of the newly embraced religion (we are certainly not dealing with a neutral transfer from "source" to "target" or with academic alternatives of a sort of polytheism). These intellectuals lived an authentic disintegration of the personality with that savage irreverence that was to unhinge the order of European thought in the period between Spinoza and Marx.

Marranism extended beyond the specific circle of sixteenth- and seventeenth-century Judaism to become a mass phenomenon, associated with a mass intellectuality and a new demand for citizenship that developed in the margin of professional displacements and traditional ideologies and in the blending of the cultures of the established residents and the immigrants to the metropolis. Marranism of the spirit and the hybridization of mass culture: in both aspects, the discomfort of the uprooted singularity reveals the intimate incoherence of the subject, its problematic relationship with the self through the distress of the encounter with the other. This, however, is where the new arises — this is the "natality" that impudently exhibits its own contingency, that betrays every predictable belonging and scandalously strains the rationality of the discussion and the project, forcing them to be, if not abandoned, at least reconfigured. The modern community, possible insofar as it is impossible, depends on simulation and betrayal, certainly not on transparency and fidelity to origins.

Citizenship

The fundamental right of humans is to signify nothing. It is the contrary of nihilism, the meaning that mutilates and fragments. This right not to have meaning is in any case the most misrecognized, the most openly trampled under foot.
Georges Bataille, L'Expérience intérieure, variation

Community is the outer side of democracy, just as citizenship is its inner side. *Dèmos*, which confers on democracy the name that has not yet been articulated, is an ancient Indo-European term associated with a family of meanings such as distribution, division (of men, food, and territory), and gathering at a banquet (*dàiomai, dàinumi, daizo*). *Daìs* is the meal in common with one, single portion. *Daìmon* is the one who gives by destiny; it is fortune, a god. This is not far from the kind of distribution involved in *nemein* and *nomos*, but this is not so tied to the idea of the occupation of the land and enclosure, law and numeration. This term is rather at the ambiguous limit between *communication* and *communion*, which is the being-in-common of singular-

ities and also the repartitioning of territory and property subsumed under an immanent collectivity. By *community* I mean not the counterutopic community that is
always mourned as recently lost, but the thought of the being-in-common of singularities, of their alterity.[10] In turning toward this community, democracy creates
its very experience from its impossibility, from the impossibility of constraining the
excess of desire to fit in an immanent representation.

The more peculiar modern condition is the *briefness of habit* and,
symmetrically, the *instantaneity of tradition*, the absolutely optional character of the
attribution of a past, a style, a root. Here, we are faced with the contradiction between
contingency and the desire for schematic stabilization, the incongruency between
authority and the precariousness of rule. In this empty interval the tensions are generated and balanced, freedom remains open and productive, and tradition can be
chosen or invented. Instead making the community present by endowing it with an
organic content, by hastening the communication of singularities in mystical communion, means eliding the distribution that is the origin of singularities, in which
the community arrives without any essence preceding it.

The community is not a myth of the past or the future; it is the
interruption of myth, the absence that leaves open the space of an infinite birth of
the new singularity. The very character of being far away and the impossibility of
realization of the utopia guarantees the plurality of experience if it does not provoke an immediatistic adjustment.[11] Unlike the *nomos*, the *demos* is not anchored in
the myth of a rigid localization; it can receive the utopia in its own specific horizon, provided that it not make the utopia a pretext for a totalizing condensation.
Demos is symbolized by the nihilism of the sea and the sky, by the disorder of the
imaginary and by the generosity of the threshold and the reception rather than by
the ordered equilibrium of the earth, rooting, and separation. Democracy rests under
the sign of Janus, the exiled god of thresholds and beginnings, not under Terminus,
god of confines and outcomes.

On the inner side of democracy, then, citizenship cannot be configured in the secular forms of myth: democracy value and substantiality of right.
Instead, citizenship is founded on the interruption of right, that is, the abstract primacy of law and equality, the creation of a barrier of the minimal right that holds
back the expansive thrust of the differences within a field of compatibility without
condensing them into a compulsory unity. If citizenship means, prior to any formalization, living a city, it should be experienced without being reduced to institutional
terms, and it should be brought back to the forms of life that subtend and redefine
it. It is precisely the city of deserters of institutions that demands nonrepresenta-

tive recognition, not exacerbating the conflicts in overordered regulations but facilitating spaces of freedom and the satisfaction of needs.

In this sense, more than a juridical concept, citizenship is a plural style of life, a mosaic that demonstrates a unitary tonality composed of differences, changeable depending on the angle of illumination. The communication that takes place inside the limit of representative fusion in the mysticism of the social is truly *fraternity*, that enigmatic appendix to equality and liberty, the ground on which the game of democracy is played. This is a fraternity among subjects of communication not mediated in the objectification of discourse, as in Bataille's understanding of the self-dissolving subjects of sovereignty in the instantaneity of emotion, laughter, or tears.[12] It is reciprocal with respect to the "similar" that function as incomposable "others" but are not even rooted in their foundation, members of an impossible community. Such is the relationship that follows from the representative self-recognition of the individual in work as "social" and in the State as "political."

Rimbaud's phrase "I is an other [Je est un autre]" is declared with respect to the outside, faced with the unequalness of a subject that is not itself, that *does not belong* to a territory, a race, an ideology. Such a reduced sociality no longer defers to the "great animal" whose idolatry is exorcized by Simone Weil. Actually, that sociality is defused of its mythic potential of being both the manufactured and instantaneously consumed tradition and the utopia that is realized and disinvested in the continuity of the present or repelled beyond the possible horizon.

A completely different meaning is instead taken on by the individuation of the citizen-individual brought about by the social rights State, the rule of law, which administratively distributes legality so as to reintegrate the underprivileged classes within the fiction of a guaranteed community in exchange for renouncing the virtual subversiveness of difference. The dissolution of the ideology that linked juridical right and labor is thus compensated for by a new disciplinary level, in such a way that the abandonment of legislative universalism in favor of considerations of the concrete case does not bring about any opening for the singularity. We have instead a dissemination of the definition of citizen and its control, with the same logic that at the level of production parcels out the workers in order to achieve greater performance efficiency and higher levels of competitiveness.[13]

The political contract is thought of in the Welfare State, or the social State, as the beyond of the wage contract, and hence it guarantees the reproduction of the actual submission that is compensated with variable levels of assistance. With the fiscal and financial crisis of the welfare model, the filtering of demand becomes all the more rigid when assistance is less available and, simultaneously, a juridical-moral construction of responsibility for the new typologies is introduced: the person infected with HIV (resignedly domestic or savage); the drug user, depending on whether or not he or she accepts treatment; the underaged or the weak; the immigrant authorized for indemnity; the dying elderly or the unborn embryo; and so forth. Subjects are reindividuated outside of any singularity and any human respect as ethical subjects, in suspect affinity with the fundamentalist fantasies that are rampant and seeking protection from the State.[14]

      This reduction of citizenship to the sum of provisions and entitlements (disposable goods and legitimate claims of access to them), which combines the extension of the area of already existing entitlement of rights and the creation of new rights, does not adequately assimilate the emergence of "defective" instances that privilege voluntary over obligatory service and defend difference against discrimination and pressures of comformity or assimilation.[15] Elusive categories such as "the society of the two-thirds" and "the majority class" are attempts to bring back into an institutional framework the scandalous phenomena of "no-go areas," behaviors or territories that defy the logic of the police and the marketplace, and ask to be recognized and legitimated above all at the material and symbolic level.

      In contemporary juridical debates, on the other hand, there is emerging a new set of guarantees that transcends the logic of both the liberal notion of right and the social State, that protects differences and satisfies their need for recognition outside the logics of the marketplace and equal rights. It is a question of configuring in political language the instances that are born outside of institutional representation and that potentially remain extraneous to them. Their own negotiability derives precisely from the fact that the most radical demands always remain external to the political system of interests, and yet there is no real intention of suppressing that system for any significant period of time.[16] Furthermore, the elasticity of complex societies serves to eliminate the tensions on the surface of the everyday, banalizing them with an "inauthentic" transposition that debunks any idea of taking power.

      This apolitical condition, this extraneousness to politics, is linked together with extreme conflict thanks to social fragmentation; it is expressed, that is, in violent but brief movements, without stable relapses or lasting organized sediments. Even the "hyperbolic" citizenship "without quality" that Etienne Balibar likens to the excess of the usual institutional schemes has the mark of intermittence. We can only get used to this shortness of breath and this "inauthenticity" of collective desires.

The tension between the inner and outer sides of democracy—insoluble in an explicit, institutional community—invests everyday experience, the inauthentic forms of politics. The ineffable gathers itself in worlds that surround it, not in silence. For this reason, the alternative models of the social State are not indifferent, and there is still value to a minimal penal law that protects the freedom of the citizens against the imposition of substantial truths, arbitrary as they are uncontrolled, against a disciplinary imposition of values on the part of the State even though it is democratically supported by a majority.[17] The differences, in fact, because of their connection to the existential sphere, do not allow themselves to be placed in a minority; they can find space only where right is not ethically overdetermined and where there exists no moral obligation to obey the laws or to conform to a style of life—where in fact, conflict and dissidence are legitimated not simply because of tolerance, but because the mechanism itself of the interpretation of right and the formation of law is a continuous process of delegitimation as a result of the changing of norms and established views.

Nonsubstantial rules that are not founded upon themselves or in the name of an *auctoritas* representative of either the common good or the development of productive forces—in other words, rules that are easily contested and modifiable without claims of ontological or ethical value—are the most appropriate for coordinating heterogeneous forms of life by way of distributing revenue and freedom in a roughly equitable way. Wittgenstein has already spoken sufficiently about their useful viscosity: any emergency legislation carries the threat of making the system more rigid. Power always claims to make others happy, whereas freedom mistrusts the good and harmony. Bataille's right to the lack of meaning is the determined opposite of the "most important and most disregarded" need of which Weil speaks: the need of being rooted, the condition of meaning, obedient participation in necessity and justice.[18] The cult of belonging—the having roots in spirit or in a territory—indefatigably reproduces a nostalgia of the myth that impedes the process of bringing it to a conclusion in the interruption.

Withdrawal and Defection

Decisive thinkers of the West, from Aristotle to Hegel and on to Lacan, have continually come back to Sophocles' *Antigone* as a primary reference point dealing with law and life, the abstract and the concrete of the city.[19] Lacan departs from the usual counterposition between Creon's firm dedication to positive law and Antigone's obedience to the unwritten laws of the heart. He departs from this in order to identify instead in the imperious *Wunsch*, in nondomesticable desire, the only plausible categorical imperative, which universally prescribes the particularism of every subject. What is thus excluded as a humanistic falsehood is the idea that it is possible to direct action toward the Good following the Aristotelian or utilitarian tradition. The end toward which actions are directed or, better yet, the end around which subjects revolve, is the Thing, the emptiness of Being to which every desire is referred. An opposition of natural desire, which would be positive, to the interdictive negativity of the law is thus not possible—we would still be dealing with a supreme Good that is transferred from the place of the final cause to that of the efficient cause, no longer a point of arrival but unconscious derivation, a psychoanalytic transcription of originary innocence.

Lacan, however, does not entertain even a generic anthropological pessimism, because in fact he formulates being faithful to one's own desire as the sole ethical principle and betraying that principle as the sole fault. The human is neither good nor bad, but rather a creature absorbed in the game of desire and forced to direct itself strategically in that game. Creon and Antigone are equally bound to rigid principles; in their opposition they are not content with the "first death," but yearn for either the complete annihilation of the enemy's body (Creon) or self-destruction in the dreadful form of being buried alive (Antigone). Antigone acts in the name of a yearning for absolute death, a fidelity toward her brother, which is (like the punishment imposed by Creon) beyond the just limit—*ektos atas.*

Lacan has reformulated the Heideggerian reflections on the historicity of *Dasein* and its dispersion in inauthentic everydayness, thus helping resolve the ambiguity whereby Heidegger maintained both the preferability of the authentic and its fungibility with the inauthentic. The decision (being-toward-death) constituted in Heidegger the anguished fidelity to the existence of its own repetitive possibilities. The temporality of authentic historicity is the depresentification of todayness, the disaccustomness for the deresponsibilizing "*da*" of everydayness. The Lacanian reformulation inserts fidelity into desire in the game involving Eros and Thanatos (which is a compulsion for repetition) and makes concrete the alternation between unveiling and veiling; the claim of authenticity of either term is a mere rigidification.

This rigidity (the opposite of which is the strategic plasticity of the subject) brings together desire and law, which remain nonetheless distinct. In fact, the rule of the good is the birth of an overarching power; having goods at one's disposal means having the right to deprive others of them and *defend* one's own (in the double meaning of the French *defendre*: "to defend" and "to prohibit") from desire. The first concern of the victors—from Alexander to Hitler to "real socialism"—is to develop utilitarian practices by repressing the sovereign ones. The preamble of the victors is a vague discourse on liberation, which is followed by the essential: continue working, do not even think of having the chance to make manifest the slightest desire. The morality of power in the service of goods goes something like this: "As far as desires are concerned, come back again later, they can wait."[20] This is the role of Creon, who cares about everyone's well-being and who distinguishes between friends and enemies in accordance to the common interests of the city and perhaps of the entire planet.

The ethics of psychoanalysis—the only ethics conceivable apart from Kantian ethics and its paradoxical opposite in de Sade—rests instead in this question: Have you acted in conformity with the desire that inhabits you? This question evidently leaves the problem entirely open. On the other hand, does not the possible, which by definition is the field of politics, consist perhaps in the fact that humans do not know what they put into motion with this question?[21]

Antigone's charity has a radically destructive character; hers is an absolute individuality that guards over the validity of crime (the two siblings are Oedipus's cursed descendants) by making use of the rigidity of the law. Between the two extremes that reciprocally prop each other up there is actually no space for politics, yet any savage claim to power is given a chance. This extremist call from the outside does not deligitimate the reign of power and goods, but it arranges it on more mild and efficient positions: after the excesses of the emergency one goes back to work, better than before.

Searching for a new political model becomes more difficult when we take for granted a mythicized opposition between the "social" and the "natural" elements of existence. This temptation, which accompanies it from its remote origins, weighs on the apolitical. Radical extraneity is a potential that rises up at the limit of its own dissolution and subtraction, but the combination of this potential with power is prosaically ambiguous, letting power work in peace.

The strategy of "leaving be" includes two possibilities: the anarchic alternative and the free market alternative (the latter being a social extension of the spontaneous functioning of the laws of nature). Already at the end of the eighteenth century, the most extreme proponents of free market economics coincided with political anarchism in the sense that the utopia of the perfect market would lead to the dissolution of State institutions. The order of nature became the naturalness of the bourgeois order, and the powers of domination dreamed of resolving themselves, in Whig England in the form of freedom of commerce and discussion, and in physiocratic France in enlightened administrative despotism—two modalities of the neutralization of politics.

The modern apolitical does not take part in the course of the world. On the contrary, it tends to subtract itself from it. In withdrawing from evil, the standard variants of an entirely interior freedom show up: ascetic puritanism and the libertinism of those who refuse to acknowledge the law. The renunciation of the laws of the city on the part of those who are elected permits the continued general operativity of the laws, although discredited and weakened, and it actually risks having need of laws in order to either transgress them or ignore them in the form of quietism.

A definite break from all this is difficult: the unilateral simplifications stand against each other, paralyzing each other, like the abstract primacy of the law in Creon and the inhuman fidelity of Antigone. The twentieth-century movement back and forth between ethical or economic naturalism on one hand and planning on the other demonstrates the incompatibility of this alternative at the level of mass society. The acknowledgment of the artificial and contingent character of the rules that constitute both subjectivity and social cohabitation instead allows for the combination of perspectives that are otherwise antinomic, for modulating the alternative between law and desire according to a good strategic complementarity instead of a destructive confrontation.

What ought to be a priority in citizenship is not the rigidity of rights composed within a holistic representation, but rather the existence of interfaces for communication between heterogeneous systems, directions that safeguard diversity without renouncing confrontation and a minimal redistribution of wealth. This is the only way to find a nonauthoritarian path leading away from the crisis of the social State and the effects of mass migrations. We are here talking about citizenship of a city already invaded by "barbarians," occupied by besiegers from outside and by internal deserters, who cannot and will not live too much below the civil and economic standards of the conquered. On the contrary, the diversity of the internal barbarians and the activities of the immigrants are already profitably put to work under the laws already in force (which are also slowly being transformed into an empty shell). More than discussing the compatibilities that one hopes would result from a public regulation of differences, it is useful to insist on the substantial unrepresentability of the new social orders of the invaded metropolis, site of an order that is not very stable or formalizable. Flight and strategies of concealment are more interesting than integration in this phase, and the contradictory combination of both instances even more so: how to remain oneself and not be inferior (even if unequal) when compared to others, how to reconcile collective solidarity and the independence of vital spheres—the desire (*cupiditas*) of the singular and the power of the multitude (*multitudo*), to use Spinozian terms[22]—and yet conserve a specific dimension of the antagonistic productivity of the masses.

Clearly, one cannot close one's eyes to the fact that multitude, masses, and the collective allude to a "social" whose notion is constructed in distinction from the "natural" or the "political." Once the opposition between the state of nature and that of society is considered a mere methodological fiction, the social is recuperated within the political State as the (positive or negative) phase of nature, the concrete with respect to the abstract. The disappearance of the foundation, which has left "nature" without divine legality and has left "the political" an orphan without representativeness, corrodes the social, which loses the features of authenticity, immediacy, and expressivity that had accompanied its triumphant entry into the scene. That the social, as a second nature, is artificial was already very clear in the nineteenth century (consider Baudelaire, for example). The great and consolidated antagonistic classes were the last epiphanies of its essential expressivity, the illusion, that is, that all of society or one of its leading sectors could lift up again the banners of human emancipation that were left to fall by the politico-juridical universalism of the French Revolution. The fact that both the State and society necessarily collapse does not mean that they lose empirical reality. The claim of foundation and the dispute of authenticity and ethicality disappear: in the end, it is still Antigone versus Creon.

Nonetheless, the social remains as the empirical receptacle of disintegrated and heterogeneous forms of life, the shadows of community. The debate on citizenship reflects the intertwining of these two aspects. In the difference between individual defection and collective exodus, between arbitrary discontinuity and rupture in the decisive points of the system, there continues to operate phantasmatically a principle of essence that, although limited and unfoundable, continues to come forward. The term *social*, with all the stirring ambiguities of its history, seems to indicate the point of contact between the defecting individual and the mode of production, the effects of the objective structures on the individual (in staying and leaving, in departure and arrival). This is both an obstacle and a point of support for the freedom of the individual. It is above all a question of the objective forms wherein the defection can realize itself, if we can even imagine the passage from the laws of wage slavery to the rules of an activity that is free from the very form of work, its coercion, equivalence, and abstractness. The "social" envelops the antinomies of rule and freedom, form and representation, and the effectiveness of the abstract and the irreducibility of the concrete, but the resulting aporia can be reduced with an appropriate shuffling of terms, as we have seen with the construction of the community between communication and communion. Here we can bring together the critique of humanism with the rejection of an economistic reading of the modes of production, that is, the refusal of a constitution of the social as the projection of the natural individual within the "objective" backdrop of technology.

An Anecdote on the Order of Representation

In the Museum of the History of German Jewry, housed in Berlin's Martin Gropius-Bau, with a view of what is left of the Berlin Wall and the ruins of the torture chambers of the Gestapo headquarters in Prinz-Albrecht-Strasse, there hangs a synoptic image of the persecutions. The last punitive measure was a January 1945 decree prohibiting all Jews in the Reich territory from stopping in the heated waiting rooms of the railway stations. Naturally, at that time there were no longer living Jews in Germany, nor was there coal for heating or railway stations that were in operation. Nonetheless, the State imaginarily reconstructed by way of decree the scenario of persecution; it legally revived the victims and the executioners for an infinite torture. One has to be appalled more by the stupidity than by the ferociousness of the decree. Here we have the impression of being admitted into the very essence of domination, into the meticulous perversity of bureaucracy, where the logic of exclusion survives beyond the concrete capacity to achieve it. The gloomy determination of Sophocles' Creon or de Sade's characters to want a "second death" for their victims yields here to a metaphysical farce of horror. And yet the Nazi perversion that wanted to extinguish difference[23] belongs to the logic of representation just as much as the grotesque liberal position that overlooks difference, thus equally prohibiting the rich and the poor from sleeping under bridges. This idolatrous adoration of pure means could indifferently refer to power or money, with variable effects on the concrete political regimes.[24]

Conversely, withdrawing from politics, the secular equivalent of gnostic estrangement from worldly evil, is the limit of a series of partial defections, which in principle can be reintegrated by way of flexible strategies of subjectivization and by the identification of diversities on the part of civil liberties. The apolitical is caught in the dilemma between the reabsorption of its potentialities within the overarching power and the resistance of its singularities against the representative alienation.

Such vicissitudes are amplified by the dynamics of socialization, by the changing constitution of the multitude. Every attempt to represent the multitude in institutions has failed—from Rousseau's transparent community to the regulated market of happiness and resources in the social Welfare State, from "spontaneous" free market harmony to the "transitional" dictatorship of the proletariat. Not even the homogeneous subject of a constituent power can be easily determined (if not as the myth of spontaneity). One could instead imagine a network of rules that guarantee the free unfolding of individual and group differences, thus favoring the objective tendencies toward the unraveling of disciplinary and hierarchical mechanisms of the capitalist mode of production. A procedural version of democracy, a minimal repressive law, and a simultaneous provision of extended rights serve as a bank for the radical autonomy of sectors reluctant to deal with labor and the State. The political defines a margin of social processes without expecting to express them or create them. Experiments in *nonrepresentative democracy* could at this point be more ambitiously undertaken, based not on an aggregate of voluntary social pacts (the political equivalents of the centrality of labor, the representation of the social nexus in voting and in money), but on forms of life that incorporate what Marx calls the "general intellect." These are not to be understood as fixed aggregates, existing romantic communities, or vital spheres that are prior to systematic colonization, but rather as linguistic games with multiple and variable participants, profoundly shaped by the abstract; and, in fact, they are themselves the potent figures of social knowledge, the effects and articulations of modern technology and complexity.

Strategies of this kind mark, in any case, the overcoming of a tradition that has constantly imprisoned revolutionary impulses in mechanisms of power, which are disappointing especially when they are successful. Up until now, in fact, the "victories" of the workers' movement have produced more failures than have the defeats. If a negotiating regime of citizenship involving an acknowledgment of difference that does not falsify that difference is to be possible, it is probably the most arduous challenge for those who are already living in or along the border of advanced societies. The other challenge, which is even more uncertain, is that regarding the majority of the world that remains outside.

The image of the city has thus been transformed imperceptibly: undoubtedly still a metaphor for modernity, no longer a chaotic herald of an unavoidable future, but rather the apocalypse of the present, a senseless and unsurpassable hell. In the final identification with the developed world, what is absent is the possibility that the city could allude to the unification of humanity (assuming, on the contrary, profound ditches and nonamalgamated mixtures) as well as the idea that it, in the terms of the 1960s, is besieged by a "campaign" that is the bearer of alternative values that are and deserve to be destined for victory.

The Western city is the originary place of conflict and also the last site where it remains after the defeat of liberation movements in the underdeveloped areas and the failure of experiments in "real" socialism. It now includes the residual emancipatory and revolutionary instances and the physical bearers of both the abysmal misery of the Third World and the differential misery of the Second. The exodus here runs in the opposite and complementary direction in centrifugal thrusts toward the margins from within the city; furthermore, it is not a metaphorical exodus, but an actual material passage from one world to another. The encounter of the two hybridly symmetrical movements, of differentiation with the loss of ancient values and solidarity on the one hand and ethnic uprooting and ghettoization on the other, is an explosive mix that could make a multinational and multicultural society extremely unpleasant. Our sole chance of converting such an amorphous conflictuality into creativity lies in subtracting the entire society from the unproductive discipline of work, within which the hierarchies are formed and in whose margins the less integrable forms of life decompose.

Translated by Paul Colilli

Notes

1. See Augusto Illuminati, "Ananmorfosi della politica," in *Racconti morali* (Naples: Liquor, 1989).

2. Maurice Blanchot, *La Communauté inavouable* (Paris: Les Édition de minuit, 1983), 57.

3. See Hannah Arendt, *Lectures on Kant's Political Philosophy* (Chicago: University of Chicago Press, 1982). Also see her *The Life of the Mind* (San Diego, Calif.: Harcourt Brace Jovanovich, 1978), in particular the section titled "Thinking." On the theory of action, see chapter 4 of Arendt's *The Human Condition* (Chicago: University of Chicago Press, 1958), although I certainly do not share her views on the ontology of the subject.

4. Leibniz-Thomasius, *Correspondance*, trans. Richard Bodéüs (Paris: Vrin, 1993), 104.

5. The idea of *cosmo-polis* as an analogy between the rational structure of the world and the rational structure of society, along with the specific role of Leibniz, is treated in Stephen Toulmin, *Cosmopolis: The Hidden Agenda of Modernity* (New York: Free Press, 1990), especially 101–4, 120ff., 143ff., 152ff., 182, 270–73.

6. Blanchot, *La Communauté inavouable*. Page numbers for quotes from this work appear in parentheses in the text.

7. See Jean-Luc Nancy, *La Communautée désoeuvrée* (Paris: Christian Bourgois, 1986), 36–37, 42–43, 50, 53–56, 64–65, 68–73, 132–41, 177–78, 223–24, 256–61.

8. See also Jean-Luc Nancy's *L'Expérience de la liberté* (Paris, Galilee, 1988), 119–20, 123–24, 207, where the experience of freedom as reciprocal exposition of the "ones" to "others"—*our* freedom—founds the community, but only by means of an infinite resistance to any appropriation of essence, collective or individual.

9. In *The Coming Community*, trans. Michael Hardt (Minneapolis: University of Minnesota Press, 1993), Giorgio Agamben hypothesizes that from the dissolution of meaning and the classes, from nihilistic and petit bourgeois homologation on a planetary scale, there arises an unprecedented opportunity for all of humanity: "If instead of continuing to search for a proper identity in the already improper and senseless form of individuality, humans were to succeed in belonging to this impropriety as such, in making of the proper being-thus not an identity and an individual property but a singularity without identity, a common and absolutely exposed singularity—if humans could, that is, not be-thus in this or that particular biography, but be only *the* thus, their singular exteriority and their face, then they would for the first time enter into a community without presuppositions and without subjects, into communication without the incommunicable" (65).

10. See the definitions provided by Nancy in *La Communautée désoeuvrée*, chaps. 2–3, in particular 33–35, 256ff.

11. See ibid., 117–18, 132–41, 145–54, 177–78.

12. See Georges Bataille, *La Souveraineté*, in *Ouvres complètes*, vol. 8 (Paris: Gallimard, 1976), 243–456.

13. The reunification of a dispersed sociality is imaginarily assured on one hand by the competitive tension itself (which is a particular form of competitive communication) and on the other by the captious bureaucratic fabric that manages all citizenship in ad hoc fashion, defined by means of a rigid definition of inherency. On the first aspect, see Lorenzo Cillario, *L'uomo di vetro' nel lavoro organizzato* (Bologna: Editoriale Mongolfiera, 1990), a stimulating text that shows how improved cybernetic surveillance makes the personnel not only an appendix of the machine but also transparent to it, thus bringing about a division of labor among parts of the same person by using psychic and neurotic disassociation as factors for competitive efficiency.

14. The constitution of precarious identities that are created and administered by bureaucratic logic does not take away representativeness; on the contrary, it is an assumption of contractual power, of social visibility in market regimes. See Massimo De Carolis, "Libertà di abitare un mondo senza abitudini," *Luogo comune*, no. 1 (November 1990): 36–37.

15. See Ralf Dahrendorf, *The Modern Social Conflict: An Essay on the Politics of Liberty* (Berkeley: University of California Press, 1988), especially chaps. 1–3. Among the entitlements are all of the constitutionally guaranteed and categorical rights that one enjoys by dint of the mere fact of being part of a society, but also (in a more unstable and revocable way) the rights of access to the market and, foremost, the level of the actual wage or a minimal income and the security of housing. The provisions are the disposable goods, but also other material and immaterial elements that enter into a definition of "well-being" (services, education, information, and so forth). Their combination produces an assortment of life opportunities, whose increase toward the highest number of people is the defining objective of liberal politics. Dahrendorf misunderstands or deplores precisely the phenomena of separation and ghettoization that are not conceivable in a merely institutional politics of the extension of rights.

16. See the essays in Massimo Ilardi, ed., *La città senza luoghi* (Genoa: Costa and Nolan, 1990), especially the essay by Marco Grispigni, " 'Qualcosa di travolgente': I

conflitti impolitici," 93–118. Grispigni discusses the paradoxical presence in metropolitan conflicts of surprising levels of both rootedness and negotiability. The abandonment of utopia facilitates negotiations and produces an indifference to political mediation. The politics of "no future," the loss of memory, and the formation of single-issue interest groups all find here a convincing unitary composition. In Hirschmann's terms, the solution prevails over the protest according to a social logic that is dominated by the categories of the market and in which the provisions appear clearly more interesting than the entitlements.

On the juridical plane, in Hans Kelsen's work one can at times identify a precedent for absorbing self-regulation into the law, thus assuring a constitution that is external to the processes of the creation of norms. On the opposition between instrumental right and reflexive right, see G. Bronzini, "Il vocabolario dei diritti e il gergo dei movimenti," *Luogo comune*, no. 1 (November 1990): 56.

17. Luigi Ferrajoli suggests that "after the political conquest of universal suffrage, the expansion of democracy can come about not only with the multiplication in the non-political centers where the 'who' and 'how' of decisions are formally democratized, but even more so with the extension of the structural and functional ties imposed on all powers—democratic and bureaucratic, public and private—for the substantial protection of still new vital rights, and together with the elaboration of new civil liberties techniques appropriate for the assurance of greater effectiveness." Luigi Ferrajoli, *Diritto e ragione: Teoria del garantismo penale* (Rome: Laterza, 1989), 906–7.

18. See the beginning of the second part of Simone Weil's *The Need for Roots* (New York: Putnam, 1952), in which she comes to the regrettable conclusion that the acceptance of physical labor is, after the acceptance of death, the most perfect form of the virtue of obedience, the form of everyday death and spiritual center of a well-ordered social life.

19. For Lacan's references to *Antigone*, see the last two parts (and especially chaps. 19, 20, 21) of *Éthique de la psychanalyse* (Paris: Seuil, 1986). My interpretation of this text relies on the essay by G. Bottiroli, "Il desiderio di Antigone: La psicoanalisi come pensiero extra-morale," *Il piccolo Hans*, no. 63 (Fall 1989).

20. See Lacan, *Éthique de la psychanalyse*, 269–70, 363. In Arendt's terms, tyrants aim to exclude citizens from the public sphere by offering work and business as a substitute for action. See *The Human Condition*, 160.

21. See Lacan, *Éthique de la psychanalyse*, 272.

22. Here I am following Antonio Negri's reading of Spinoza in *The Savage Anomaly* (Minneapolis: University of Minnesota Press, 1993), in particular

187–98. The force of Negri's analysis depends on a unilateral undertaking of the positivity of modern society (which the *multitudo* prefigures) and thus on the possibility of a constituent and revolutionary movement from the base against the State's imposition of the abstract.

23. This is predicated on a symbiosis of nationalism and racism within the State. Etienne Balibar has written very well on this relationship in his essays in *Race, Nation, Class: Ambiguous Identities* (London: Verso, 1991).

24. "Power is the pure means. For this reason it is the highest end for all of those who have not understood." Simone Weil, *Cahiers*, vol. 3 (Paris: Plon, 1974), 123.

FOURTEEN

Virtuosity and Revolution: The Political Theory of Exodus

Paolo Virno

Action, Work, Intellect

Nothing appears so enigmatic today as the question of what it means to act. This issue seems both enigmatic and out of reach—up in the heavens, one might say. If nobody asks me what political action is, I seem to know; but if I have to explain it to somebody who asks, this presumed knowledge evaporates into incoherence. And yet what notion is more familiar in people's everyday speech than action? Why has the obvious become clothed in mystery? Why is it so puzzling? The answer is not to be found in the customary realm of ready-made responses: the present unfavorable power balance, the continuing echo of past defeats, the resignation that postmodern ideology endlessly foments. All these do count, of course, but in themselves they explain nothing. Rather, they confuse, because they foster a belief that we are going through a dark tunnel at the end of which everything will go back to being the way it was. That is not the case. The fact is that the paralysis of action relates back to very basic aspects of the contemporary experience. It is there that we have to excavate, in the knowledge that these aspects represent not some unfortunate deviation but an unavoidable backdrop. In order to break the spell, we need to elaborate a model of action that will enable action to draw nourishment precisely from what is today creating its blockage. The interdiction itself has to be transformed into a laissez-passer.

According to a long tradition of thought, the realm of political action can be defined fairly precisely by two boundaries. The first relates to labor, to its taciturn and instrumental character, to that automatism that makes of it a repetitive and predictable process. The second relates to pure thought, to the solitary and nonappearing quality of its activity. Political action is unlike labor in that its sphere of intervention is social relations, not natural materials. It modifies the context within which it is inscribed, rather than creates new objects to fill it. Unlike intellectual reflection, action is public, geared to exteriorization, to contingency, to the hustle and bustle of the multitude. This is what the long tradition teaches us. But we cannot necessarily go along with this definition any longer. The customary frontiers separating Intellect, Work, and Action (or, if you prefer, theory, poiesis, and praxis) have given way, and everywhere we see the signs of incursions and crossovers.

In the pages that follow, I will propose first that Work has absorbed the distinctive traits of political action and second that this annexation has been made possible by the intermeshing between modern forms of production and an Intellect that has become public — in other words, that has erupted into the world of appearances. Finally, what has provoked the eclipse of Action has been precisely the symbiosis of Work with "general intellect," or "general social knowledge," which, according to Marx, stamps its form on "the process of social life itself."[1] I will then advance two hypotheses. The first is that the public and worldly character of the *nous* — or the material potentiality (*potenza*) of general intellect — has to be our starting point for a redefinition of political praxis and its salient problems: power, government, democracy, violence, and so on. To put it briefly, a coalition between Intellect and Action is counterposed to the coalition between Intellect and Work. Second, whereas the symbiosis of knowledge and production produces an extreme, anomalous, but nonetheless flourishing legitimation for a pact of obedience to the State, the intermeshing between general intellect and political Action enables us to glimpse the possibility of a non-State public sphere.

Activity without Work

The dividing line between Work and Action, which was always hazy, has now disappeared altogether. In the opinion of Hannah Arendt — whose positions I would here seek to challenge — this hybridization is due to the fact that modern political praxis has internalized the model of Work and come to look increasingly like a process of making (with a "product" that is, by turns, history, the State, the party, and so forth).[2] This diagnosis, however, must be inverted and set on its feet. The important thing is not that political action may be conceived as a form of producing, but that the producing has embraced within itself many of the prerogatives of action. In the post-Fordist era, we have Work taking on many of the attributes of Action: unforeseeability, the ability to begin something new, linguistic "performances," and an ability to range among alternative possibilities. There is one inevitable consequence to all this. In relation to a Work that is loaded with "actionist" characteristics, the transition to Action comes to be seen as somehow falling short, or, in the best of cases, as a superfluous duplication. It appears to be falling short, for the most part: in its structuring according to a rudimentary logic of means and ends, politics offers a communicative network and a cognitive content that are weaker and poorer than those to be found within the present-day process of production. Action appears as less complex than Work, or as too similar to it, and either way it appears as not very desirable.

In "Results of the Immediate Process of Production" (but also, in almost identical words, in *Theories of Surplus Value*), Marx analyzes intellectual labor and distinguishes two principal kinds. On the one hand, there is the immaterial activity that has as its result "commodities which exist separately from the producer..., e.g. books, paintings and all products of art as distinct from the artistic achievement of the practising artist." On the other hand, Marx defines those activities in which "the product is not separable from the act of producing"[3] — in other words, activities that find their fulfillment in themselves, without being objectivized in a finished work existing outside and beyond them. The second kind of intellectual labor may be exemplified by "performing artists," such as pianists or dancers, but also includes more generally various kinds of people whose work involves a *virtuosic performance*, such as orators, teachers, doctors, and priests. In short, this second kind of intellectual labor refers to a wide cross section of human society, ranging from Glenn Gould to the impeccable butler of the classic English novel.

Of the two categories of intellectual labor, for Marx only the first appears to fit fully with the definition of "productive labor" (wherein productive labor is defined only as work that procures surplus value, not work that is merely useful or merely tiring). Virtuosos, who limit themselves to playing a "musical score" and leave no lasting traces, on the one hand "are of microscopic significance when compared with the mass of capitalist production" and on the other are to be considered as "wage-labour that is not at the same time productive labour."[4] Although it is easy to understand Marx's observations on the quantitative irrelevance of vir-tuosos, one experiences some perplexity at his observation that they are "non-productive." In principle, there is nothing to say that a dancer does not give rise to a surplus value. However, for Marx, the absence of a finished work that lives on beyond the activity of performance puts modern intellectual virtuosity on a par with actions undertaken in the provision of a personal service: services that are seen as being nonproductive, because in order to obtain them one spends income, not capital. The "performing artist," put down and parasitic, is thus consigned to the limbo of service work.

      The activities in which "the product is not separable from the act of producing" have a mercurial and ambiguous status that is not always and not completely grasped by the critique of political economy. The reason for the diffi-culty is simple. Well before becoming swallowed up within capitalist production, virtuosity was the architrave of ethics and politics. Furthermore, it was what quali-fied Action, as distinct from (and in fact opposed to) Work. Aristotle writes that the aim of production is different from production itself, whereas the aim of action could not be, inasmuch as virtuous conduct is an end in itself.[5] Related immedi-ately to the search for the "good life," activity that manifests itself as a "conduct," and that does not have to pursue an extrinsic aim, coincides precisely with political praxis. According to Arendt, the performing arts, which do not lead to the creation of any finished work, "have indeed a strong affinity with politics. Performing artists—dancers, play-actors, musicians, and the like—need an audience to show their vir-tuosity, just as acting men need the presence of others before whom they can ap-pear; both need a publicly organized space for their 'work,' and both depend upon others for the performance itself."[6]

      The pianist and the dancer stand precariously balanced on a watershed that divides two antithetical destinies: on the one hand, they may become examples of "wage-labour that is not at the same time productive labour"; on the other, they have a quality that is suggestive of political action. Their nature is essentially amphibian. So far, however, each of the potential developments inher-ent in the figure of the performing artist—poiesis or praxis, Work or Action—seems to exclude its opposite. The status of waged laborer tends to militate against political vocation, and vice versa. From a certain point onward, however, the alter-native changes into a complicity—the *aut-aut* gives way to a paradoxical *et-et*: the virtuoso works (in fact she or he is a worker par excellence) not despite the fact, but precisely because of the fact that her or his activity is closely reminis-cent of political praxis. The metaphorical tearing apart comes to an end, and in this new situation we find no real help in the polar oppositions of Marx and Arendt.

Within post-Fordist organization of production, activity-without-a-finished-work moves from being a special and problematic case to becoming the prototype of waged labor in general. There is not much point, here, in going back over the detailed analyses that have already been conducted in other essays in this volume: a few basic points will have to suffice. When labor carries out tasks of overseeing and coordination, in other words when it "steps to the side of the production process instead of being its chief actor,"[7] its function consists no longer in the carrying out of a single particular objective, but in the modulating (as well as the varying and intensifying) of social cooperation, in other words, that ensemble of relations and systemic connections that as of now are "the great foundation-stone of production and of wealth."[8] This modulation takes place through linguistic services that, far from giving rise to a final product, exhaust themselves in the communicative inter-action that their own "performance" brings about.

Post-Fordist activity presupposes and, at the same time, unceas-ingly re-creates the "public realm" (the space of cooperation, precisely) that Arendt describes as the indispensable prerequisite of both the dancer and the politician. The "presence of others" is both the instrument and the object of labor; therefore, the processes of production always require a certain degree of virtuosity, or, to put it another way, they involve what are really political actions. Mass intellectuality (a rather clumsy term that I use to indicate not so much a specific stratum of jobs, but more a quality of the whole of post-Fordist labor power) is called upon to exercise the art of the possible, to deal with the unforeseen, to profit from opportunities. Now that the slogan of labor that produces surplus value has become, sarcastically, "politics first," politics in the narrow sense of the term becomes discredited or paralyzed.

In any case, what other meaning can we give to the capitalist slogan of "total quality" if not the attempt to set to work all those aspects that tra-ditionally it has shut out of work — in other words, the ability to communicate and the taste for Action? And how is it possible to encompass within the productive pro-cess the entire experience of the single individual, except by committing her or him to a sequence of variations on a theme, performances, improvisations? Such a se-quence, in a parody of self-realization, represents the true acme of subjugation. There is none so poor as the one who sees her or his own ability to relate to the "presence of others," or her or his own possession of language, reduced to waged labor.

Public Intellect, the Virtuosos' Score

What is the "score" that post-Fordist workers have unceasingly had to play from the moment they were called upon to give proof of virtuosity? The answer, stripped to basics, is something like this: the *sui generis* "score" of present-day labor is Intellect *qua* public Intellect, general intellect, global social knowledge, shared linguistic ability. One could also say that production demands virtuosity and thus introjects many traits that are peculiar to political action, precisely and solely because Intellect has become the principal productive force, premise, and epicenter of every poiesis.

Hannah Arendt rejects out of hand the very idea of a public intellect. In her judgment, reflection and thought (in a word, the "life of the mind") bear no relation to that "care for common affairs" that involves an exhibition to the eyes of others. The insertion of intellect into the world of appearances is first sketched by Marx in the concept of "real abstraction," and then, more important, that of general intellect. Whereas real abstraction is an empirical fact (the exchange of equivalents, for example) that has the rarefied structure of pure thought, general intellect marks rather the stage in which pure thought as such comes to have the value and the incidence typical of facts (we could say the stage at which mental abstractions are immediately, in themselves, real abstractions).

I should add, however, that Marx conceives general intellect as "a scientific capacity" objectified within the system of machines, and thus as fixed capital. He thereby reduces the external or public quality of intellect to the technological application of natural sciences to the process of production. The crucial step consists rather in highlighting to the full the way in which general intellect, rather than being a *machina machinarum*, comes to present itself finally as a direct attribute of living labor, as a repertoire of a diffuse intelligentsia, as a "score" that creates a common bond among the members of a multitude. Furthermore, we are forced into this position by our analysis of post-Fordist production: here a decisive role is played by conceptual constellations and schemes of thinking that cannot ever be recuperated within fixed capital, given that they are actually inseparable from the interaction of a plurality of living subjects. Obviously, what is in question here is not the scientific erudition of the particular worker. What comes to the fore — to achieve the status of a public resource — is only (but that "only" is everything) the more general aspects of the mind: the faculty of language, the ability to learn, the ability to abstract and correlate, and access to self-reflection.

By *general intellect* we have to understand, literally, intellect in general. Now, it goes without saying that Intellect-in-general is a "score" only in the broadest of senses. It is certainly not some kind of specific composition (let us say, Bach's Goldberg Variations) as played by a top-notch performer (let us say Glenn Gould, for example), but rather a simple *faculty*. It is the faculty that makes possible all composition (not to mention all experience). Virtuosic performance, which never gives rise to a finished work, in this case cannot even presuppose it. It consists in making Intellect resonate *precisely as* attitude. Its only "score" is, *as such*, the condition of possibility of all "scores." This virtuosity is nothing unusual, nor does it require some special talent. One need only think of the process whereby someone who speaks draws on the inexhaustible potential of language (the opposite of a defined "work") to create an utterance that is entirely of the moment and unrepeatable.

Intellect becomes public when it joins together with Work; however, once it is conjoined with Work, its characteristic publicness is also inhibited and distorted. Ever anew called upon to act as a force of production, it is ever anew suppressed as public sphere, as possible root of political Action, as different constitutional principle.

General intellect is the foundation of a kind of social cooperation that is broader than the social cooperation based specifically on labor—broader and, at the same time, entirely heterogeneous. Whereas the interconnections of the process of production are based on a technical and hierarchical division of functions, the acting-in-concert implied by general intellect takes as its starting point a common participation in the "life of the mind," in other words a prior sharing of communicative and cognitive attitudes. The *excess* cooperation of Intellect, however, rather than eliminating the coercions of capitalist production, figures as capital's most eminent resource. Its heterogeneity has neither voice nor visibility. Rather, because the exteriority of Intellect, the fact that it appears, becomes a technical prerequisite of Work, the acting-in-concert outside of labor that it engenders in its turn becomes subjected to the kinds of criteria and hierarchies that characterize the factory regime.

The principal consequences of this paradoxical situation are twofold. The first relates to the form and nature of political power. The peculiar publicness of Intellect, deprived of any expression of its own by that labor that nonetheless claims it as a productive force, manifests itself indirectly within the realm of the State through the *hypertrophic growth of administrative apparatuses*. Administration has come to replace the political, parliamentary system at the heart of the State, but it has done this precisely because it represents an authoritarian concretion of general intellect, the point of fusion between knowledge and command, the reverse image of excess cooperation. It is true that for decades there have been indications of a growing and determining weight of the bureaucracy within the "body politic," the predominance of decree over law. Now, however, we face a situation that is qualitatively new. What we have here is no longer the familiar process of rationalization of the State, but rather a Statization of Intellect. The old expression *raison d'État* for the first time acquires a nonmetaphorical meaning. If Hobbes and the other great theoreticians of "political unity" saw the principle of legitimation of absolute power in the *transfer* of the natural right of each single individual to the person of the sovereign, nowadays we might speak of a *transfer* of Intellect, or rather of its immediate and irreducible publicness, to State administration.

The second consequence relates to the effective nature of the post-Fordist regime. Because the public realm opened by Intellect is every time anew reduced to labor cooperation, in other words to a tight-knit web of hierarchical relations, the interdictive function that comes with "presence of others" in all concrete operations of production takes the form of *personal dependency*. Putting it another way, virtuosic activity comes across as universal *servile labor*. The affinity between the pianist and the waiter that Marx glimpsed finds an unexpected confirmation in which all wage labor has something of the "performing artist" about it. When "the product is not separable from the act of producing," this act calls into question the self of the producer and, above all, the relationship between that self and the self of the one who has ordered it or to whom it is directed. The setting-to-work of what is common, in other words, of Intellect and Language, although on the one hand renders fictitious the impersonal technical division of labor, on the other hand, given that this commonality is not translated into a "public sphere" (that is, into a political community), leads to a stubborn personalization of subjugation.

Exodus

The key to political action (or rather the only possibility of extracting it from its present state of paralysis) consists in developing the publicness of Intellect outside of Work, and in opposition to it. The issue here has two distinct profiles, which are, however, strictly complementary. On the one hand, general intellect can only affirm itself as an autonomous public sphere, thus avoiding the "transfer" of its own potential into the absolute power of Administration, if it cuts the linkage that binds it to the production of commodities and wage labor. On the other hand, the subversion of capitalist relations of production henceforth develops only with the institution of a non-State public sphere, a political community that has as its hinge general intellect. The salient characteristics of the post-Fordist experience (servile virtuosity, the valorization even of the faculty of language, the necessary relation with the "presence of others," and so forth) postulate as a conflictual response nothing less than a radically new form of democracy.

I use the term *Exodus* here to define mass defection from the State, the alliance between general intellect and political Action, and a movement toward the public sphere of Intellect. The term is not at all conceived as some defensive existential strategy—it is neither exiting on tiptoe through the back door nor a search for sheltering hideaways. Quite the contrary: what I mean by *Exodus* is a full-fledged model of action, capable of confronting the challenges of modern politics—in short, capable of confronting the great themes articulated by Hobbes, Rousseau, Lenin, and Schmitt (I am thinking here of crucial couplings such as command/obedience, public/private, friend/enemy, consensus/violence, and so forth). Today, just as happened in the seventeenth century under the spur of the civil wars, *a realm of common affairs* has to be defined from scratch. Any such definition must draw out the opportunities for liberation that are to be found in taking command of this novel interweaving among Work, Action, and Intellect, which up until now we have only suffered.

Exodus is the foundation of a Republic. The very idea of "republic," however, requires a taking leave of State judicature: if Republic, then no longer State. The political action of the Exodus consists, therefore, in an *engaged withdrawal*. Only those who open a way of exit for themselves can do the founding; but, by the opposite token, only those who do the founding will succeed in finding the parting of the waters by which they will be able to leave Egypt. In the remainder of this essay, I shall attempt to circumstantiate the theme of Exodus—in other words, action as *engaged withdrawal* (or founding leave-taking)—through consideration of a series of key words: Disobedience, Intemperance, Multitude, Soviet, Example, Right of Resistance, and Miracle.

The Virtue of Intemperance

"Civil disobedience" is today the sine qua non of political action—but only if it is conceived differently and freed from the terms of the liberal tradition within which it is generally encapsulated. Here I am not talking about rescinding particular laws because they are incoherent with or contradict other fundamental norms, for example, with the provisions of the Constitution; in such a case, nonobedience would imply only a deeper loyalty to State command. Quite the contrary, through myths that may be its single manifestations, the radical Disobedience that interests me here must bring into question the State's very faculty of command.

According to Hobbes, with the institution of the body politic we put an obligation on ourselves to obey even *before* we know what that obedience is going to entail: "Our obligation to civill obedience, by vertue whereof the civill Lawes are valid, is before all civill Law."[9] This is why one will find no specific law that says explicitly that one is not to rebel. If the unconditional acceptance of command were not already *presupposed*, the actual provisions of the law (including, obviously, the one that says, "Thou shalt not rebel") would have no validity. Hobbes maintains that the original bond of obedience derives from natural law, in other words, from a common interest in self-preservation and security. He hastens to add, however, that this natural law, or the Superlaw that requires obedience to all the commands of the sovereign, becomes effectively a law only when one emerges from the state of nature, in other words, when the State is already instituted. What we have here is a paradox: the obligation to obedience is both cause and effect of the existence of the State; it is maintained by that of which it is also the foundation; it simultaneously precedes and follows the formation of the "supreme power."

Political Action takes as its target the preliminary and contentless obedience that provides the only basis for the subsequent development of the baleful dialectic of acquiescence and "transgression." In contravening a particular decree on the dismantling of the health service, or on the banning of immigration, one goes right back to the hidden presupposition of every imperative prescription and saps the force of that prescription. Radical Disobedience is also "before all civill Law," inasmuch as it not only violates the laws, but also challenges the very foundation of their validity.

In order to justify the prior obligation to obedience, an end-of-the-millennium Hobbes, rather than appealing to a "natural law," would have to invoke the technical rationality of the process of production—in other words, "general intellect" *precisely as* despotic organization of waged labor. In the same way as we saw with "natural law," the "law of general intellect" also has a paradoxical structure: whereas on the one hand it seems to provide the basis of the State Administration's powers of command, demanding the respect of any decision that it may happen to take, on the other hand, it appears as a real *law* only because (and after) Administration *already* exercises an absolute command.

Radical Disobedience breaks this circle within which public Intellect figures simultaneously as both premise and consequence of the State. It breaks it with the double movement to which I referred previously. Most particularly, it highlights and develops positively the aspects of general intellect that are at odds with the continued existence of waged labor. On this basis, it sets in motion the practical potentiality of Intellect against the decision-making faculty of Administration. Delinked from the production of surplus value, Intellect becomes no longer the "natural law" of late capitalism, but the matrix of a non-State Republic.

The breeding ground of Disobedience consists of the social conflicts that manifest themselves not only and not so much as *protest*, but most particularly as *defection* — or, to put it in the terms used by Albert O. Hirschman, not as voice but as exit.[10]

Nothing is less passive than flight. The "exit" modifies the conditions within which the conflict takes place, rather than presupposes it as an irremovable horizon; it changes the context within which a problem arises, rather than deals with the problem by choosing one or another of the alternative solutions already on offer. In short, the "exit" can be seen as a free-thinking inventiveness that changes the rules of the game and disorients the enemy. One has only to think of the mass flight from the factory regime set in motion by the workers of North America halfway through the nineteenth century as they headed off to the "frontier" in order to colonize low-cost land. They were seizing the truly extraordinary opportunity of making their own conditions of departure *reversible*.[11]

Something similar happened in the late 1970s in Italy, when a youthful workforce, contradicting all expectations, decided that it preferred temporary and part-time jobs to regular jobs in big factories. Albeit only for a brief period, occupational mobility functioned as a political resource, bringing about the eclipse of industrial discipline and permitting a certain degree of self-determination. In this case too, preestablished roles were deserted and a "territory" unknown to the official maps was colonized.

Defection stands at the opposite pole to the desperate notion of "You have nothing to lose but your chains." It is postulated, rather, on the basis of a latent wealth, on an abundance of possibilities — in short, on the principle of the *tertium datur*. But how are we to define, in the post-Fordist era, the virtual abundance that favors the escape option at the expense of the resistance option? What I am talking about here is obviously not a spatial "frontier" but an abundance of knowledges, communication, and acting-in-concert implied by the publicness of general intellect. The act of collective imagination that we call "defection" gives an independent, affirmative, high-profile expression to this abundance, thus stopping its being transferred into the power of State administration.

Radical Disobedience involves, therefore, a complex ensemble of *positive actions*. It is not a resentful omission, but a committed undertaking. The sovereign command is not carried out, because, above all, we are too busy figuring out how to pose differently the question that it would interdict.

We have to bear in mind the distinction — fairly clear in ancient ethics, but subsequently almost always overlooked — between "intemperance" and "incontinence." Incontinence is a vulgar unruliness, disregard for laws, a giving way to immediate appetite. Intemperance is something very different — it is the opposition of an intellectual understanding to given ethical and political standards. As a guiding principle of action, a "theoretical" premise is adopted in place of a "practical" premise, with consequences for the harmony of societal life that may be dangerous and deviant. The intemperate person, according to Aristotle, is possessed of a vice, because he or she counterposes two kinds of discourse that are essentially diverse.[12] The intemperate is not ignorant of the law, nor does he or she merely oppose it; rather, the intemperate seriously discredits it, inasmuch as he or she derives a public conduct from that pure Intellect that should operate within its own realm and should not interfere with the affairs of the *polis*.

In Intemperance the Exodus has its cardinal virtue. The preexisting obligation of obedience to the State is not disregarded for reasons of incontinence, but in the name of the systematic interconnection between Intellect and political Action. Each constructive defection plays upon the visible reality of general intellect, drawing from it practical consequences that break with "civil laws." In the intemperate recourse to Intellect-in-general there is finally outlined a possibility of a *nonservile virtuosity*.

Multitude, General Intellect, Republic

The decisive political counterposition is what opposes the Multitude to the People. The concept of "people" in Hobbes (but also in a large part of the democratic-socialist tradition) is tightly correlated to the existence of the State and is in fact a reverberation of it: "The *People* is somewhat that is *one*, having *one will*, and to whom one action may be attributed; none of these can properly be said of a Multitude. The *People* rules in all Governments," and reciprocally, "the King is the *People*."[13] The progressivist notion of "popular sovereignty" has as its bitter counterpoint an identification of the people with the sovereign, or, if you prefer, the popularity of the king. The multitude, on the other hand, shuns political unity, is recalcitrant to obedience, never achieves the status of juridical personage, and is thus unable to make promises, to make pacts, or to acquire and transfer rights. It is anti-State, but, precisely for this reason, it is also antipopular: the citizens, when they rebel against the State, are "the *Multitude* against the *People.*"[14]

For the seventeenth-century apologists for sovereign power, "multitude" was a purely negative defining concept: a regurgitation of the state of nature within civil society, a continuing but somewhat unformed leftover, a metaphor of possible crisis. Liberal thinking, then, tamed the unrest provoked by the "many" through the dichotomy between public and private: the Multitude is "private" both in the literal sense of the term, being *deprived* of both face and voice, and in the juridical sense of being extraneous to the sphere of common affairs. In its turn, democratic-socialist theory produced the dichotomy "collective/individual": on the one hand, the collectivity of "producers" (the ultimate incarnation of the People) comes to be identified with the State, be it with Reagan or with Honecker; on the other, the Multitude is confined to the corral of "individual" experience — in other words, condemned to impotence.

We can say that this destiny of marginality has now come to an end. The Multitude, rather than constituting a "natural" ante-fact, presents itself as a historical *result*, a mature arrival point of the transformations that have taken place within the productive process and the forms of life. The "Many" are erupting onto the scene, and they stand there as absolute protagonists while the crisis of the society of Work is being played out. Post-Fordist social cooperation, in eliminating the frontier between production time and personal time, not to mention the distinction between professional qualities and political aptitudes, creates a new species, which makes the old dichotomies of "public/private" and "collective/individual" sound farcical. Neither "producers" nor "citizens," the modern *virtuosi* attain at last the rank of Multitude.

What we have here is a lasting and continuing reality, not some noisy intermezzo. Our new Multitude is not a whirlpool of atoms that "still" lacks unity, but a form of political existence that takes as its *starting point* a One that is radically heterogeneous to the State: public Intellect. The Many do not make alliances, nor do they transfer rights to the sovereign, because they already have a shared "score"; they never converge into a "general will" because they already share a "general intellect."

The Multitude obstructs and dismantles the mechanisms of political representation. It expresses itself as an ensemble of "acting minorities," none of which, however, aspires to transform itself into a majority. It develops a *power* that refuses to become *government.*

Now, it is the case that each of the "many" turns out to be inseparable from the "presence of others," inconceivable outside of the linguistic cooperation or the "acting-in-concert" that this presence implies. Cooperation, however, unlike the individual labor time or the individual right of citizenry, is not a
"substance" that is extrapolatable and commutable. It can, of course, be subjected,
but it cannot be represented or, for that matter, delegated. The Multitude, which
has an exclusive mode of being in its "acting-in-concert," is infiltrated by all kinds
of Kapos and Quislings, but it does not accredit stand-ins or nominees.

   The States of the developed West are today characterized by a
political nonrepresentability of the post-Fordist workforce. In fact, they gain strength
from it, drawing from it a paradoxical legitimation for their authoritarian restructuring. The tangible and irreversible crisis of representation offers an opportunity
for them to eliminate any remaining semblance of "public sphere"; to extend enormously, as observed above, the prerogatives of Adminstration at the expense of the
politico-parliamentary process; and thus to make an everyday reality of the state of
emergency. Institutional reforms are set in motion to prepare the requisite rules
and procedures for governing a Multitude upon whom it is no longer possible to
superimpose the tranquilizing physiognomy of the "People."

   As interpreted by the post-Keynesian State, the structural weakening of representative democracy comes to be seen as a tendency toward a restriction of democracy *tout court*. It goes without saying, however, that an opposition to
this course of events, if conducted in the name of values of representation, is pathetic
and pointless — as useful as preaching chastity to sparrows. Democracy today has
to be framed in terms of the construction and experimentation of forms of *nonrepresentative and extraparliamentary democracy*. All the rest is vacant chitchat.

The democracy of the Multitude takes seriously the diagnosis that Carl Schmitt
proposed, somewhat bitterly, in the last years of his life: "The era of the State is
now coming to an end. . . . The State as a model of political unity, the State as titleholder of the most extraordinary of all monopolies, in other words, the monopoly
of political decision-making, is about to be dethroned."[15] And the democracy of the
Multitude would make one important addition: the monopoly of decision making
can only really be taken away from the State if it ceases once and for all to be a
monopoly. The public sphere of Intellect, or the Republic of the "many," is a *centrifugal force*: in other words, it excludes not only the continued existence, but also
the reconstitution in any form of a unitary "political body." The republican con-
spiracy, to give lasting duration to the antimonopoly impulse, is embodied in those

democratic bodies that, being nonrepresentative, prevent, precisely, any reproposition of "political unity."

Hobbes had a well-known contempt for "irregular politicall systemes," precisely because they served to adumbrate the Multitude within the heart of the People: "Irregular Systemes, in their nature, but Leagues, or sometimes meer concourse of people, without union to any particular designe, [not] by obligation of one to another, but proceeding onely from a similitude of wills and inclinations."[16] Well, the Republic of the "many" consists precisely of institutions of this kind: *leagues, councils, and soviets*. Except that, contrary to Hobbes's malevolent judgment, here we are not dealing with ephemeral appearances whose insurgence leaves undisturbed the rights of sovereignty. The leagues, the councils, and the soviets—in short, the organs of nonrepresentative democracy—give, rather, political expression to the "acting-in-concert" that, having as its network general intellect, already always enjoys a publicness that is completely different from what is concentrated in the person of the sovereign. The public sphere delineated by "concourse" in which "obligation of one to another" does not apply, determines the "solitude" of the king, in other words, reduces the structure of the State to a very private *peripheral band*, which is overbearing but at the same time marginal.

The Soviets of the Multitude interfere conflictually with the State's administrative apparatuses, with a view to eating away at its prerogatives and absorbing its functions. They translate into republican praxis, in other words, into a care for common affairs, those same basic resources—knowledge, communication, a relationship with the "presence of others"—that are the order of the day in post-Fordist production. They emancipate *virtuosic cooperation* from its present connection with waged labor, showing with positive actions how the one goes beyond the other.

To representation and delegation, the Soviets counterpose an operative style that is far more complex, centered on *Example* and *political reproducibility*. What is exemplary is a practical initiative that, exhibiting in a particular instance the possible alliance between general intellect and Republic, has the authoritativeness of the *prototype*, but not the normativity of command. Whether it is a question of the distribution of wealth or the organization of schools, the functioning of the media or the workings of the inner city, the Soviets elaborate actions that are paradigmatic and capable of blossoming into new combinations of knowledge, ethical propensities, technologies, and desires. The Example is not the empirical application of a universal concept, but it has the singularity and the qualitative completeness that, normally, when we speak of the "life of the mind," we attribute to an *idea*. It is, in short, a "species" that consists of one sole individual. For this reason, the Example may be politically *reproduced*, but never transposed into an omnivorous "general program."

The Right to Resistance

The atrophy of political Action has had as its corollary the conviction that there is no longer an "enemy," but only incoherent interlocutors, caught up in a web of equivocation, and not yet arrived at clarification. The abandonment of the notion of "enmity," which is judged as being too crude and anyway unseemly, betrays a considerable optimism: people think of themselves, in other words, as "swimming with the current" (this is the reproof that Walter Benjamin directed against German Social Democracy in the 1930s).[17] And the benign "current" may take a variety of different names: progress, the development of productive forces, the choice of a form of life that shuns inauthenticity, general intellect. Naturally, we have to bear in mind the possibility of failing in this "swimming," in other words, not being able to define in clear and distinct terms the precise contents of a politics adequate to our times. However, this caution does not annul but corroborates the fundamental conviction: as long as one learns to "swim," and thus as long as one thinks well about possible liberty, the "current" will drive one irresistibly forward. However, no notice is taken of the interdiction that institutions, interests, and material forces may oppose the good swimmer. What is ignored is the catastrophe that is often visited precisely and only on the person who has seen things correctly. But there is worse: when one fails to define the specific nature of the *enemy*, and the places in which its power is rooted and where the chains that it imposes are tightest, one is not really even in a position to indicate the kinds of positive instances for which one might fight, the alternative ways of being that are worth hoping for.

The theory of the Exodus restores all the fullness of the concept of "enmity," while at the same time highlighting the particular traits that it assumes once "the epoch of the State comes to an end." The question is, how is the friend-enemy relationship expressed for the post-Fordist Multitude, which, while on the one hand tending to dismantle the supreme power, on the other is not at all inclined to become State in its turn?

In the first place, we should recognize a change in the *geometry of hostility*. The "enemy" no longer appears as a parallel reflection or mirror image, matching point by point the trenches and fortifications that are occupied by the "friends"; rather, it appears as a segment that intersects several times with a sinusoidal *line of flight* —

and this is principally for the reason that the "friends" are evacuating predictable positions, giving rise to a sequence of *constructive defections*. In military terms, the contemporary "enemy" resembles the pharaoh's army: it presses hard on the heels of the fleeing population, massacring those who are bringing up the rear, but never succeeding in getting ahead of it and confronting it. Now, the very fact that hostility becomes *asymmetrical* makes it necessary to give a certain autonomy to the notion of "friendship," retrieving it from the subaltern and parasitic status that Carl Schmitt assigns it. The characteristic of the "friend" is not merely that of sharing the same "enemy"; it is defined by the relations of solidarity that are established in the course of flight—by the necessity of working *together* to invent opportunities that up until that point have not been computed, and by the fact of their common participation in the Republic. "Friendship" always extends more broadly than the "front" along which the pharaoh unleashes his incursions. This overflowingness, however, does not at all imply an indifference to what happens on the line of fire. On the contrary, the asymmetry makes it possible to take the "enemy" from the rear, confusing and blinding it as we shake ourselves free.

Second, one has to be careful in defining today the degree or *gradation of hostility*. By way of comparison, it is useful to recall Schmitt's proverbial distinction between *relative enmity* and *absolute enmity*.[18] The wars among the European States in the eighteenth century were circumscribed and regulated by criteria of conflict in which each contender recognized the other as a legitimate titleholder of sovereignty and thus as a subject of equal prerogatives. These were happy times, Schmitt assures us, but they are irrevocably lost in history. In our own century, proletarian revolutions have removed the brakes and impediments from hostility, elevating civil war to an implicit model of every conflict. When what is at stake is State power—in other words, sovereignty—enmity becomes *absolute*. But can we still stand by the Mercalli scale elaborated by Schmitt? I have my doubts, given that it leaves out of account the truly decisive subterranean shift: a kind of hostility that does not aspire to shift the monopoly of political decision making into new hands, but that demands its very elimination.

The model of "absolute" enmity is thus seen to be deficient—not so much because it is extremist or bloody, but, paradoxically, because it is not radical enough. The republican Multitude actually aims to destroy what is the much-desired prize of the victor in this model. Civil war sits best only with ethnic blood feuds, in which the issue is still *who* will be the sovereign, whereas it is quite inappropriate for conflicts that undermine the economic-juridical ordering of the capitalist State and challenge the very fact of sovereignty. The various different "acting minorities" multiply the non-State centers of political decision making, without, however, posing the formation of a new *general will* (in fact, removing the possible basis of this). This then entails a perpetuation of an intermediary state between peace and war. On the one hand, the battle for "the most extraordinary of all monopolies" is premised on either total victory or total defeat; on the other, the more radical scenario (which is *antimonopolistic*) alternates between negotiation and total rejection, between an intransigence that excludes all mediation and the compromises necessary for carving out free zones and neutral environments. It is neither "relative" in the sense of the *ius publicum Europaeum* that at one time moderated the contests between sovereign States, nor is it "absolute" in the manner of civil wars; if anything, the enmity of the Multitude may be defined as *unlimitedly reactive*.

The new geometry and the new gradation of hostility, far from counseling against the use of arms, demands a precise and punctilious redefinition of the role to be fulfilled by violence in political Action. Because the Exodus is a *committed* withdrawal, the recourse to force is no longer gauged in terms of the conquest of State power in the land of the pharaohs, but in relation to the *safeguarding* of the forms of life and communitarian relations experienced en route. What deserve to be defended at all costs are the works of "friendship." Violence is not geared to visions of some hypothetical tomorrow, but functions to ensure respect and a continued existence for things that were mapped out yesterday. It does not innovate, but acts to prolong things that are already there: the autonomous expressions of the "acting-in-concert" that arise out of general intellect, organisms of nonrepresentative democracy, forms of mutual protection and assistance (welfare, in short) that have emerged outside of and against the realm of State Administration. In other words, what we have here is a *violence that is conservational*.

We might choose to label the extreme conflicts of the post-Fordist metropolis with a premodern political category: the *ius resistentiae* — the Right to Resistance. In medieval jurisprudence, this did not refer to the obvious ability to defend oneself when attacked. Nor did it refer to a general uprising against constituted power: there is a clear distinction between this and the concepts of *seditio* and *rebellio*. Rather, the Right of Resistance has a very subtle and specific meaning. It authorizes the use of violence each time that an artisanal corporation, or the community as a whole, or even individual citizens, see certain of their *positive prerogatives* altered by the central power, prerogatives that have been acquired de facto or that have developed by tradition. The salient point is therefore that it involves the preservation of a transformation that has already happened, a sanctioning of an already existing and commonplace way of being. Given that it is a close relation of radical Disobedience and of the virtue of Intemperance, the *ius resistentiae* has the feel of a very up-to-date concept in terms of "legality" and "illegality." The founding of the Republic eschews the prospect of civil war, but postulates an unlimited Right of Resistance.

Waiting for the Unexpected

Work, Action, Intellect: following the line of a tradition that goes back to Aristotle and that was still "common sense" for the generation that arrived in politics in the 1960s, Hannah Arendt sought to separate these three spheres of human experience and show their mutual incommensurability. Albeit adjacent and sometimes overlapping, the three different realms are essentially unrelated. In fact, they exclude themselves by turns: while one is making politics, one is not producing, nor is one involved in intellectual contemplation; when one works, one is not acting politically and exposing oneself to the presence of others, nor is one participating in the "life of the mind"; and anyone who is dedicated to pure reflection withdraws temporarily from the work of appearances, and thus neither acts nor produces. "To each his own" seems to be the message of Arendt's *The Human Condition*, and every man for himself. Although she argues passionately for the specific value of political Action, fighting against its entrapment in mass society, Arendt maintains that the other two fundamental spheres, Work and Intellect, remain unchanged in their qualitative structures. Certainly, Work has been extended enormously, and certainly, Thought seems feeble and paralyzed; however, the former is still nonetheless an organic exchange with nature, a social metabolism, a production of new objects, and the latter is still a solitary activity, by its nature extraneous to the cares of common affairs.

As must be obvious by now, however, what I am arguing here is radically opposed to the conceptual schema proposed by Arendt and the tradition by which it is inspired. Allow me to recapitulate briefly. The decline of political Action arises from the qualitative changes that have taken place both in the sphere of Work and in the sphere of Intellect, given that a strict intimacy has been established between them. Conjoined to Work, Intellect (as an aptitude or "faculty," not as a repertory of special understandings) becomes *public*, appearing, worldly. In other words, what comes to the fore is its nature as a shared resource and a common good. By the same token, when the potentiality of general intellect comes to be the principal pillar of social production, so Work assumes the aspect of an activity without a finished work, becoming similar in every respect to those *virtuosic performances* that are based on a relationship with a "presence of others." But is not virtuosity the characteristic trait of political action? One has to conclude, therefore, that post-Fordist production has absorbed within itself the typical modalities of Action and, precisely by so doing, has decreed its eclipse. Naturally, this metamorphosis has nothing liberatory about it: within the realm of waged labor, the virtuosic relationship with the "presence of others" translates into *personal dependence*; the "activity-without-finished-work," which nonetheless is strongly reminiscent from close up of political praxis, is reduced to an extremely modern *servitude*.

Earlier in this essay, then, I proposed that political Action finds its redemption at the point where it creates a coalition with public Intellect (in other words, at the point where this Intellect is unchained from waged labor and, rather, builds its critique with the tact of a corrosive acid). Action consists, in the final analysis, in the articulation of general intellect as a non-State public sphere, as the realm of common affairs, as Republic. The Exodus, in the course of which the new alliance between Intellect and Action is forged, has a number of fixed stars in its own heaven: radical Disobedience, Intemperance, Multitude, Soviet, Example, Right of Resistance. These categories allude to a political theory of the future, a theory perhaps capable of facing up to the political crises of the late twentieth century and outlining a solution that is radically *anti-Hobbesian*.

Political Action, in Arendt's opinion, is a new beginning that interrupts and contradicts automatic processes that have become consolidated into fact. Action has, thus, something of the *miracle*, given that it shares the miracle's quality of being surprising and unexpected.[19] Now, in conclusion, it might be worth asking whether, even though the theory of Exodus is for the most part irreconcilable with Arendt, there might be some usefulness in her notion of Miracle.

Here, of course, we are dealing with a recurrent theme in great political thinking, particularly in reactionary thought. For Hobbes, it is the role of the sovereign to decide what events merit the rank of miracles, or transcend ordinary law. Conversely, miracles cease as soon as the sovereign forbids them.[20] Schmitt takes a similar position, inasmuch as he identifies the core of power as being the ability to proclaim states of exception and suspend constitutional order: "The exception in jurisprudence is analogous to the miracle in theology."[21] On the other hand, Spinoza's democratic radicalism confutes the theological-political value of the miraculous exception. There is, however, an ambivalent aspect in his argumentation. In fact, according to Spinoza, a miracle, unlike the universal laws of nature that are identified with God, expresses only a "limited power"; in other words, it is something specifically human. Instead of consolidating faith, it makes us "doubt God and everything," thus creating a predisposition to atheism.[22] But are not these very elements — a solely human power, a radical doubt regarding constituted power, and political atheism — some of the characteristics that define the anti-State Action of the Multitude?

In general, the fact that in both Hobbes and Schmitt the miracle is the preserve of the sovereign in no sense runs counter to the connection between Action and Miracle; rather, in a sense, it confirms it. For these authors, it is only the sovereign who acts politically. The point is therefore not to deny the importance of the state of exception in the name of a critique of sovereignty, but rather to understand what form it might assume once political Action passes into the hands of the Many. Insurrections, desertions, invention of new organisms of democracy, applications of the principle of the *tertium datur*: herein lie the Miracles of the Multitude, and these miracles do not cease when the sovereign forbids them.

Unlike what we have in Arendt, however, the miraculous exception is not an ineffable "event," with no roots, and entirely imponderable. Because it is contained within the magnetic field defined by the mutually changing interrelations of Action, Work, and Intellect, the Miracle is rather something that is *awaited but unexpected*. As happens in every oxymoron, the two terms are in mutual tension, but inseparable. If what was in question was only the salvation offered by an "unexpected," or only a long-term "waiting," then we could be dealing, respectively, with the most insignificant notion of causality or the most banal calculation of the relationship between means and ends. Rather, it is an exception that is especially surprising to the one who was awaiting it. It is an anomaly so potent that it completely disorients our conceptual compass, which, however, had precisely signaled the place of its insurgence. We have here a discrepancy between cause and effect, in which one can always grasp the cause, but the innovative effect is never lessened.

Finally, it is precisely the explicit reference to an *unexpected waiting*, or the exhibition of a necessary incompleteness, that constitutes the point of honor of every political theory that disdains the benevolence of the sovereign.

Translated by Ed Emory

Notes

1. The following is the complete passage: "The development of fixed capital indicates to what degree general social knowledge has become a *direct force of production*, and to what degree, hence, the conditions of the process of social life itself have come under the control of the general intellect and been transformed in accordance with it. To what degree the powers of social production have been produced, not only in the form of knowledge, but also as immediate organs of social practice, of the real life process." Karl Marx, *Grundrisse: Foundations of the Critique of Political Economy*, trans. Martin Nicolaus (New York: Random House, 1973), 706.

2. Hannah Arendt, *The Human Condition* (Chicago: University of Chicago Press, 1958), in particular "The Traditional Substitution of Making for Acting," 220–30.

3. Karl Marx, "Results of the Immediate Process of Production," in *Capital*, vol. 1, trans. Ben Fowkes (New York: Vintage, 1977), 1048.

4. Ibid., 1044–45.

5. Aristotle, *Nicomachean Ethics*, book 6 (Indianapolis: Hackett, 1985), 1139b.

6. Hannah Arendt, *Between Past and Future: Six Exercises in Political Thought* (New York: Viking, 1961), 154.

7. Marx, *Grundrisse*, 705.

8. Ibid.

9. Thomas Hobbes, *De Cive* (Oxford: Oxford University Press, 1983), chap. 14, sec. 21, 181.

10. Albert O. Hirschman, *Exit, Voice, and Loyalty: Responses to Decline in Firms, Organizations, and States* (Cambridge: Harvard University Press, 1970).

11. Marx discusses the North American "frontier" and its economic and political importance in the final chapter of the first volume of *Capital*, titled "The Modern Theory of Colonization." Marx writes: "There, the absolute numbers of the population increase much more quickly than in the mother country, because many workers enter the colonial world as ready-made adults, and still the labour-market is always understocked. The law of the supply and demand of labour collapses completely. On the one hand, the old world constantly throws in capital, thirsting after exploitation and 'abstinence'; on the other, the regular reproduction of the wage-labourer as a wage-labourer comes up against the most mischievous obstacles, which are in part insuperable. And what becomes of the production of redundant wage-labourers, redundant, that is, in proportion to the accumulation of capital? Today's wage-labourer is tomorrow's independent peasant or artisan, working for himself. He vanishes from the labour-market—but not into the workhouse. This constant transformation of wage-labourers into independent producers who work for themselves instead of for capital, and enrich themselves instead of the capitalist gentlemen, reacts in its turn very adversely on the conditions of the labour-market. Not only does the degree of exploitation of the wage-labourer remain indecently low. The wage-labourer also loses, along with the relation of dependence, the feeling of dependence on the abstemious capitalist." *Capital*, vol. 1, trans. Ben Fowkes (New York: Vintage, 1977), 935–36.

12. Aristotle, *Nicomachean Ethics*, book 7, 1147a25–b20.

13. Hobbes, *De Cive*, 151.

14. Ibid., 152.

15. Carl Schmitt, *Der Begriff des Politischen: Text von 1932 mit eimen Vorwort und drei Corollarien* (Berlin: Duncker and Humblot, 1963), 10.

16. Thomas Hobbes, *Leviathan* (Cambridge: Cambridge University Press, 1991), chap. 22, 163.

17. See Walter Benjamin, "Theses on the Philosophy of History," in *Illuminations* (New York: Schocken, 1968), in particular thesis XI, 258–59.

18. See Schmitt, *Der Begriff des Politischen*, 102–11.

19. See Arendt, *Between Past and Future*, 168–70.

20. See Hobbes, *Leviathan*, chap. 37.

21. Carl Schmitt, *Political Theology: Four Chapters on the Concept of Sovereignty* (Cambridge: MIT Press, 1985), 36.

22. Baruch Spinoza, *Theologico-Political Treatise*, in *The Chief Works of Benedict de Spinoza*, vol. 1, trans. R. Elwes (New York: Dover, 1951), 81–97.

FIFTEEN

Constituent Republic

Antonio Negri

To Each Generation Its Own Constitution

When Condorcet suggested that each generation might produce its own political constitution, on the one hand he was referring to the position of constitutional law in Pennsylvania (where constitutional law was on the same footing as ordinary law, providing one single method for creating both constitutional principles and new law), and on the other he was anticipating article XXVIII of the French revolutionary Constitution of 1793: "Un peuple a toujours le droit de revoir, de reformer et de changer sa Constitution. Une génération ne peut assujetter à ses lois les générations futures [A people always has the right to revise, reform, and change its constitution. A generation may not subject future generations to its own laws]."

Standing at the threshold of a new era of developments in State and society, to be brought about by revolution, scientific innovation, and capitalism, Condorcet understood that any preconstituted blockage of the dynamic of production and any restraint of liberty that goes beyond the requirements of the present necessarily lead to despotism. To put it another way, Condorcet understood that, once the constituent moment is past, constitutional fixity becomes a reactionary fact in a society that is founded on the development of freedoms and the development of the economy. Thus a constitution should not be granted legitimacy on the basis of custom and practice, or the ways of our ancestors, or classical ideas of order.

On the contrary, only life in a constant process of renewal can form a constitution—in other words, can continually be putting it to the test, evaluating it, and driving it toward necessary modifications. From this point of view, Condorcet's recommendation that "each generation should have its own constitution" can be put alongside that of Niccolò Machiavelli, who proposed that each generation (in order to escape the corruption of power and the "routine" of administration) "should return to the principles of the State"—a "return" that is a process of building, an ensemble of principles, not an inheritance from the past but something newly rooted.

Should our own generation be constructing a new constitution? When we look back at the reasons the earlier creators of constitutions gave for why constitutional renewal was so urgent, we find the same reasons entirely present in our own situation today. Rarely has the corruption of political and administrative life been so deeply corrosive; rarely has there been such a crisis of representation; rarely has disillusionment with democracy been so radical. When people talk about "a crisis of politics," they are effectively saying that the democratic State no longer functions—and that in fact it has become irreversibly corrupt in all its principles and organs: the division of powers; the principles of guarantee; the single individual powers; the rules of representation; the unitarian dynamic of powers; and the functions of legality, efficiency, and administrative legitimacy. There has been talk of an "end of history," and if such a thing exists we might certainly identify it in the end of the constitutional dialectic to which liberalism and the mature capitalist State have tied us. To be specific, since the 1930s, in the countries of the capitalist West, there has begun to develop a constitutional system that we would call the "Fordist" constitution, or the laborist Welfare State constitution. This model has now gone into crisis. The reasons for the crisis are clear when one takes a look at the changes in the subjects that had forged the original agreement around the principles of this constitution: on the one hand there was the national bourgeoisie, and on the other was the industrial working class, which was organized in both the trade unions and the socialist and communist parties. Thus the liberal-democratic system functioned in such a way as to match the needs of industrial development and the sharing out of global income between these classes. Constitutions may have differed more or less in their forms, but the "material constitution"—the basic convention covering the distribution of powers and counterpowers, work and income, rights and freedoms—was substantially homogeneous. The national bourgeoisies renounced fascism and guaranteed their powers of exploitation within a system of distributing national income that—reckoning on a context of continuous growth—

enabled the construction of a welfare system for the national working class. For its part, in return, the working class renounced revolution.

At the point when the crisis of the 1960s concluded in the emblematic events of 1968, the State built on the Fordist constitution went into crisis: the subjects of the original constitutional accord in effect underwent a change. On the one hand, the various bourgeoisies became internationalized, basing their power on the financial transformation of capital and turning themselves into abstract representations of power; on the other, the industrial working class (in the wake of radical transformations in the mode of production, such as the victory for the automation of industrial labor and the computerization of social labor) transformed its own cultural, social, and political identity. A multinational and finance-based bourgeoisie (which sees no reason it should bear the burden of a national welfare system) was matched by a socialized, intellectual proletariat—which, on the one hand, has a wealth of new needs and, on the other, is incapable of maintaining a continuity with the articulations of the Fordist compromise. With the exhaustion of "real socialism" and the etching of its disaster into world history at the end of 1989, even the symbols—already largely a dead letter—of a proletarian independence within socialism were definitively destroyed.

The juridico-constitutional system based on the Fordist compromise, strengthened by the constituent agreement between the national bourgeoisie and the industrial working class, and overdetermined by the conflict between the Soviet and U.S. superpowers (symbolic representations of the two conflicting parties on the stage of each individual nation) has thus run out its time. There is no longer a long-term war between two power blocs at the international level, within which the civil war between classes might be cooled down by means of immersion in the Fordist constitution and/or in the organizations of the Welfare State. There no longer exist, within individual countries, the subjects who could constitute that constitution and who might legitimate its expressions and its symbols. The whole scenario is now radically changed.

So what is the new constitution that our generation must construct?

Arms and Money

Machiavelli says that in order to construct the State, the prince needs "arms and money." So what arms and what money are going to be required for a new constitution? For Machiavelli, the arms are represented by the people (*il popolo*), in other words the productive citizenry, who, within the democracy of the commune, become a people in arms. The question is, what "people" could be counted on today for the creation of a new constitution? Do we have a generation opening itself to a new institutional compromise that will go beyond the Welfare State? In what terms would it be disposed to organize itself, to "arm" itself, to this end? And what about the question of "money"? Is the multinational finance bourgeoisie willing to consider a new constitutional and productive compromise that will go beyond the Fordist compromise—and if so, on what terms?

Within the social system of post-Fordism, the concept of "the people" can and must be redefined. And not only the concept of "the people," but also the concept of "the people in arms"—in other words, that fraction of the citizenry that by its work produces wealth and thus makes possible the reproduction of society as a whole. This is the group that can claim that its own hegemony over social labor be registered in constitutional terms.

The political task of arriving at a definition of the post-Fordist proletariat is by now well advanced. This proletariat embodies a substantial section of the working class that has been restructured within processes of production that are automated and computer controlled—processes that are centrally managed by an ever-expanding intellectual proletariat, which is increasingly directly engaged in labor that is computer related, communicative, and, in broad terms, educational or formative. The post-Fordist proletariat, the "people" represented by the "social" worker (*operaio sociale*), is imbued with and constituted by a continuous interplay between technico-scientific activity and the hard work of producing commodities, by the entrepreneuriality of the networks within which this interaction is organized, and by the increasingly close combination and recomposition of labor time and life time. There, simply by way of introduction, we have some possible elements of the new definition of the proletariat, and what becomes clear is that, in all the sections in which this class is being composed, it is essentially *mass intellectuality*. Plus—and this is crucial—we have another element: within the scientific subsumption of productive labor, within the growing abstraction and socialization of production, the post-Fordist labor form is becoming increasingly cooperative, independent, and autonomous. This combination of autonomy and cooperation means that the entrepreneurial power of productive labor is henceforth completely in the hands of the post-Fordist proletariat. The very development of productivity is what constitutes this enormous independence of the proletariat, as an intellectual and cooperative base, as economic entrepreneuriality. The question is, Does it also constitute it as political entrepreneuriality, as political autonomy?

We can attempt an answer to this question only once we have asked ourselves what exactly we mean by "money" within this historic development. In other words, in today's world, what happens to the bourgeoisie as a class and to the productive functions of the industrial bourgeoisie? Well, if what we have said about the new definition of a post-Fordist proletariat is true, it follows that the international bourgeoisie has now lost its productive functions, that it is becoming increasingly parasitic—a kind of Roman Church of capital. It now expresses itself only through financial command, in other words, a command that is completely liberated from the demands of production. "Money" operates here in the postclassical and post-Marxian sense, "money" as an alienated and hostile universe, "money" as a general panacea—the opposite of labor, intelligence, and the immanence of life and desire. "Money" no longer functions as mediation between labor and commodity; it is no longer a numeric rationalization of the relationship between wealth and power; it is no longer a quantified expression of the nation's wealth. In the face of the entrepreneurial autonomy of a proletariat that has materially embraced within itself also the intellectual forces of production, "money" becomes the phony reality of a command that is despotic, external, empty, capricious, and cruel.

It is here that the potential of a new fascism reveals itself—a postmodern fascism, which has little to do with Mussolinian alliances, with the illogical schemata of Nazism, or the cowardly arrogance of Petainism. Postmodern fascism seeks to match itself to the realities of post-Fordist labor cooperation, and seeks at the same time to express some of its essence in a form that is turned on its head. In the same way that the old fascism mimicked the mass organizational forms of socialism and attempted to transfer the proletariat's impulse toward collectivity into nationalism (national socialism or the Fordist constitution), so postmodern fascism seeks to discover the communist needs of the post-Fordist masses and transform them, gradually, into a cult of differences, the pursuit of individualism, and the search for identity—all within a project of creating overriding despotic hierarchies aimed at constantly, relentlessly, pitting differences, singularities, identities, and individualities one against the other. Whereas communism is respect for and synthesis of singularities, and as such is desired by all those who love peace, the new fascism (as an expression of the financial command of international capital) would produce a war of all against all; it would create religiosity and wars of religion, nationalism and wars of nations, corporative egos and economic wars.

We should be careful, however, to distinguish what is really fascist from what is not. It may be dangerous to cry wolf too early and too often. For example, despite the numerous villifications in Italy and around Europe, Silvio Berlusconi is not a fascist—he is a boss. Berlusconi is a new figure of the collective capitalist, an emblem of capitalist command over society: in him communication and production have become the same thing. The Italian "revolution" that brought him to power is not fascist, but reactionary. It is not fascist to revise the Constitution of 1947 and subordinate the liberal-representative system to a presidential machine—that is only Gaullism. It is not fascist to expand and strengthen the autonomy of the various regions—that can, at the most, become a kind of egoism. It is not fascist to set in motion, from the point of view of the majority and through institutional pressures, a reactionary wave against the emancipation of social practices (against abortion, homosexuality, and so forth)—that is only clericalism. All of this was set in motion by the Berlusconi government, but it is not fascism. It is the social, economic, cultural, and political vision of a conservative Right. Berlusconi interprets, constructs, renews, and celebrates a reactionary community. He develops and perfects the new postmodern and communicative capitalism, showing Italian society what it has already become in the past twenty years: a society in which the enormous corruption that involved businessmen and politicians was nothing compared to the corruption that infiltrated the thought and ethical consciousness of the multitude. It may be true, then, in these terms, that this reactionary "revolution" is laying the groundwork for a future postmodern fascism.

So, let us return to the question of "the arms of the people." We are asking, What is this constitution that our new generation has to build? This is another way of asking, What are the balances of power, the compromises, that the new postmodern proletariat and the new multinational capitalist class have to institute, in material terms, in order to organize the next productive cycle of the class struggle? But if what we have said so far is true, does this question still make sense? What possibility exists now for constitutional compromise, in a situation where a huge degree of proletarian cooperation stands at the opposite pole to a huge degree of external and parasitic command imposed by multinational capital, a situation in which money stands in opposition to production?

Does it still make sense to ask ourselves how rights and duties might be measured in a reciprocal way, given that the dialectic of production no longer has workers and capital mixing in the management of the productive relationship? We would probably all agree that the question makes no sense. The "arms" and the "monies" are no longer such that they can be put together in order to construct the State. Probably the Welfare State represents the final episode of this history of accords between those who command and those who obey (a history that—

if we are to believe Machiavelli—was born with the "dualism of power" that the Roman tribunes installed in relation to the Republic). Today everything is changing in the fields of political science and constitutional theory: if it is the case that those who once were the "subjects" are now more intelligent and more "armed" than kings and ruling classes, why should they go looking for a mediation with the members of those classes?[1]

State Forms: What Constituent Power Is Not

From Plato to Aristotle and, with some modifications, through to the present day, the theory of "State forms" has come down to us as a theory that is unavoidably dialectical. Monarchy and tyranny, aristocracy and oligarchy, democracy and anarchy, handing over from one to the other, are thus the only alternatives within which the cycle of power develops. At a certain point in the development of the theory, Polybius, with undoubted good sense, proposed that these forms should be considered not as alternatives, but rather as complementary. (Here he referred to the constitution of the Roman Empire, to show that there were instances in which different State forms not only did not counterpose each other, but could also work together as complementary functions of government.) The theorists of the American Constitution, along with those of the popular-democratic Constitutions of Stalinism, thus all contentedly recognized themselves as Polybians! Classical and contemporary constitutionalism, wherein all the apologists of the Rights State (*Rechsstaat*) happily wallow, is nothing other than Polybian! Monarchy, aristocracy, and democracy, put together, form the best of republics!

However, the alleged scientific value of this dialectic of State forms does not go much beyond the well-known classical apologetics of Menenius Agrippus, whose position was as reactionary as any other, given that it implied a conception of power that was organic, unmoving, and animal (inasmuch as it required the various social classes to work together to construct an animal functionality). Should we write it off as being of no value then? Perhaps. At the same time, however, there is a value in recognizing these theories for what they are, because the way they have survived over the centuries, the effects they have had on history, and the daily effect of inertia that they exert provide useful reminders of the power of mystification.

The ideology of revolutionary Marxism too, albeit overturning the theory of State forms, nonetheless ended up affirming its validity. The "abolition of the State," *pace* Lenin, assumes the concept of State as it exists within bourgeois theory, and poses itself as a practice of extreme confrontation with that reality. In other words, all these concepts—"transition" as much as "abolition," the "peaceful road" as much as "people's democracy," the "dictatorship of the proletariat" as much as the "cultural revolution"—all these are bastard concepts, because they are impregnated with a conception of the State, its sovereignty, and its domination, because they consider themselves as necessary means and unavoidable processes to be pursued in the seizure of power and the transformation of society. The mystificatory dialectic of the theory of State forms turns into the negative dialectic of the abolition of the State, but the theoretical nucleus remains, in the absolute and reactionary way in which the power of the State is affirmed. "All the same old shit," as Marx put it.

It is time to emerge from this crystallization of absurd positions—which are given a value of truth solely by their extremism. It is time to ask ourselves whether there does not exist, from a theoretical and practical point of view, a position that avoids absorption within the opaque and terrible essence of the State. In other words, we should ask ourselves whether there does not exist a viewpoint that, renouncing the perspective of those who would construct the constitution of the State mechanistically, is able to maintain the thread of genealogy, the force of constituent praxis, in its extensiveness and intensity. This point of view exists. It is the viewpoint of daily insurrection, continual resistance, constituent power. It is a breaking-with, it is refusal, it is imagination, all as the basis of political science. It is the recognition of the impossibility, nowadays, of mediating between "arms" and "money," the "people in arms" and the multinational bourgeoisie, production and finance. As we begin to leave Machiavellianism behind us, we are firmly of the opinion that Machiavelli would have been on our side. We are beginning to arrive at a situation where we are no longer condemned to think of politics in terms of domination. The very form of the dialectic—that is, mediation as the content of domination in its various different forms—is thus brought into question. In my opinion, it is definitively in crisis. We have to find ways of thinking politically beyond the theory of "State forms." To pose the problem in Machiavellian terms, we have to ask, Is it possible to imagine constructing a republic on the basis of the arms of the people, and without the money of the prince? Is it possible to entrust the future of the State solely to popular "virtue," and not also to "fortune"?

Constructing the Soviets of Mass Intellectuality

In the period that we have now entered, in which immaterial labor is tending to become hegemonic, and that is characterized by the antagonisms produced by the new relationship between the organization of the forces of production and multinational capitalist command, the form in which the problem of the constitution presents itself, from the viewpoint of mass intellectuality, is that of establishing how it might be possible to build its Soviets. In order to define the problem, let us begin by recalling some of the conditions that we have assumed thus far. The first of these conditions derives from the tendential hegemony of immaterial labor and thus from the increasingly profound reappropriation of technico-scientific knowledge by the proletariat. On this basis, technico-scientific knowledge can no longer be posed as a mystified function of command, separated from the body of mass intellectuality.

The second condition derives from what I referred to above as the end of all distinction between working life and social life, between social life and individual life, between production and forms of life. In this situation, the political and the economic become two sides of the same coin. All the wretched old bureaucratic distinctions between trade union and party, between vanguard and mass, and so on, seem definitively to disappear. Politics, science, and life function together; it is within this framework that the real produces subjectivity.

The third point to consider arises from what has been said above: on this terrain the alternative to existing power is constructed positively, through the expression of potentiality (*potenza*). The destruction of the State can be envisaged only through a concept of the reappropriation of administration—in other words, a reappropriation of the social essence of production, the instruments of comprehension of social and productive cooperation. Administration is wealth, consolidated and put at the service of command. It is fundamental for us to reappropriate this, reappropriating it by means of an exercise of individual labor posed within a perspective of solidarity, within cooperation, in order to administer social labor, in order to ensure an ever-richer reproduction of accumulated immaterial labor.

Here, therefore, is where the Soviets of mass intellectuality are born. And it is interesting to note how the objective conditions of their emergence are in perfect accord with the historical conditions of the antagonistic class relationship. In this latter terrain, as I proposed above, there is no longer any possibility of constitutional compromise. The Soviets will therefore be defined by the fact that they will express immediately potentiality, cooperation, and productivity. The Soviets of mass intellectuality will give rationality to the new social organization of work, and they will make the universal commensurate to it. The expression of their potentiality will be without constitution.

The constituent Republic is thus not a new form of constitution: it is neither Platonic nor Aristotelian nor Polybian, and perhaps it is no longer even

Machiavellian. It is a Republic that comes before the State, that comes outside of the State. The constitutional paradox of the constituent Republic consists in the fact that the constituent process never closes, that the revolution does not come to an end, that constitutional law and ordinary law refer back to one single source and are developed unitarily within a single democratic procedure.

Here we are, finally, at the great problem from which everything starts and toward which everything tends: the task of destroying separation, inequality, and the power that reproduces separation and inequality. The Soviets of mass intellectuality can pose themselves this task by constructing, outside of the State, a mechanism within which a democracy of the everyday can organize active communication, the interactivity of citizens, and at the same time produce increasingly free and complex subjectivities.

All the above is only a beginning. Is it perhaps too general and abstract? Certainly. But it is important that we begin once again to talk about communism — in this form — in other words, as a program that, in all its aspects, goes beyond the wretched reductions that we have seen being enacted in history. And the fact that this is only a start does not make it any the less realistic. Mass intellectuality and the new proletariat that have been constructed in the struggles against capitalist development and through the expression of constitutive potentiality (*potenza*) are beginning to emerge as true historic subjects.

The event, the untimely, the *Angelus novus* — when they arrive — will appear suddenly. Thus our generation *can* construct a new constitution. Except that it will not be a constitution. And perhaps this event has already occurred.

Translated by Ed Emory

Note

1. If there is a terrain on which arms and money, production and command, do actually clash, it is the terrain of communication. If the question of a new constitution, in the traditional sense of the term, still makes sense, it is at this level that its meaning is to be found. But in fact here one finds oneself not so much having to resolve a new problem as having to recover an issue that, in previous compromises, the proletariat had, in a manner of speaking, left to one side. And anyway, how can the problem of communication be resolved in constitutional terms? The problem of communication is a problem of truth, and how is it possible to effect a compromise on truth? How is it possible to have two advertisements making statements that are opposite and contradictory in relation to an identical object? How is it possible to arrive at compromise in the sphere of image and symbol? Some might object that the constitutional problem of communication touches only indirectly on the problem of truth and touches directly on the problem of the means of expression — so that a compromise, as well as relations of force, is entirely possible. This objection, however, is only relatively valid, or rather it is valid up until the moment when one enters into a phase of civil war. And given that, in the postmodern, everything drives toward civil war, it really is hard to understand at what point a compromise on communication might be reached.

Appendix: A Future History

SIXTEEN

Do You Remember Revolution?

Lucio Castellano,

Arrigo Cavallina,

Giustino Cortiana,

Mario Dalmaviva,

Luciano Ferrari Bravo,

Chicco Funaro,

Antonio Negri,

Paolo Pozzi,

Franco Tommei,

Emilio Vesce, and

Paolo Virno

Rebibbia Prison, Rome, 1983

Looking back to reexamine the 1970s, one thing at least is clear to us: the history of the revolutionary movement, first the extraparliamentary opposition and then Workers' Autonomy, was not a history of marginals, fringe eccentricity, or sectarian fantasies from some underground ghetto. On the contrary, it should be clear that this history (part of which is now the object of our trial) is inextricably linked to the overall development of the country and the decisive passages and ruptures that have marked its history.

Adopting this point of view (which in itself might be obvious, but in times like these is seen as reckless if not directly provocative), we want to propose a series of historical-political theses on the past decade that go beyond our own immediate defense concerns in the trial. The problems we are posing are not addressed to the judges, but rather to all those involved in the struggles of these years—to the comrades of 1968, to those of 1977, and to all the intellectuals who "dissented" (is that how we say it now?), judging rebellion to be rational. We hope that they may intervene in their turn to break the vicious circle of memory distortion and new conformism. We think that the time has come for a realistic reappraisal of the 1970s. We need to clear the way for the truth and for our own political judgment against the distortions spread by the State and the *pentiti* (literally, "the penitent ones," that is, the accused who turned State's evidence and named names). It is both possible and necessary today to accept and assign responsibility fully: this is one of the fundamental steps needed to enter the stage of "postterrorism."

That we have had nothing to do with terrorism is obvious. That we have been "subversive" is equally obvious. Between these two truths lies the key issue at stake in our trial. Clearly the judges are inclined to equate subversion and terrorism, and we will thus argue our defense with the appropriate technical-political means. The historical reconstruction of the 1970s, however, cannot be conducted only in the courtroom. An honest and far-reaching debate must be pursued in parallel to the trial among the social subjects who have been the real protagonists of the "great transformation" of these years. This debate is vitally necessary if we are to confront adequately the new tensions facing us in the 1980s.

The specific characteristic of the "Italian '68" was a combination of new, explosive social phenomena—in many respects typical of the mature, industrialized countries—together with the classic paradigm of communist political revolution. The radical critique of wage labor and its refusal on a mass scale was the central driving force behind the mass struggles, the matrix of a strong and lasting antagonism, and the material content of all the future hopes that the movement represented. This nourished the mass challenge directed against professional roles and hierarchies, the struggles for equal pay, the attack on the organization of social knowledge, and the qualitative demands for changes in the structure of everyday life—in short, the general striving toward concrete forms of freedom. In other Western capitalist countries (such as Germany and the United States), these same forces of transformation were developed as molecular mutations of social relations, without directly and immediately posing the problem of political power, that is, an alternative management of the State. In France and Italy, due to institutional rigidities and a somewhat simplified way of regulating conflicts, the question of State power—and its "seizure"—immediately became central.

In Italy especially, the wave of mass struggles from 1968 onward marked, in many respects, a sharp break with the "laborist" and State socialist traditions of the established working-class movement, and at the same time gave new life to the communist political model in the body of the new movements. The extreme polarization of the class confrontation and the relative poverty of institutional political mediations (with a welfare system that was overly centralized) created a situation in which struggles for higher wages and more freedom became linked to the Leninist goal of "smashing the State machine."

Between 1968 and the early 1970s, the problem of finding a political outlet for the mass struggles was on the agenda of the entire Left, both old and new. Both the Italian Communist Party (PCI) and the unions on one hand and the extraparliamentary revolutionary groups on the other were working for a drastic change in the power structure, one that would carry through and realize the change in the relation of forces that had already occurred in the factories and the labor market. There was a prolonged battle for hegemony within the Left about the nature and quality of this political outlet.

The revolutionary groups, which held a majority in the high schools and universities, but with roots also in the factories and service industries, realized that the recent wave of struggles and social transformations coincided with a sharp rupture from the framework of legality in which the movements had hitherto existed. They emphasized this aspect of the situation in order to prevent any institutional recuperation of the movements within structures of command and profit. The extension of the struggles to the entire social terrain and the building of forms of counterpower were seen as necessary steps against the blackmail of economic crisis. The Communist Party and the unions, on the other hand, saw the breaking up of the Center-Left coalition and the establishment of "structural reforms" as the natural outcome of the mass struggles of 1968. A new "framework of compatibility" and a more dense and articulated network of institutional mediations would, in their view, guarantee a more central role for the working class in the renewal of economic growth.

Even though the most bitter polemics took place between the extraparliamentary groups and the historical Left, there were also very significant struggles within the two camps. It is sufficient to recall, for example, the polemics of the Communist Party right wing against the Turin engineering workers' federation (FLM) on the question of a "new unionism" that they saw in the movement, or, on the other side, the sharp differences between the workerist current and the Marxist-Leninist line. These divisions, however, revolved around one basic problem: how to translate into terms of political power the upheaval in social relations that had developed from the wave of struggles since 1968.

In the early 1970s, the extraparliamentary Left posed the problem of the use of force, the problem of violence in terms that were completely within the revolutionary communist tradition. The Left saw it as one of the means necessary for a struggle on the terrain of power. There was no fetishism of the use of violence. On the contrary, it was strictly subordinated to the advancement of mass actions. There was, however, a clear acceptance of its relevance. There was no real continuity between the interplay of social conflicts and the question of political power. After the violent clashes in the late 1960s in Battipaglia, near Naples, and in Corso Traiano in Turin, the State's monopoly of the use of force appeared as an unavoidable obstacle that had to be confronted systematically.

The programs and slogans of this period thus conceptualized the violent breaking of legality in offensive terms, as the manifestation of a different form of power. Slogans such as "Take over the city" or "Insurrection" synthesized this perspective, which was considered inevitable, albeit not in any immediate sense. On the other hand, in concrete terms of the mass movements themselves, organization within the framework of illegality was much more modest, with strictly defensive and contingent goals: the defense of picket lines, housing occupations, demonstrations—in short, security measures to prevent possible right-wing reaction (which was seen as a real threat after the fascist bombing of a rally at Piazza Fontana in Milan in December 1969).

On one hand, then, there was a theory of attack and rupture based on the combination of a communist outlook and the "new political subject" that emerged from 1968, but on the other hand there were only minimal realizations of this in practice. It should be clear nonetheless that following the "Red Years" of 1968–69 thousands of militants—including trade union groups—considered normal and commonplace the "illegal" organization of struggles, along with public debates on the forms and timing of confrontation with the repressive structures of the State.

In these years, the role of the first clandestine armed organizations—the Partisan Action Groups (GAP) and the Red Brigades—was completely marginal and outside the general outlook and debate of the movement. Clandestine organization itself, the obsessive appeal to the partisan tradition of the wartime resistance and the reference to the highly skilled sectors of the working class that accompanied it, had absolutely nothing in common with the organization of violence in the class vanguards and revolutionary groups of the movement. The Partisan Action Groups, linked to the old anti-Fascist resistance and the communist tradition of organizing at "dual levels" (mass and clandestine) that goes back to the 1950s, proposed the need for preventive measures against what they saw as an imminent Fascist coup. The Red Brigades, on the other hand, were formed from a confluence of Marxist-Leninists in the city of Trento, ex-Communist Party members from the Milan region, and those who came out of the Communist Youth Federation in the Emilia area.

Throughout this early phase, the Red Brigades looked for support and contacts among the Communist Party rank and file, and not at all in the revolutionary movement. Their operations were characterized by anti-Fascism and "armed struggle in support of reforms."

Paradoxical though it may seem, the adoption on the part of the revolutionary groups in the movement of a perspective of struggle that included illegality and violence made the gap between this and the strategy of "armed struggle" and clandestine organization even wider and more unbridgeable. The sporadic contacts that existed between the groups and the first armed organizations only confirmed the gulf in cultural perspective and political line that divided them.

In the period 1973–74, the political context within which the movement had developed began to disintegrate. Within a short period of time, there were multiple ruptures in the movement, sharp changes in political perspective, and changes in the very conditions of the conflict itself. These changes were due to a number of interacting factors. The first was the change in the policy of the Communist Party, which now perceived a closing down of possibilities at the international level, making the need to find an immediate "political solution" to the social turmoil within the confines of the given conditions.

This led to a split, which became increasingly deep, among the political and social forces that since 1968 had, in spite of internal differences, shared the common goal of constructing an alternative on the terrain of power that would reflect the radical and transformative content of the struggles. A large part of the Left, notably the Communist Party and its federated unions, now began to draw nearer to the terrain of government and became increasingly opposed to wide sectors of the movement.

The extraparliamentary opposition now had to redefine itself in relation to the governmental "compromise" that the Communist Party was seeking. This redefinition led to a crisis and a progressive loss of identity for the groups. The struggle for hegemony on the Left that had to some extent justified the existence of the revolutionary groups now seemed to have been resolved unilaterally in a way that closed the debate altogether. From that point on, the old question of finding a "political outlet," an alternative management of the State, was identified with the moderate politics of the Communist Party. Those extraparliamentary organizations that still followed this perspective were forced to try to go along with the Communist Party, influencing the outcome of the compromise as best they could — for example, participating in the 1975 (local) and the 1976 (national) elections. Other groups instead found that they had reached the limits of their own reason for being and before long found no alternative but to disband.

The second factor in this change of the movement in the period 1973–74 was the fact that the central figure of the factory struggles, the assembly line workers of the major factories, began, with the union-employer contracts of 1972–73, to lose its central role as an offensive and organizing protagonist. The restructuring of large-scale industries had begun.

       The increasing use of layoffs and the first partial implementation of new technologies radically changed the terms of production, blunting the thrust of previous forms of struggle, including the mass strike. The homogeneity of the shop floor and its capacity to exercise power over the overall process of production were undercut by new machinery and the reorganization of the working day. The representative functions of the factory councils and their internal divisions into Left and Right withered almost immediately. The power of the assembly line worker was not weakened by what is traditionally imagined as an "industrial reserve army" or competition from the unemployed. The point is that industrial reconversion tended toward investment in sectors outside the sphere of mass production. This made now central sectors of labor power that previously had been relatively marginal and had less organizational experience behind them (such as women, youth, and highly educated workers). The terrain of confrontation began to shift from the factory to the overall mechanisms of the labor market, public spending, the reproduction of the proletariat and young people, and the distribution of income independent of remuneration for work.

In the third place, a change occurred within the subjectivity of the movement, its culture, and its outlook toward the future. There was a complete rejection of the entire tradition of workers' movements, including the idea of "seizing power," the canonical goal of the "dictatorship of the proletariat," the residual baggage of "real socialism," and any project of State management.

       The links that had existed within the post-1968 movements between the new aspirations and the model of a communist political revolution were now completely broken. Power was seen as a foreign enemy force in society, to be defended against; there was no use conquering or overturning power, one could only reduce it and keep it at bay. The key to this new outlook was the affirmation of the movement itself as an alternative society, with its own richness of communication, its own free productive capacities, its own forms of life. The dominant form of struggle for the new social subjects became a project of conquering and managing its own "spaces." Waged labor was no longer seen as the primary terrain of socialization, but rather as something episodic, contingent, and unvalued.

The feminist movement, with its practices of communalism and separatism, its critique of politics and power, its deep distrust of any "general" and institutional representation of needs and desires, and its love of differences, was emblematic of this new phase of the movement. It provided the inspiration, explicitly or implicitly, for the various itineraries of proletarian youth in the mid-1970s. The referendum on divorce in 1974 gave a first indication of the tendency that came to be called "the autonomy of the social."

It was no longer possible to regard the Left in terms of a family tree, even referring to a family in crisis. The new mass subjectivity was alien to the workers' movement; their languages and objectives no longer had any common ground. The very category of "extremism" no longer explained anything, but only confused the situation. One can only be "extremist" in relation to something similar, but it was precisely the points of resemblance that were fast disappearing.

All three of these factors that characterized the situation between 1973 and 1975, but particularly the last one, contributed to the birth of the organization called Workers' Autonomy. Autonomy was formed in opposition to the Communist Party project of "compromise," in response to the crisis and failure of the revolutionary groups, and as a step beyond the factory-centered perspective, in order to interact conflictually with the restructuring of production that was taking place. Above all, however, Autonomy expressed the new subjectivity of the movement, the richness of its differences, and its radical separation from formal politics and mechanisms of representation. It did not seek any "political outlet" or solution, but looked rather toward the concrete and articulated exercise of power on the social terrain.

In this sense, localism was a defining characteristic of the experience of Autonomy. With the rejection of any perspective of an alternative management of the State, there could be no centralization of the movement. Every regional collective that was part of Autonomy traced the concrete particularity of class composition in that area, without experiencing this as a limitation, but rather as its reason for being. It is therefore literally impossible to try to reconstruct a unitary history of these movements among Rome, Milan, the Veneto region, and the South.

From 1974 to 1976, the practice of mass illegality and violence became more intense and more common. This form of antagonism, however, which had been practically unknown in the previous phase of the movement, had no coherent plan against the State, and it was not preparation for any "revolutionary break." This is its essential characteristic. In the big cities violence arose in response to immediate needs, as part of an effort to create "spaces" that could be independently controlled, and as a reaction to cuts in public spending.

In 1974, the self-reduction of transport fares, organized by the unions in Turin, relaunched a form of mass illegality that had been practiced before, notably during rent strikes. From that point on, and in relation to a whole range of public services, this form of "guaranteed income" was widely put into practice. The unions had intended this self-reduction to be a symbolic gesture, but the movement transformed it into a generalized, material form of struggle.

Even more important than these practices of self-reduction, however, was the occupation of housing in San Basilio, Rome, in October 1974. It was a turning point, a spontaneous "militarization" of the population as a defensive response to violent police aggression. Another decisive step came with the mass demonstrations in Milan in the spring of 1975 after two activists (Varelli and Zibecchi) had been killed by fascists and police. Violent street confrontations were the point of departure for a whole series of struggles against the government's austerity measures, the first steps in the so-called politics of sacrifice. The period 1975–76 witnessed what in certain respects is a "classic" response to the decline of the Welfare State: the passage from self-reduction to direct appropriation, from a defensive struggle in the face of rising costs to an offensive struggle for the collective satisfaction of needs, aimed at overturning the mechanisms of the crisis.

Appropriation (of which the greatest example at the time seemed to be the looting that took place during the night of the New York blackout) became part of collective practice in all aspects of metropolitan life: free or "political" shopping, occupation of buildings for open activities, the "serene habit" of young people not paying for movies and concerts, and the refusal of overtime and the extension of coffee breaks in the factories. Above all, it was the appropriation of free time, liberation from the constraints of factory command, and the search for a new community.

By the mid-1970s, two distinct tendencies in class violence had become apparent. These may be approximately defined as two different paths in the birth of the so-called militarization of the movement. The first path was the movement of violent resistance against the restructuring of production taking place in the large and medium-sized factories. Here the protagonists were above all worker militants, formed politically in the period 1968–73, who were determined to defend at all costs the material basis on which their bargaining strength had depended. Restructuring was seen as a political disaster. Above all, those factory militants who were most involved in the experience of the factory councils tended to identify the restructuring with defeat, and this was confirmed by repeated union concessions to management on work conditions. To preserve the factory as it was and maintain a favorable relation of force—these were their aims. It was around this set of problems and among the members in this political/trade-union base that the Red Brigades, from 1974–75 onward, found support and were able to take root.

The second path of illegality, in many ways diametrically opposed to the first, was made up of all those "social subjects" who were the result of the restructuring, the decentralization of production, and the mobility in the labor force. Violence here was the product of the absence of guarantees, the situation of part-time and precarious forms of employment, and the immediate impact of the social organization of capitalist command.

      This new proletariat that was emerging from the process of restructuring violently confronted local government controls and the structures of income, fighting for self-determination of the working day. This second type of illegality, which we can more or less identify with the Autonomy movement, was never an organic project, but was defined rather by the complete identity between the form of struggle and the attainment of specific objectives. There were thus no separate military structures that specialized in the use of force.

      Unless we accept Pier Paolo Pasolini's view of violence as natural to certain social strata, it is impossible to deny that the diffuse violence of the movement in these years was a necessary process of self-identification. It was a positive affirmation of a new and powerful productive subject, born out of the decline of the centrality of the factory and exposed to the full pressure of the economic crisis.

The movement that exploded in 1977, in its essentials, expressed this new class composition and was by no means a phenomenon of marginalization. What was described at the time as a marginal "second society" was already becoming the "first society" from the point of view of its productive capacities, its technical-scientific intelligence, and its advanced forms of social cooperation. The new social subjects reflected or anticipated in their struggles the growing identity between new productive processes and forms of communication, represented, for example, in the new reality of the computerized factory and the advanced tertiary sector. The movement of 1977 was itself a rich, independent, and conflictual productive force. The critique of waged labor now took an affirmative direction, creatively asserting itself in the form of "self-organized entrepreneurship" and in the partial success of managing "from below" the mechanisms of the welfare system.

This "second society" that took center stage in 1977 was asymmetrical in its relation to State power. There was no longer a frontal counterposition, but rather a sort of evasion, or rather, concretely, a search for spaces of freedom and income in which the movement could consolidate and grow. This asymmetrical relation was very significant, a great achievement, and it demonstrated the substance of the social processes in play. But it needed time—time and mediation, time and negotiation.

Instead, the forces of the "Historic Compromise" (between the Communist Party and the Christian Democratic Party) reacted to the movement entirely negatively, denying it any time or space and reimposing a symmetrical relation of opposition between the struggles and the State. The movement was subjected to a frightening process of acceleration, blocked in its potential articulations and deprived of any mechanisms of mediation. This was quite different from the process in other European countries, most notably Germany, where the repressive operation was accompanied by forms of bargaining with the mass movements and hence did not directly corrode their reproduction. The Italian Historic Compromise government cast the repressive net exceedingly widely, negating the legitimacy of any forces outside of or opposed to the new corporative and trade-unionist regulation of the social conflicts. In Italy, the repression had such a general scope that it was aimed directly against spontaneous social forces. The government's systematic recourse to politico-military measures made necessary in a certain sense a general political struggle, often in the form of a pure and simple struggle for survival. The emancipatory practices of the movement and its efforts to improve the quality of life and directly satisfy social needs were marginalized and confined to the ghetto.

The organizations of Autonomy found themselves caught in a dilemma between confinement to a social ghetto and direct confrontation with the State. Autonomy's "schizophrenia" and its eventual defeat can be traced to the attempt to close this gap, maintaining roots in the social network of the movement while at the same time confronting the State.

This attempt quickly proved to be quite impossible and failed on both fronts. On the one hand, the political acceleration imposed on the movement in 1977 led to the Autonomy organizations losing contact with the social subjects, who, rejecting traditional politics, followed their own various solutions (sometimes individual, sometimes collective) in order to work less, live better, and maintain their own spaces for freely creative production. On the other hand, this same acceleration pushed the autonomous organizations into a series of splits over the question of militarization. The contacts with the militarist groups were rejected and there soon developed a separate tendency in the movement, pushing for the formation of armed organizations. The dilemma was not resolved, but only became deeper. The whole form of Autonomy, its organization, its discourse on power, and its conception of politics, was thrown into crisis by both the question of the "ghetto" and that of militarization.

We should add that at the time, Autonomy underestimated all the weaknesses of its own politico-cultural model, which relied on the continual and linear expansion and radicalization of the movement. The model sought to weave together old and new: "old" anti-institutional extremism and new emancipatory needs. The separateness and alterity that distinguished the new subjects and their struggle were often read by Autonomy as a negation of any political mediation, even mediation that might support this alterity. The immediate antagonism was seen as precluding any discussion, any negation, and any "use" of the institutions.

From the end of 1977 through 1978, there was a growth and multiplication of formations operating at a specifically military level, while the crisis of the autonomous organizations became more acute. Many saw in the equation "political struggle equals armed struggle" the only adequate response to the trap in which the movement was caught by the politics of the Historic Compromise. In a first phase — in a scenario repeated numerous times — groups of militants within the movement made the so-called leap to armed struggle, conceiving this choice as an "articulation" of the movement's struggles, as a sort of "servicing structure." The very form of organization specifically geared to armed actions, however, proved to be structurally incompatible with the practices of the movement. They could only sooner or later go along separate ways. The numerous armed groups that proliferated in the period 1977–78 thus ended up resembling the model of the Red Brigades (which they had initially rejected) or even joining them. The Red Brigades, precisely insofar as they were conducting a "war against the State" totally detached from the dynamics of the movement, ended by growing parasitically in the wake of the defeat of the mass struggles.

In Rome especially, from the end of 1977 onward, the Red Brigades made a large-scale recruitment from the movement, which was in deep crisis. Precisely in that year, Autonomy had come up against all its own limitations, opposing State militarism with a wide series of street confrontations, which only produced a dispersion of the potential the movement represented. This repressive straitjacket and the real errors of the autonomists in Rome and some other areas opened the way for the expansion of the Red Brigades. The Red Brigades had been external to and bitterly critical of the mass struggles of 1977, but paradoxically they now gathered the fruits of those struggles, reinforcing their own organization.

The defeat of the movement of 1977 began with the kidnapping and murder of Aldo Moro, the prominent Christian Democrat politician, in 1978. The Red Brigades, in a sort of tragic parody of the way the official Left had developed its policies in the mid-1970s, pursued their own "political outlet" in complete separation from and outside of developments of currents of resistance in society at large. The "culture" of the Red Brigades, with its own courts, jails, prisoners, and trials — along with its practice of an "armed fraction," totally within the logic of a separate sphere of "politics" — played against the new subjects of social antagonism as much as against the institutional framework.

With the Moro operation, the unity of the movement was definitively broken. There began a twilight phase, characterized by Autonomy's frontal attack against the Red Brigades, while large sectors of the movement retired from the struggle. The emergency measures instituted by the State and the Communist Party were not successful as far as "antiterrorism" was concerned; on the contrary, the State tended to select its victims from among those publicly known as "subversives," who were used as scapegoats in a general witch-hunt. Autonomy soon found itself facing a violent attack, starting in the factories of the North. The "autonomous collectives" in the factories were denounced by trade-union and Communist Party watchdogs as probable terrorists and were weeded out. During the period of the Moro kidnapping, when the autonomists launched a struggle at the Alfa Romeo plant against Saturday work, the official Left responded with military "antiterrorist" tactics, demonizing them. Thus began the process of the expulsion of a new generation of autonomous militants from the factories, a process that reached its climax with the mass layoffs at the Fiat auto plant in Turin in the autumn of 1979.

After the Moro assassination, in the desolation of a militarized civil society, the State and the Red Brigades fought each other like opposite reflections in the same mirror. The Red Brigades rapidly went down the path already set for them; the armed struggle became terrorism in the true sense of the word, and thus began the campaigns of annihilation. Police, judges, magistrates, factory managers, and trade unionists were killed solely on the basis of their "function," as we have since learned from those who turned State's evidence, the *pentiti*. The repressive wave of arrests and imprisonment against the movement of Autonomy in 1979 eliminated the only political network that was in a position to fight against this logic of terrorist escalation. Thus between 1979 and 1981 the Red Brigades were able to recruit, for the first time, not only militants from the lesser armed combatant organizations, but also more widely from the scarcely politicized youth, whose discontent and anger were now deprived of any political mediation.

Those who have named names in exchange for remission of sentences, the *pentiti*, are only the other side of the terrorist coin. These informants are only a conditioned reflex of terrorism itself, and testify to its total alienation from the fabric of the movement. The incompatibility between the new social subject and the armed struggle is demonstrated in a horrible and destructive way in the verbal statements made by the informants. The system of remission for State informants (set up by law in December 1979) is a judicial "logic of annihilation" based on indiscriminate vendettas. The public destruction of the collective memory of the movement is conducted by manipulating the individual memories of the witnesses. Even when they tell the truth, they abolish the real motivations and contexts of what they describe, establishing hypothetical links, effects without causes, interpreted according to theorems constructed by the prosecution.

The sharp, definitive defeat of the political organizations of the movement at the end of the 1970s by no means coincided with any defeat of the new political subjects that had emerged in the eruption of 1977. These new social subjects have carried out a long march through the workplaces, the organization of social knowledge, the "alternative economy," local services, and administrative apparatuses. They have proceeded by keeping themselves close to the ground, avoiding any direct political confrontation, scoping out the terrain between the underground ghetto and institutional negotiations, between separateness and coalition. Though under pressure and often forced into passivity, this underground movement today constitutes, even more than in the past, the unresolved problem of the Italian crisis. The renewal of struggles and debates on the working day, the pressure on public spending, the question of protection of the environment and choice of technologies, the crisis of the party system, and the problem of finding new constitutional formulas of government—behind all these questions lies the density and living reality of a mass subject, still entirely intact and present, with its multiple demands for income, freedom, and peace.

Now that the Historic Compromise and the phase of terrorism have both come to an end, the same question is again, as in 1977, on the agenda: how to open spaces of mediation that can allow the movement to express itself and grow. Struggle and political mediation, struggle and negotiation with the institutions—this perspective, in Italy as in Germany, is both possible and necessary, not because of the backwardness of the social conflict but, on the contrary, because of the extreme maturity of its contents.

We must now take a clear stand, to take up once more and develop the thread of the movement of 1977. This means opposing both the militarism of the State and any new proposal of "armed struggle." There is no "good" version of armed struggle, no alternative to the elitist practice of the Red Brigades; armed struggle is in itself incompatible with and antithetical to the new movements. A new productive power, both individual and collective, that is outside and opposed to the framework of waged labor has emerged. The State is going to have to settle accounts with this power, and not only in its administrative and economic calculations. This new social force is such that it can be at one and the same time separate, antagonistic, and capable of seeking and finding its own mediations.

Translated by Michael Hardt

Editors' Note

An English translation of this text appeared in Antonio Negri, *Revolution Retrieved* (London: Red Notes, 1988), 229–43. We consulted that translation in the preparation of this work, and we are grateful to the Red Notes collective for their generous collaboration.

SEVENTEEN

Do You Remember Counterrevolution?

Paolo Virno

What does the word *counterrevolution* mean? We should not understand it as meaning only a violent repression (although, certainly, that is always part of it), nor is it a simple restoration of the ancien régime, that is, the reestablishment of the social order that had been torn by conflicts and revolts. Counterrevolution is literally *revolution in reverse*. In other words, it is an impetuous innovation of modes of production, forms of life, and social relations that, however, consolidate and again set in motion capitalist command. The counterrevolution, just like its symmetrical opposite, leaves nothing unchanged. It creates a long state of emergency in which the temporal succession of events seems to accelerate. It actively makes its own "new order," forging new mentalities, cultural habits, tastes, and customs—in short, a new common sense. It goes to the root of things, and works methodically.

But there is more: the counterrevolution enjoys the very same presuppositions and the very same (economic, social, and cultural) tendencies that the revolution would have been able to engage; it occupies and colonizes the territory of the adversary; it gives different responses to the *same* questions. In other words, it reinterprets in its own way the set of material conditions that would merely make imaginable the abolition of waged labor and reduces these conditions to profitable *productive forces*. (This hermeneutical task was facilitated to an extent in Italy by the use of maximum-security prisons.) Furthermore, the counterrevolution inverts the very mass practices that seemed to refer to the withering of State power and the immanence of radical self-government, transforming them into depoliticized passivity or plebiscitory consensus. This is why a critical historiography, reluctant to worship the authority of "simple facts," must try to recognize, in every step and every aspect of the counterrevolution, the silhouette, the contents, and the qualities of a potential revolution.

The Italian counterrevolution began in the late 1970s and continues still in the mid-1990s. Contained within it are numerous stratifications. Like a chameleon, it has several times changed its appearance: the "Historic Compromise" between the Christian Democrats and the Communist Party, the triumphant socialism led by Bettino Craxi, and the political reform of the system that has followed the collapse of the Soviet Union and the other regimes in Eastern Europe are some of its guises. It is not difficult nonetheless to recognize with the naked eye the leitmotif that runs throughout these phases. The unitary nucleus of the Italian counterrevolution of the 1980s and 1990s incorporates several elements: (1) the full affirmation of the post-Fordist mode of production (electronic technologies, decentering and flexibility of laboring processes, knowledge and communication as principal economic resources, and so forth); (2) the capitalist management of the drastic reduction of socially necessary labor time (through a labor market characterized by structural unemployment, part-time employment, long-term job insecurity, forced early retirements, and so forth); and (3) the dramatic crisis, which is in several respects irreversible, of representative democracy. The First Republic, which was established after the Second World War, has come to a close. The Second Republic sets down its roots in the material foundation of these new elements. The Second Republic must attempt to make its form and procedures of government adequate to the transformations that have *already* come about in the sites of production and the labor market. With the Second Republic, the post-Fordist counterrevolution finally finds its own constitution and, thus, reaches its completion.

In the historical-political theses that follow, I will attempt to extrapolate some salient aspects from the Italian developments of the past fifteen years—specifically, those aspects that offer an immediate empirical background to the theoretical discussions presented in this book. When, during this historical analysis, I find a concrete event to be exemplary (or, really, when I find it makes forseeable an "epistemological break" or a conceptual innovation), I will pause to explore it through an excursus, the function of which will be similar to the foreground of a cinematographic scene.

Thesis 1

Post-Fordism in Italy was given its baptism by the so-called movement of '77. In those social struggles, a working population characterized by its mobility, low job security, and high student participation, and animated by a hatred for the "ethic of work," frontally attacked the tradition and culture of the historical Left and marked a clean break with respect to the assembly line worker. Post-Fordism was born of this turmoil.

The masterpiece of the Italian counterrevolution was its having transformed these collective tendencies, which in the movement of '77 were manifested as intransigent antagonism, into professional prerequisites, ingredients of the production of surplus value, and leavening for a new cycle of capitalist development. The Italian neoliberalism of the 1980s was a sort of inverted 1977. The converse, however, is also true — that old period of conflicts continues still today to represent the other face of the post-Fordist coin, the rebellious side. The movement of '77 constitutes (to use Hannah Arendt's beautiful expression) a "future at our backs," the *remembrance* of the potential class struggles that may take place in *the next phase*, a future history.

First Excursus: Work and Nonwork, or the Exodus of '77

Like every authentic innovation, the movement of '77 suffered the insult of being taken for a phenomenon of *marginalization* — in addition to the accusation (which is really not contradictory but complementary to the first) of being *parasitic*. These concepts invert the reality in such a complete and precise way that they may be useful for us. In effect, those who thought that the "barefoot intellectuals" of '77 (the student-workers and worker-students, and the part-time and precarious workers of every sort) were marginal or parasitic were precisely those who thought the stable job in the factories of durable consumer goods was "central" and "productive." They were the ones who looked at these new subjects from the vantage point of the cycle of development in decline — a vantage point that today can be recognized as marginal and parasitic. If one looks closely, however, at the great transformations of the productive processes and the social working day that began during that period, it is not difficult to recognize in the protagonists of those street struggles some connection to the very heart of the productive forces.

The movement of '77 gave voice *for a moment* to the new class composition, which had begun to take form after the oil crisis and the layoffs in the large factories, in the beginning of the process of industrial reconversion. It was not the first time that a radical transformation of the mode of production was accompanied by the precocious conflictuality of the strata of labor power on the verge of becoming the central axis of the new productive schema. Recall, for example, the social danger that in the eighteenth century characterized the English vagabonds, who were *already* expelled from the fields and *on the verge of* being put to work in early manufacturing production. One could also point to the struggles of the dequalified workers in the United States in the 1910s, that is, in the period directly preceding the implementation of Fordist and Taylorist production based precisely on the systematic dequalification of labor. Every sudden metamorphosis of the organization of production is destined in principle to reevoke the pains of "primitive accumulation," having to transform a relationship among "things" (that is, new technologies, different allocations of investments, and labor power with certain specific prerequisites) into a social relationship. Precisely in this passage, however, there can sometimes arise the *subjective turn* of what will later become the unquestionable course of events.

The struggles of '77 assumed as their own the fluidification of the labor market, making it a terrain of social aggregation and a point of strength. The mobility among different jobs, and between work and nonwork, determined (rather than disrupted) homogeneous practices and common habits that characterized subjectivities and conflicts. Against this background there began to emerge the tendency that in subsequent years was analyzed by Ralf Dahrendorf, Andre Gorz, and many others: the reduction of traditional manual labor, the growth of intellectual labor at a mass level, and increased unemployment due to investment (that is, due to economic development, not its obstacles). The movement thus gave this tendency a sort of *partial representation*: it made it visible for the first time, baptized the tendency in a way, but distorted its physiognomy, giving it an antagonistic face. What was essential was the recognition of a possibility—conceiving waged labor as an *episode* in our lives rather than a *prison*. There followed then an inversion of expectations: refusing to strive to enter the factory and stay there, and instead searching for any way to avoid and flee it. Mobility became no longer an imposed condition but a positive demand and the principal aspiration; the stable job, which had been the primary objective, was now seen as an exception or a parenthesis.

In large part it was these tendencies, and not the violence of the struggles, that made the young people of '77 incomprehensible for the traditional elements of the workers' movement. They made the growth in the area of nonwork and its instability into a collective path, a *conscious migration away from factory work.* Rather than resisting the productive restructuring with all their might, they challenged its limits and directions, trying to divert it to their own advantage. Rather than closing themselves in a besieged fortress, doomed to a passionate defeat, they tested the possibilities of tempting the adversary to attack empty fortresses, abandoned long ago. The acceptance of mobility was combined with both the demand of a guaranteed income and the idea of a kind of production closer to the demands of self-realization. There thus developed a fissure in the link between production and socialization. Moments of communal association were experienced outside and against the realm of direct production. At this point, this independent sociality came to be recognized also in the workplace, as insubordination. And a decisive element of this was the option for "continuous education," that is, the continuation of school even after having found a job. This fed the so-called rigidity of the supply of labor, but, more important, it created a condition in which the positions of unstable and illegal labor were filled by subjects whose networks of knowledge and information were always *excessive* with respect to various and changing roles. This was an *excess* that could not be taken away from them and could not be reduced to the given form of laboring cooperation. Its investment and its waste were in any case tied to the possibility of populating and inhabiting in a stable way a territory situated beyond the reach of the wage.

This set of practices is obviously ambiguous. It is possible to read it, in fact, as a Pavlovian response to the crisis of the Welfare State. According to that interpretation, old and new subjects who had depended on assistance descend into the field to defend their own enclaves, carving out various pockets of public spending. They would thus embody those fictional costs that the neoliberal and antiwelfare policies sought to abolish or at least contain. The traditional Left can also defend this spurious position, with a certain embarrassment, and condemn this kind of "parasitism." Perhaps the movement of '77, however, can show the crisis of the Welfare State in a completely different light, radically redefining the relationship between labor and assistance, between real costs and "false costs," between productivity and parasitism. The exodus from the factory, which in part anticipated and in part gave a different meaning to the incipient structural unemployment, suggests in a provocative way that at the origin of the bankruptcy of the Welfare State there is, perhaps, a failure to develop sufficiently the area of nonwork. That is to say, *there is not too much nonwork, but too little.* It is a crisis, then, caused not by the assumed dimensions of assistance, but by the fact that assistance was granted, in large part, in the form of waged labor. And it was also caused, conversely, by the fact that waged labor was conceived, from a certain point on, as assistance. After all, were not the politics of full employment born in the 1930s under the golden motto, "Dig holes and then fill them up"?

The central point, which emerged in 1977 in conflictual forms and then during the 1980s continued as an economic paradox of capitalist development, is the following: manual labor, divided in various repetitive tasks, proves, due to its inflated and yet rigid costs, to be uncompetitive with automation and in general with a new sequence of applications of science to production. Labor thus shows its face of *excessive social cost*, of indirect assistance, disguised and hypermediated. Having made physical tasks radically "antieconomical," however, is the extraordinary result of years of workers' struggles — and this is certainly nothing to be ashamed of. The movement of '77, I repeat, momentarily made this result its own, demonstrating in its own way the *socially parasitic character of work under the boss*. In many respects it was a movement at the height of the neoliberalist new wave: it addressed the same problems that neoliberalism would later address, but sought different solutions. It looked for outlets but did not find them, and quickly imploded. Even remaining only a symptom, however, that movement represented the only vindication of an alternative path for the management of the phase of the end of "full employment."

Thesis 2

After having contributed both to the annihilation (including the military destruction) of the class movements and to the first phase of industrial reconversion, the historical Left was gradually excluded from the political scene. In 1979, the government of the "broad agreements" (also called the government of "national solidarity"), which was supported unreservedly by the Communist Party and its union, came to an end. The power of political initiative returned entirely to the hands of big business and the centrist parties.

As if acting out a now classic script, the reformist workers' organizations were co-opted in the direction of the State in a transitional phase, characterized by a "no longer" (no longer the Fordist-Keynesian model) and a "not yet" (not yet the full development of the network enterprise, immaterial labor, and computer technologies). The politics of the transition was aimed at containing and repressing social insubordination. Subsequently, as soon as the new cycle of development began, the mass workers of the assembly line definitively lost their weight with respect to both politics and contractual negotiations. The official Left became a powerless shell, to be discarded as soon as possible.

The decline of the Communist Party has its roots in the late 1970s. It is a "Western" story, an Italian story, tied to the new configuration of laboring processes. Only an optical illusion made it seem that this decline, which in 1990 led to the dissolution of the Communist Party and the formation of the Democratic Party of the Left (PDS), was caused by the Party's conflation with the "real socialism" of Eastern Europe and thus precipitated by the fall of the Berlin Wall. The symbolic sanction of the defeat suffered by the historical Left really occurred in the mid-1980s. In 1984, the government led by Bettino Craxi abolished the "point of contingency," that is, the mechanism by which wages were automatically adjusted for inflation. The Communist Party introduced a referendum to reestablish this important goal won by union struggles in the 1970s. The referendum took place in 1985 and lost by a landslide. The consequence of this debacle were that from that point on the Party and its union took only "realistic" positions, in collaboration with the government, on wages and the working day. From 1985 on, there was no more "social-democratic" or "trade-unionist" protection of the material conditions of dependent labor. The post-Fordist working class would have to live through its first period without being able to count on its "own" party or its "own" union. That had never happened in Europe since the days of the first industrial revolution.

Second Excursus: Scene Changes at the Fiat Auto Plant in the 1980s
The changes at the Fiat auto plant in the late 1970s and early 1980s demonstrate with exemplary clarity the ferocious "dialectic" at work among the conflictual spontaneity of the young labor force, the Communist Party, and a business about to change its physiognomy. As a sort of microcosm, Fiat anticipated and encompassed the "great transformation" that Italy was about to experience. It was one act, divided into three scenes.

Scene 1: In July 1979 production at Fiat was halted by a violent strike that in many respects resembled a real occupation of the factory. It was the culminating moment in a dispute over a comprehensive labor contract, but above all it was the final large episode of the worker *offensive* of the 1970s. The ten thousand new workers who had begun to work at Fiat only in the previous two years were some of the most active participants. These were "eccentric" workers, similar in all respects (mentalities, schooling, and metropolitan habits) to the students and workers with unstable employment who had filled the streets in 1977. The new workers defined themselves by their diligent sabotage of the rhythms of work: "slowness" was their passion. With the blockade of the Fiat plant they wanted to reaffirm the "porousness" or the elasticity of the time of production. The Communist Party and the union disavowed them, openly condemning their disaffection to work.

Scene 2: In the fall of 1979, Fiat launched a counteroffensive, firing sixty-one workers who had been the historical leaders of shop-floor struggles. It should be noted, however, that the workers were not fired with the pretext of some business reason. The official reason for the measure was the presumed involvement of the sixty-one workers with "terrorism." It mattered little that the magistrates had no concrete evidence to use in prosecuting the suspects. The company "knew," and that was enough. This episode of the sixty-one fired workers was in perfect harmony with the government of "national solidarity" and its strategy to equate all extrainstitutional social struggles with armed insurrection. The Communist Party and the union backed Fiat's decision, limiting criticism to a few formal details.

Scene 3: One year later, in the fall of 1980, Fiat unveiled a restructuring plan that called for thirty thousand layoffs. The Fordist factory was to be dismantled and would become a site for future industrial archaeology. There followed a thirty-five-day strike into which the Communist Party, which was by this time out of the government coalition, threw all its organizational power. The general secretary of the Party, Enrico Berlinguer, held an assembly at the gates of the factory—an event that in the following years was held up for worship by the militants of the official Left. *But it was already too late.* By supporting the expulsion of the sixty-one worker leaders and condemning and repressing the spontaneous struggle of the newly hired workers, the Communist Party and the union had destroyed the worker organization in the factory. In other words, they had sawed off the limb on which they, too, despite everything, were sitting. Only a dishonest or self-deceiving historiography could claim that the thirty-five-day strike was the decisive struggle, the watershed event. Really, everything had been played out earlier, between 1977 and 1979. To win the dispute, Fiat could count on its mass base: the intermediate-level workers, the foremen, and the office employees. In October 1980, Fiat organized a march in Turin against the continuation of the workers' strike and attracted a large following of forty thousand demonstrators. The Fiat restructuring plan passed.

Thesis 3

Between 1984 and 1989, the Italian economy enjoyed a brief golden age. The indexes of productivity rose continuously, exports expanded, and the stock exchange showed constant growth. The counterrevolution unfurled the standard that had been so dear to Napoleon III after 1848: *Enrichissez-vous*, enrich yourselves. The leading sectors of the boom were electronics, the communication industry (these were the years in which Silvio Berlusconi's company, Fininvest, grew enormously), the refined chemical industry, "postmodern" textiles such as Benetton (which directly organize the commercialization of the product), and the businesses that procure services and infrastructural elements. Even the auto industry, once it was slimmed down and restructured, accumulated exceptional profits for several years.

The nature of the labor market changed drastically in these years. Employment was less institutionalized and shorter-term. There was enormous growth of the "gray zone" of semiemployment and intermittent or short-term work. This led to the rapid alternation of superexploitation and inactivity. On the whole, the demand for industrial labor diminished. Marx, when writing about "overpopulation" or the "reserve army of waged-labor" (in short, about the unemployed), distinguished three types: *fluid* overpopulation (today we would call this turnover, early retirements, and so forth), *latent* overpopulation (in which technological innovation could reduce the labor at any moment), and *stagnant* overpopulation (including illegal labor, subterranean labor, and work with no job security). One could say that beginning in the mid-1980s the concepts with which Marx analyzed the industrial reserve army now applied instead to the mode of being of the working class itself. All of the employed labor power experienced the structural condition of "overpopulation" (either fluid, latent, or stagnant). Labor power was always potentially superfluous.

The concept of "professionalism" was thus radically redefined. What is valued in and demanded of the single worker no longer includes the "virtues" traditionally acquired in the workplace as a result of industrial discipline. The really decisive competencies needed to complete the tasks demanded by post-Fordist production are those acquired outside the processes of direct production, in the "life world." In other words, professionalism has now become nothing other than a generic sociality, a capacity to form interpersonal relationships, an aptitude for mastering information and interpreting linguistic messages, and an ability to adjust to continuous and sudden reconversions. The movement of '77 was thus *put to work*. Its nomadism, its distaste for a stable job, its entrepreneurial self-sufficiency, even its taste for individual autonomy and experimentation, were all brought together in the capitalist organization of production. It is sufficient, for an example, to point to the massive growth in Italy in the 1980s of "autonomous labor," or rather, the set of microbusinesses, which were sometimes little more than family enterprises, established by those who had previously been dependent workers. This "autonomous labor" is indeed the continuation of the migration away from the factory regime that began in '77, *but* it is strictly subordinated to the variable demands of big business—or, more precisely, it is the specific mode in which the largest Italian industrial groups managed to escape from part of their production costs. Autonomous labor almost always coincides with extremely high levels of self-exploitation.

Thesis 4

The Socialist Party (PSI), led by Bettino Craxi, who was prime minister from 1983 to 1987, was for a substantial period the political organization that best understood and interpreted the productive, social, and cultural transformation taking place in Italy.

In the late 1970s and early 1980s, the Socialist Party, in an effort to guarantee its own survival, conducted a sort of guerrilla war against the consistent policy of the two major parties, the Christian Democrats and the Communists, to seek agreement on major legislative and governmental questions. This is why during the period that Aldo Moro was held captive by the Red Brigades, Craxi opposed the no-compromise line (promoted by the Communists and accepted by the Christian Democrats), supporting instead negotiations with the terrorists for the release of the hostage. For this same reason, the Socialist Party was opposed to the special laws for public order, the logic of "emergency," and the restricting of civil liberties in order to combat the clandestine armed groups. In order to get out from under the suffocating embrace of its two major partners (the Communists and the Christian Democrats), the Socialist Party postioned itself as a political element that refused to worship the "reasons of State." The idolators will never forgive them. As a result of these rather liberatarian positions, the Socialist Party gained favor from certain elements who had participated previously in the extreme Left in addition to various other social subjects that had flowered along the archipelago of the movement of '77.

For several years the Socialist Party succeeded in offering a partial political representation to the strata of dependent labor that were the specific result of capitalist reconversion of production. In particular, it influenced and attracted the "mass intellectuality"—in other words, those who work productively with knowledge, information, and communication as raw materials. I want to be clear on this point. There are several examples in different periods and different national contexts when reactionary parties were composed of peasants or unemployed people — consider, for example, the populist movement in the United States at the end of the nineteenth century. In the same way, in Italy in the 1980s, the Socialist Party was the *reactionary party of mass intellectuality*. This means that it established an effective link with the condition, the mentality, the desires, and the forms of life of this labor power, but turned it all to the right. The link was real and the turn unmistakable. If one ignores either of these aspects, the entire phenomenon becomes incomprehensible.

The Socialist Party organized the highest elements (in terms of status and income) of mass intellectuality *against* the rest of dependent labor. It articulated in a new system of hierarchies and privileges the preeminence of knowledge and information in the productive process. It promoted a culture in which "difference" became synonymous with inequality, social status, and oppression, nourishing the myth of a "popular liberalism."

Thesis 5

In contrast to what happened in France and the United States, in Italy so-called postmodern thought has had no theoretical coherence, but rather a direct *political* meaning. More precisely, it has been a kind of thought that is in part *consolatory* (because it sought to demonstrate the "necessity" of the defeat of the class movements of the 1970s) and in part *apologetic* (because it never tired of singing the praises of the present state of things, celebrating the possibilities inherent in the "society of generalized communication"). Postmodern thought offered a mass ideology to the counterrevolution of the 1980s. All the talk about the "end of history" created in Italy a euphoric resignation. The indiscriminate enthusiasm for the multiplication of lifestyles and cultural styles constituted a small metaphysical *prêt-à-porter*, completely functional to the network enterprise, the electronic technologies, and the perennial insecurity of the labor relation. The postmodern ideologues, often operating in the media, took on the role of imposing an *immediate ethico-political direction* on post-Fordist labor power, filling the function to a certain extent played traditionally by party officials.

Third Excursus: Italian Ideology

In the 1980s, the dominant ideas were multiplied, differentiated, and expressed in a thousand and one dialects, sometimes bitterly against one another. The capitalist victory at the end of the previous decade authorized an unbridled pluralism: "There is room in back" as the sign says in the bus. And yet, dealing with "Italian ideology" requires that we trace this self-satisfied fracturing back to a unitary center of gravity, to solid common presuppositions. It means investigating the intersections, the complicities, and the complementarities among positions that are apparently far apart.

How does the Italian culture of the 1980s resemble a manger scene, complete with donkeys, Magi, shepherds, holy family, and so forth — various masks for one single spectacle? One aspect is the widespread tendency to *naturalize* the various social dynamics. Once again society has been refigured as a "second nature" endowed with unnamable objective laws. What is different, and this is the really remarkable point, is that to everyday social relations are applied the models, categories, and metaphors of postclassical science: Prigogine's thermodynamics instead of Newtonian linear causality, quantum physics in the place of universal gravitation, and the sophistic biologism of Luhmann's systems theory instead of Mandeville's "fable of the bees." Historical-social phenomena are interpreted on the basis of concepts such as entropy, fractals, and autopoiesis. Social syntheses are proposed on the basis of the principle of indeterminacy and the paradigm of self-referentiality.

Postmodern Italian ideology presupposes the *sociological* use of quantum physics and the interpretation of productive forces as the causal motor of elementary particles. But where does this renewed inclination to treat society as a natural order come from? And more important, if applied to social relations, of what kind of extraordinary mutations are these indeterminist and self-referential concepts of modern natural science at once symptom and mystification? We can hazard this tentative response: the great innovation subtended by this recent and very specific naturalization of the idea of society has to do with the *role of labor*. The opacity that seems to involve the behaviors of individuals and groups derives from the declining importance of labor (industrial, manual, and repetitive labor) both in the production of wealth and in the formation of identities, "images of the world," and values. This "opacity" is certainly well-suited to an *indeterminist* representation. While the labor loses its function as primary social nexus, it becomes impossible to locate the "position" of isolated bodies, their "direction," or the result of their interactions. The indeterminism is accentuated, moreover, by the fact that post-Fordist productive activity is no longer configured as a silent chain of cause and effect, antecedents and consequents, but rather by linguistic communication, and thus by an interactive correlation in which simultaneity predominates and there is no univocal causal direction. Italian ideology ("weak thought," the aesthetic of the fragment, the sociology of "complexity," and so forth) grasps, and also degrades to *nature*, the new nexus of knowledge, communication, and production.

Thesis 6

What are the forms of resistance to the counterrevolution? And what are the conflicts rising from the new Italian social landscape, which the counterrevolution has defined so prominently? It will be useful, first of all, to make clear a negative point: in the list of these forms and conflicts the practice of the Italian Greens is *not* included. Whereas in Germany and elsewhere ecologism inherited themes and issues from 1968, in Italy instead ecologism was born *against* the class struggles of the 1970s. It was a moderate political movement, full of those who had renounced and denounced radical action. Other collective experiences of recent years will be more useful for us here: first, the "social centers" established by young people all over Italy; second, the extrasyndicalist base committees that have been established in workplaces since the mid-1980s; and third, the student movement that in 1990 paralyzed university activity for several months, critically confronting the "hard core" of post-Fordism, or rather, the centrality of knowledge in the productive process.

The social centers, which have grown all over the country since the early 1980s, have given body to a desire for *secession* — secession from the dominant forms of life, from the myths and rituals of the victors, and from the din of the media. This secession is expressed as a voluntary marginality, a self-imposed ghetto, a world apart. In concrete terms, a "social center" is a vacant building occupied by young people and transformed into the site of alternative activities, such as concerts, theater, collective cafeteria, assistance for foreign immigrants, and public debates. In some cases, the centers have given rise to small artisinal enterprises, recalling the old model of the socialist "cooperative" of the beginning of the century. In general, however, they have promoted (or really only alluded to) a sort of public sphere not filtered by the State apparatuses. By *public sphere*, I mean an environment for free discussion of questions of common interest, from the national economic crisis to the neighborhood sewage system, from the wars in the former Yugoslavia to personal drug problems. In recent years, a large number of the centers have taken advantage of the alternative computer networks that circulate political documents, whispers and cries from the social "underground," news of social struggles, and personal messages. All in all, the experience of the social centers has been an attempt to give autonomous physiognomy and positive content to the growing time of nonwork. The attempt has been inhibited, however, by the tendency to construct what in Italy is imagined as an "Indian reservation," a sort of separate and isolated community, which, almost always, has marked (and saddened) the experience.

The worker base committees known as Cobas (*Comitati di base*) were first formed among the teachers (whose memorable and victorious labor dispute stopped the schools in 1987), the railway workers, and the public service employees. Subsequently, the Cobas spread to a certain number of factories (in particular, the Alfa Romeo plant, where they undermined the traditional union (CGIL) in the internal elections). The base committees have led several relatively serious conflicts over wages and work conditions. They refuse to be considered a "new union," seeking rather to link themselves to the social centers and the students and thus attempting to sketch an outline of forms of *political* organization at the level of post-Fordist "complexity." They give voice, above all, to a demand for democracy. This democracy is aimed against the legislative measures that throughout the 1980s substantially revoked the right to strike of public workers. It is also aimed at the trade union in general, which, having been displaced by the new productive processes, has redefined itself as an authoritarian State structure, adopting methods and procedures worthy of a monopolistic trust. The fortunes of the Cobas reached their pinnacle in the fall of 1992 during the protest strikes following the economic maneuver of the Amato government (which drastically reduced "social expenditures," pensions, medical assistance, and so forth). In all the major Italian cities there were violent protests against union "collaborationism," and counterdemonstrations by the Cobas disrupted union meetings. It was a little Tiananmen, which began to settle accounts with the "State monopoly union."

Whereas the social centers and the Cobas embodied, more or less effectively, the virtues of "resistance," the student movement (called the Panther movement because its birth in February 1990 coincided with the felicitous flight of a panther from the Roman zoo) seemed to allude, at least for a moment, to a true and proper "counteroffensive" of mass intellectuality. The conjuncture between knowledge and production, which until then had demonstrated only its capitalist face, was shown suddenly as a lever that could be used to further the conflicts and a precious political resource. The universities that were occupied in protest of the government project to "privatize" instruction became, for several months, a point of reference for that *immaterial labor* (researchers, technicians, computer specialists, teachers, cultural industry employees, and so forth) that in the large cities still only appeared as dispersed in a thousand separate streams, without any collective power. The Panther movement quickly died away, however, constituting little more than a symptom or an omen. It did not succeed in identifying appropriate objectives that would guarantee the continuity of the political action. It remained paralyzed, analyzing itself, contemplating its own navel. The hypnotic self-referentiality clarified, however, an important point: in order for mass intellectuality to enter the political scene and destroy what deserves to be destroyed, it cannot limit itself to a series of refusals, but beginning with itself it must exemplify *positively* through construction and experimentation what men and women can do outside the capitalist relationship.

Thesis 7

In 1989, the collapse of "real socialism" upset the political system in Italy in a much more radical way than in the other countries of Western Europe (including Germany, despite the repercussions of reunification). This unanticipated earthquake, which coincided with heavy shocks of economic recession, prevented the full emergence of an "antidote" to the capitalist era of the 1980s, that is, a set of social struggles intent on obtaining at least a physiological reequilibrium in the distribution of income. The signals launched by the Cobas and the Panther movement, rather than reaching a critical threshold and spreading out in lasting mass practices, were covered over and submerged by the din of Italy's institutional failure. Subjects and needs that grew out of the post-Fordist mode of production, far from presenting their demands to the careless sorcerer's apprentice, had to put on deceptive masks that hid their physiognomy. The rapid undoing of the First Republic overdetermined to the point of making unrecognizable the class dynamics of "business-Italy" (to use an expression dear to Silvio Berlusconi).

The fall of the Berlin Wall was not the cause of the Italian institutional crisis, but rather the extrinsic occasion in which it appeared to flourish and in which it became obvious to every observer. The national political system was suffering from a long-term illness that had nothing to do with the East-West conflict — an illness whose incubation began in the 1970s. The system was wasting away from consumption: *the withering of representative democracy*, the rules and procedures that characterize it, and the very foundations on which it rests. The catastrophe of the regimes of Eastern Europe had a greater effect in Italy than elsewhere precisely because it offered a theatrical costume for a completely different tragedy, precisely because it was superimposed on a crisis of different origin.

The decline of the society of work is what threw the mechanisms of political representation into profound disorder. In Italy, since World War II, political representation had been based on the identity between "producers" and "citizens." The individual was represented in labor, and the labor represented in the State; that was the primary axis of industrial democracy (and also of the Welfare State). This axis was already crumbling when the governments of "national solidarity" in the late 1970s wanted to celebrate with intolerant ardor its continuing values. The axis fell to bits in the subsequent years when the great transformation of the productive structures was in full course. The merely residual weight of factory labor in the production of wealth, the determinant role that abstract knowledges and linguistic communication play in it, and the fact that the processes of socialization have their center of gravity outside of the factory and the office — all this lacerated the fundamental ties of the First Republic, which, as the Italian Constitution says, is "founded on labor." The post-Fordist workers are the ones who first removed themselves from the logic of political representation. They do not recognize themselves in a "general interest," and they are never willing to integrate themselves into the State machine. With diffidence or hatred, they remain uneasily at the edges of the political parties, considering them nothing more than cheap ventriloquists of collective identities.

This situation opens up two possibilities that are not only different but diametrically opposed. The first is the emancipation of the concept of democracy from that of representation, and thus the invention and the practice of nonrepresentative forms of democracy. This is not, clearly, the false salvation that would follow from a mere simplification of politics. On the contrary, nonrepresentative democracy demands an equally complex and sophisticated operative style. In fact, it directly conflicts with the State administrative apparatuses, corroding their prerogatives and absorbing their competencies. The attempt to translate into political action those same productive forces — communication, knowledge, science — is what carries weight in the post-Fordist productive process. This first possibility has remained and will continue to remain in the background for some time to come. The opposite possibility has instead prevailed: the structural weakening of representative democracy has come to be seen as a tendential restriction of political participation, or rather of democracy *tout court*. In Italy, those implementing the institutional reform have made themselves strong by means of the solid and irreversible crisis of representation, using this for the legitimation of an authoritarian reorganization of the State.

Thesis 8

In the course of the 1980s there were numerous and unequivocal symptoms indicating the inglorious end of the First Republic in Italy. The downfall of representative democracy was announced by several signs, including the following:

"emergency" (that is, the recourse to special laws and the formation of exceptional organisms for implementing those laws) as a stable form of government, as an accepted institutional technique for confronting, at various times, the armed clandestine struggle, the public debt, or immigration problems;

the transfer of several functions of the politico-parliamentary system to the administrative realm and hence the prevalence of bureaucratic "ordinances" over the laws;

the overarching power of the magistrate (confirmed during the repression of terrorism) and its role as a substitute for politics given by this power; and

the anomolous behaviors of President Cossiga, who in the final years of his tenure began to act "as if" Italy were a presidential (rather than a parliamentary) republic.

After the fall of the Berlin Wall, all the symptoms of the imminent crisis were condensed in the campaign (supported almost unanimously by all the institutional parties from the Right to the Left) to gain public support for the liquidation of the most visible symbol of representative democracy: the proportional criterion of elections to the legislative assembly. In 1993, after a referendum abrogated the old norms, a majoritarian electoral system was introduced. This fact, together with the judiciary operation called *mani pulite* (clean hands), which has brought accusations of corruption against a large part of the political class, accelerated or completed the undoing of the traditional parties. Already in 1990, as I have noted, the Italian Communist Party had transformed itself into the Democratic Party of the Left, abandoning any residual reference to a class basis and proposing itself as a "light" party or a party of public opinion. The Christian Democratic Party deteriorated little by little until 1994, when it too changed its name, becoming the Popular Party. The minor parties of the center (including the Socialist Party, which in many respects had anticipated the need for radical institutional reform) disappeared almost overnight.

In any case, the salient aspect of the prolonged convulsion that has shaken the Italian political system in the early 1990s is the formation of a *new Right*. This is not a conservative right by any means, but rather one devoted to innovation, heavily invested in the notion of dependent labor, and capable of giving a partisan expression to the principal productive forces of our time.

Thesis 9

The new Right, which came to power with the political elections of 1994, is primarily constituted by two organizing subjects: the Lega Nord (Northern League), rooted exclusively in the northern parts of the country, and Forza Italia (Go Italy), the party centered around Silvio Berlusconi, the owner of several television stations, publishing houses, construction companies, and large retail stores.

The Lega Nord calls up the myth of ethnic self-determination, of roots refound: the northern population must valorize its traditions and its customs, without delegating any authority to the centralizing apparatuses of the State. Local identity (based in the region or the city) is contrasted to the empty universalism of political representation and the unbearable abstraction implied in the concept of citizenship. The local identity promulgated by the Lega Nord, however, has strongly racist overtones, particularly with respect to southern Italians and immigrants from outside the European Community. The Lega Nord proposes a form of federalism that weaves together the ancient and the postmodern: Alberto da Giussano (a medieval *condottiere* from Lombardy) is combined with ultraliberalism, and the motto "earth and blood" is thrown together with fiscal revolt. This rather strident mélange has given voice to the diffuse anti-State tendency that has matured in the course of the past decade in the most economically developed zones of the country. In time, the Lega Nord could become the mass base on which the small and medium-sized post-Fordist businesses could achieve relative autonomy from the national State. In the presence of the new quality of productive organization and in light of imminent European integration, the Italian State machine has shown itself inadequate in many respects: the *subnational* protest of the Lega Nord functions paradoxically as a support for delaying the political decision on *supernational* issues.

Forza Italia, on the other hand, replaces the traditional procedures of representative democracy with models and techniques derived from the world of business. The electorate is equated with a (television) "public," which is expected to give a consensus that is both passive and plebiscitory. Moreover, the form of the party faithfully reproduces the structure of the "network business." The "clubs" that support Forza Italia have grown on the basis of the personal initiative of professionals outside of conventional politics, such as a zealous office manager or a provincial notary who has decided to make a name for himself. These clubs have the same relationship with the party that autonomous labor and small family businesses have to the mother company: in order to market their own political product, they have to rely on a recognized brand, but in exchange they have to follow precise rules of style and conduct, bringing a good name to the company under whose label they work. As the Socialist Party did in the mid-1980s, Forza Italia has secured the loyalty of workers involved in computer and communication technologies, that is, among the social sectors that are being formed in the technological and ethical storm of post-Fordism.

The new Right recognizes, and temporarily makes its own, elements that would ultimately be worthy of our highest hopes: anti-Statism, collective practices that elude political representation, and the power of mass intellectual labor. It distorts all this, masking it in an evil caricature. And it brings to an end the Italian counterrevolution, drawing the curtain on this long intermezzo. That act is over—let the next begin!

Translated by Michael Hardt

Glossary of Concepts

Constituent power (*potere costituente*). This term refers to a form of power that continually creates and animates a set of juridical and political frameworks. Its perpetually open processes should be contrasted with the static and closed character of constituted power. The revolutionary dynamic of constituent power is itself the constitution of a republic; when the revolutionary forces are closed down or reined in to a constituted framework, the constituent moment too has passed. For an extended analysis of this concept from Machiavelli through the modern political revolutions, see Antonio Negri, *Constituent Power* (Minneapolis: University of Minnesota Press, forthcoming).

Exodus (*esodo*). In part this term refers to the biblical journey of the Jews through the desert to escape the pharaoh's army. Exodus might be understood better, however, as an extension of the "refusal of work" to the whole of capitalist social relations, as a generalized strategy of refusal or defection. Structures of social command are combated not through direct opposition, but by means of withdrawal. Exodus is thus conceived as an alternative to dialectical forms of politics, where all too often the two antagonists locked in contradiction end up resembling each other in a static mirror reflection. Dialectical politics constructs negations, but exodus operates through subtraction. The State will crumble, then, not by a massive blow to its head, but through a mass withdrawal from its base, evacuating its means of support. It is important, however, that this politics of withdrawal also simultaneously constitute a new society, a new republic. We might conceive this exodus, then, as an engaged withdrawal or a founding leave-taking, which both refuses this social order and constructs an alternative. Paolo Virno gives an extended analysis of exodus in his essay in this volume, "Virtuosity and Revolution: The Political Theory of Exodus."

General intellect (*intelleto generale*). This term is taken from a single reference by Marx, in which he uses the English term. (See Karl Marx, *Grundrisse: Foundations of the Critique of Political Economy*, trans. Martin Nicolaus [New York: Random House, 1973], 706.) Marx uses the term to refer to the general social knowledge or collective intelligence of a society at a given historical period. Fixed capital, in particular "intelligent" machines, can thus embody this general intellect as well as humans. Just as collective corporeal power is necessary to complete certain tasks of production (for example, to move the huge stones for the Pyramids), so too collective intellectual power is employed directly in production. Furthermore, as information technologies and cybernetic machines have become more important as means of production, general intellect has become increasingly not just a direct force, but the primary force of social production.

Immaterial labor (*lavoro immateriale*). Commodities in capitalist society have come to be less material, that is, more defined by cultural, informational, or knowledge components or by qualities of service and care. The labor that produces these commodities has also changed in a corresponding way. Immaterial labor might thus be conceived as the labor that produces the informational, cultural, or affective element of the commodity. One central characteristic of the new forms of labor that this term tries to capture is that the labor is increasingly difficult to quantify in capitalist schemata of valorization: in other words, labor time is more difficult to measure and less distinct from time outside of work. Much of the value produced today thus arises from activities outside the production process proper, in the sphere of nonwork. For an extended analysis of this concept, see Maurizio Lazzarato's essay in this volume, "Immaterial Labor."

Mass intellectuality (*intelletualità di massa*). This term refers to the collective intelligence and accumulated intellectual powers that extend horizontally across society. It does not refer to a specific group or category of the population (such as a new intelligentsia), but rather to an intellectual quality that defines to a greater or lesser degree the entire population. Intellectuality is not a phenomenon limited to the individual or the closed circle of trained intellectuals; it is a mass phenomenon that depends on a social accumulation and that proceeds through collective, cooperative practices. Gramsci says that all men are intellectuals but not all in society have the function of intellectuals. Today technico-scientific knowledges and practices are spreading to invest all spheres of life to a greater extent. Capital has learned from Gramsci's insight and put it to work. The post-Fordist workforce produces increasingly on the basis of its collective intelligence, its mass intellectuality.

Power (*potere, potenza*). The English term *power* corresponds to two distinct terms in Italian, *potenza* and *potere* (which roughly correspond to the French *puissance* and *pouvoir*, the German *Macht* and *Vermögen*, and the Latin *potentia* and *potestas*, respectively). *Potenza* can often resonate with implications of potentiality as well as with decentralized or mass conceptions of force and strength. *Potere*, on the other hand, refers to the might or authority of an already structured and centralized capacity, often an institutional apparatus such as the State. In some cases in this volume we have translated both terms as "power" and included the original Italian term in parentheses; in other cases we have used other terms to avoid confusion, translating *potenza*, for example, as "potentiality" or *potere* as "sovereign power."

Refusal of work (*rifiuto di lavoro*). The refusal of work was a popular slogan in Italy beginning with radical workers' groups in the 1960s and then spreading throughout the social movements of the 1970s. It should be understood principally in opposition to the glorification of work that has permeated some veins of the socialist tradition. (Consider Stachanov, for example, the mythical Soviet miner who did the work of several men for the glory of his country.) For these workers, communism does not mean any sort of liberation *of* work but rather a liberation *from* work. The destruction of capitalism involves also the destruction (not the affirmation) of the worker *qua* worker. This refusal of work should not be confused with a denial of one's own creative and productive powers. It is a refusal rather of the capitalist command that structures the relations of production and binds and distorts those powers. This refusal, then, is also an affirmation of our productive forces or creative capacities outside of capitalist relations of production. A classic source for this concept is Mario Tronti's "The Strategy of Refusal," in "Autonomia: Post-political Politics" (special issue) *Semiotext(e)* 3, no. 3 (1980): 28–34.

Self-valorization (*autovalorizzazione*). Marx understood capitalist valorization as the process by which capital creates surplus value in the labor process. "If the [labor] process is not carried beyond the point where the value paid by the capitalist for the labour-power is replaced by an exact equivalent, it is simply a process of creating value; but if it is continued beyond that point, it becomes a process of valorization" (*Capital*, vol. 1 [New York: Vintage, 1977], 302). Surplus labor and the value it creates are thus what define the process of valorization. *Valorization* can also refer more generally to the entire social structure of value that is grounded in the production and extraction of surplus value. In contrast, self-valorization (which appears in the *Grundrisse*) refers to an alternative social structure of value that is founded not on the production of surplus value but on the collective needs and desires of the producing community. In Italy, this concept has been deployed to describe the practices of local and community-based forms of social organization and welfare that are relatively independent of capitalist relations of production and State control. Self-valorization is also conceived in a more philosophical framework as the social processes that constitute an alternative and autonomous collective subjectivity within and against capitalist society. See Antonio Negri, *Marx beyond Marx* (New York: Autonomedia, 1984).

Contributors

.

Giorgio Agamben

teaches philosophy at the University of Verona and the Collège Internationale de Philosophie in Paris. His books in English include *Language and Death* (Minnesota, 1991), *Stanzas* (Minnesota, 1993), *Infancy and History*, *The Coming Community* (Minnesota, 1993), and *The Idea of Prose*.

Massimo De Carolis

teaches philosophy at the University of Salerno. He has written extensively on the philosophy of language, and his most recent book is *Tempo di esodo*. He is an editor of the journal *Luogo comune*.

Alisa Del Re

spent several years in exile in France. She now teaches political science at the University of Padua. She has written on sexual difference, domestic labor, and the Welfare State. Her most recent book is *Les Femmes et l'état-providence*.

Michael Hardt

is assistant professor of literature at Duke University. He is author of *Gilles Deleuze* (Minnesota, 1993) and, with Antonio Negri, *Labor of Dionysus* (Minnesota, 1994). He is an editor of the journal *Futur antérieur*.

Augusto Illuminati

is professor of philosophy at the University of Urbino. He has written several books on the history of political philosophy, including works on Kant and Rousseau. His most recent book is *Esercizi politici: Quattro sguardi su Hannah Arendt*. He is an editor of the journal *Luogo comune*.

Maurizio Lazzarato

went into exile in France in the early 1980s. He is completing a doctoral dissertation at the University of Paris VIII on communication paradigms, information technologies, and immaterial labor. He is an editor of the journal *Futur antérieur*.

Antonio Negri

was imprisoned on political charges from 1979 to 1983 and has lived since his release in exile in Paris. He was a professor of political science at the University of Padua and now teaches at the University of Paris VIII. His works include *Marx beyond Marx, Revolution Retrieved, The Savage Anomaly* (Minnesota, 1991), and *The Politics of Subversion*. He is coauthor, with Félix Guattari, of *Communists Like Us* and, with Michael Hardt, *Labor of Dionysus* (Minnesota, 1994). He is an editor of the journal *Futur antérieur*.

Franco Piperno

is professor of physics at the University of Calabria. He was a major leader of the radical student and worker movements of the 1960s and 1970s. In order to escape arrest in the late 1970s, he fled first to France and then to Canada, where he lived for seven years. He has written extensively on the problems of time in physics, economics, and linguistics.

Marco Revelli

teaches in the Department of Political Studies at the University of Turin. He has written on right-wing ideology in the twentieth century and on the recent history of the Fiat auto plant in Turin.

Rossana Rossanda

was a member of Parliament for the Italian Communist Party when in 1969 she was expelled from the Party and worked to found *il manifesto*, which was first a political organization and now remains an independent daily newspaper published in Rome. She writes regularly for the newspaper and has published numerous books on political movements and feminism in Italy.

Carlo Vercellone

has lived in exile in Paris since the early 1980s. He is completing a doctoral dissertation at the University of Paris VIII on regulation theories in economics and the history of the Italian Welfare State.

Paolo Virno

spent three years in prison in the early 1980s under preventive detention for political charges and was then absolved of any crime. He has worked as an editor of the culture pages of the newspaper *il manifesto*. His published works focusing on philosophy and politics include *Convenzione e materialismo*, *Mondanità*, and *Parole con parole*. He is an editor of the journal *Luogo comune*.

Adelino Zanini

teaches a seminar on contemporary philosophy. He has written books on the history of economic thought, including works on Schumpeter and Keynes. His latest book, *Il moderno come residuo*, is a philosophical analysis of modernity.

Index